FILTERS AND REFLECTIONS

FILTERS AND REFLECTIONS
Perspectives On Reality

Edited by Zachary Jones, Brenda Dunne,
Elissa Hoeger, and Robert Jahn

ICRL Press
Princeton, New Jersey

ICRL Press
468 N. Harrison St.
Princeton, NJ 08540-3511

ISBN 13: 978-1-936033-01-0
ISBN 10: 1-936033-01-1

Annotated Table of Contents

Mind and Biological Evolution

177

Antonio Giuditta (*Department of Biological Sciences,
University of Naples Federico II, Naples, Italy*)

An alternative representation of biological evolution is proposed that draws on the neo-Lamarkian tradition and has the potential for transcending the current impasse between neo-Darwinism and Creationism. By attributing consciousness to all living systems, it is proposed that organisms have the capability of exchanging information with their environments in ways that contribute to their adaptive responses, thereby influencing their structures, functions, and behaviors, and inducing variations that can be transmitted to their progeny.

Complexity, Interdependence, and Objectification

187

Vasileios Basios (*Interdisciplinary Centre for Nonlinear Phenomena and Complex Systems, University of Brussels, Brussels, Belgium*)

Many of the fundamental aspects of complex physical systems highlight the observer's participatory role in determining their workings. These fundamental complexity issues not only bear a formal resemblance to, but also reveal a profound connection with, quantum mechanics, and point to a common origin on a deeper level of description, suggesting that any description of a complex whole is only a partial objectification that is projected onto, and even redefines, its constituent parts.

The Human Shape of Cosmological Structure: Topological Association of Quantum Mechanics and Consciousness

209

Zachary Jones (*Tempe, Arizona*)

The ancient alchemists adhered to the Hermetic principle: "What is below is like that which is above, to accomplish the miracles of one thing." In this essay, the author describes the concept of a "macroscope," a model that synthesizes scale-independent forms in a way that reveals the activity of a self-reflective consciousness and provides access to aspects of reality beyond the reach of direct experience.

Editorial Introduction

I attribute my first interests and explorations in the realm of anomalous studies and 'frontier' science to my exposure to water dowsing at the age of four. There are few things more powerful than to know that there exists a world around you, unseen to the common senses but immediate and knowable with a tuning of the mind. At that age, the power of this awareness transcended the threshold across which Santa Claus and others turned into 'fairy tales.' Home was given to a healthy appetite for mystery, which has remained to this day a wellspring for the investigation of the most significant matters.

Nearly two decades later, the Princeton Engineering Anomalies Research (PEAR) Laboratory had established itself as the center and icon for landmark scientific studies in the field of anomalies research and my pursuit of dowsing research led me to its door. With the mentorship of PEAR staff and associates, I became conversant with the breadth of literature in the field, and its contemporary measurement limitations.

Had I not received such outstanding feedback and guidance at that time, I am very likely to have gone the more common route of learning investigative models that are insufficient to the standards of science and inadequate to encompass the structure of anomalous effects. From then on my investigations took a significant turn, and one such line of my explorations is included in this book.

The book itself was conceived several years ago in response to the substantial feedback that greeted Robert Jahn and Brenda Dunne's article, "Sensors, Filters, and the Source of Reality." Among the responses was a common element that many people felt they had been trying to say similar things in the language and from the viewpoint of their respective fields of study.

Jahn and Dunne invited a spectrum of essays on this theme, knowing that the ideas within the "Filters" paper would properly mature only when considered from many points of view. Several interim efforts of organization and editorship preceded my coming to serve as editor for the book. I extend my sincere appreciation to Elissa Hoeger, without whose sharp eye the editorial ride would have been much more bumpy, and my thanks to Nicholas Rose and Vincent Herzog for their early efforts to assemble the collection of papers.

I have boundless appreciation for all of the authors, who have spent much time and energy on the preparation and editing of their essays. None of this, of course, would exist without the passion and determination of Brenda Dunne and Bob Jahn. They have served as mother and father to a generation of researchers (junior and senior) dedicated to advancing the PEAR work beyond its initial conception.

Today the PEAR laboratory has wrapped itself in the new garments of the International Consciousness Research Laboratories (ICRL). This transition reflects the involvement of a network comprised of some of the planet's most progressive researchers. May this work support them and those who will follow a similar path.

ZACHARY JONES
Tempe, February 4, 2009

Foreword:
The Power of Weakness

By their founding of the International Consciousness Research Laboratories (ICRL) in the early 1990s, Brenda Dunne and Bob Jahn convened a group of researchers from diverse scholarly heritages to explore the issue of consciousness from a variety of perspectives, in an environment of warm companionship that fostered open-minded attention to alternative conceptualizations. Each of us was challenged to interpret the presentations of the others through the filters of one's own particular domain of expertise, which included such wide-ranging topics as anomalies research, zero-point energy, archaeology, psychotherapy, solitons, biophotonics, and others. The overarching theme of "consciousness" itself posed a filter through which each of us had now to re-consider the implications of our own specific research and as a result, each of our subjective reactions also differed somewhat from those of the others, yet each discovered nuances of individual assumptions and associations not previously recognized. These in turn opened us to a much broader picture of "reality," *e.g.* the interconnectivity of an imaginable, but never completely realizable unity with the rest of the world. In these conferences, our attention was inexorably drawn to the role that consciousness filters play in forming personal experience and in coloring interpersonal communications, as well as to the fundamental importance of a basic kind of uncertainty in their establishment, utilization, and alteration.

In its essence, filtering involves clarifying and falsifying at the same time, correcting and misleading, cleaning and polluting, distributing and concentrating, adding and extinguishing, clouding information while at the same time improving it, with no certainty whether one or the opposite of any of these possibilities happens in any given case. This is as trivial as it is surprising, since we are never justified to claim that we are in possession of the perfect and total truth. All information inevitably becomes filtered in one or the other direction. As soon as I try to convince somebody that I understand "reality" completely and unfiltered, that reality already belongs to the past and cannot reflect the immediate and relevant truth. As soon as I assign the label "truth" to connected spatio-temporal happenings, I am obliged to lie at the same time, simply in view of well-known uncertainties as described by and originating from the inaccuracies of quantum mechanics or of chaos theory.

From the perspective of my own field of biophotonics, for example, we find that once we understand the possibilities of coherence in biological systems, we enter a completely new world. Biophotons are quanta which are permanently emitted from biological systems far from thermal equilibrium. In order to emphasize the quantum nature of the phenomenon and to distinguish it from common bioluminescence, we call this radiation "biophotons." The field addresses basic questions of biophysics and related subjects, along with questions of the role of biophotons in regulation of biological functions, cell growth and differentiation, relevance of delayed luminescence, coherence in biological systems, and supermolecular processes in living tissues. Over the years it has been possible to demonstrate that biophotons are signals of intercellular communication, with the coherence of the emissions serving as indicators of this information exchange.

While technically non-functional, at a sufficiently high level coherence is capable of enhancing a system's performance; producing awareness of long-distance interactions (which play an important role in nonlinear relationships through the overlapping of information and randomness); and in developing what we may call "consciousness" in internal structures. In other words, consciousness itself can be regarded as an evolutionary process based on coherent states, raising a completely new perspective of how information is filtered from the ocean of potential information and how coherence among individual consciousnesses can affect the perception and integration of that shared information. This, in essence, is the operational principle that underlies and guides all of ICRL's activities.

Is it possible that any event can be looked upon as an isolated one, completely separated from the "external" world? Is this thinkable at all? Or are we forced always to take into account, under all possible circumstances, that the world is a permanent whole entity? Do events even exist that may perfectly carry through the randomness of mathematical statistics? We know from experience that this is never the case, but that there are always undeterminable aberrations from "ideal" randomness. Most of us would claim by using their "common sense" that according to the mathematical limit law (*Grenzwertsatz* in German) an infinite number of independent trials will lead to a fully chaotic accumulation of all the interactions, which can never provide any information out of randomness that cancels possible frequencies of the stochastic varieties of single events. As a model, theoretically this is trivial and therefore also true. But is such a situation realistic at all? Do we know the "ultraweak" influences of the external world that affect all the single, but never completely random, events and that cannot simply be eliminated without leaving traces of long-range interactions? They accumulate in every single case with an unknown probability to leave macroscopic traces of mysterious information.

For example, one can show that resonance phenomena will always lead to situations where it is impossible to find a mathematical cut-off procedure where events at infinite distances can be truly separated from their interactions with local processes. Quantum theory may even amplify this information transfer from infinity by resonance processes. The classical approach leads to the curious situation that the shifting of a gram mass of only one centimetre dimension at Sirius distorts by gravitational forces the molecules in the brain to such an extent that it is impossible to describe it by accurate continuous movement of the molecules for more than a few seconds. This is not a problem of chaos theory alone, but implies the impossibility of determining whether randomness gets a further macroscopic stimulus by far distant interactions that can never be investigated thoroughly and accurately. Another example: Does the Weber-Fechner-law with its logarithmic dependency on the strengths of stimuli lead to a completely different awareness of distant events compared to that usually detected by linear dependencies of our known detector systems? In accordance with this law, fish are able to detect signals of about 10^{-12} W/m^2. This electromagnetic reception which, for instance, allows fish to find their way back to their locations of birth over hundreds of kilometres, seems to function in all living systems. It is quite likely that these macroscopic interactions include information that cannot be expressed in terms of theoretical models that exclude *ab initio* other sources, such as those termed "mind-mind" or "matter-mind" interactions.

A further very important point comes into play just here. Is it actually unimaginable that these subjective feelings escape "objective" proof in such a way that a definite attitude of non-expectation (impartiality) is necessary to make them subjects of scientific investigation? How could this field become the subject of scientific exploration at all? How does it interfere with what we call "consciousness"? Maybe this kind of investigation is the only way to get a reliable and relevant scientific description of the awareness of consciousness, which should be not confused with the term "consciousness" itself. There are manifold unanswered questions connected to these phenomena. However, what could be confirmed with certainty at the present time?

The establishment of ICRL by Brenda Dunne and Bob Jahn opened a completely new door for exploring what we may understand about "reality," "truth," objectivity, subjectivity, or consciousness about consciousness, and the interaction of our mind with the world. The term "filtering," which tries to explain the deep duality of "truth," is just the right expression to underline the importance of this book and is, in essence, the operational principle that underlies and guides all of ICRL's activities.

FRITZ-ALBERT POPP
International Institute of Biophysics
Neuss, August 14, 2007

Prologue

When our article "Sensors, Filters, and the Source of Reality" (henceforth SFSR), on which this anthology is based, was first published in 2004 it evoked some critical commentary from a few of our colleagues. Their point was that whereas this had introduced some interesting conceptual propositions to complement our prior theoretical efforts, they found it excessively academic and abstract in its language and style. Why, they suggested, did we not compose a version cast in more common vocabulary, and featuring more specific and familiar examples and metaphors that might more readily be assimilated by a less sophisticated readership? Our somewhat petulant response, predicated in part by literary exhaustion and in part by an aversion to popularized writing in any technical venue, was to challenge these individuals to attempt their own representations of this mind/filter/Source taxonomy. This possibility intrigued some of our ICRL associates, several of whom volunteered to explore the implications of the paper for their own fields and to contribute a summary thereof. The result is this anthology that presents under one cover an assortment of personal and professional perspectives on the SFSR thesis.

An initial logistical naïveté regarding fidelity of author commitments and composition skills, editorial and publication vicissitudes, and the inescapable subtleties and complexities of the subject itself, while never succeeding in totally derailing the project, nevertheless conspired to delay it by a dreary sequence of false starts, detours, redefinitions, and changes of editors. Notwithstanding, the obdurate patience of the contributors and editorial staff, and the inexorable fascination of the topic have finally prevailed in assembling a delightful myriad of perspectives that illustrate the broad range of subjective and objective filters applied by the authors in their own daily lives, not least of all in the creation of their particular representations of such processes.

Even casual examination of the table of contents reveals that this potpourri of essays spans a wide topical and stylistic terrain ranging from pleasantly homespun and whimsical narrations to highly sophisticated philosophical and technical argumentations (some of which far exceed the original article in their density, abstraction, and profundity of expression!). Yet the common central theme permeates all of them: the experiences of "reality" we extract from the ineffable ontological "Source" are so strongly conditioned by the biological, cultural, and psychical filters we consciously and unconsciously impose, that we may legitimately be regarded as co-creators of those experiences.

But an even subtler and more portentous implication also emerges: the individual and collective effects of such proliferate and incessant filtering may influence the character of the Source itself. As proposed in SFSR, the complex ensemble of resonant oscillations of the two-way information channels connecting individual and collective Consciousness to its Source may instill an evolutionary progression in the latter that is in turn reflected back to the cultural and biological development of the former. *Via* this epistemic feedback loop we become creatures of our desires, for better or for worse.

After perusing the original SFSR article and the several variations on that theme contributed by this panel of authors, readers might want to take inventory of their own armamentaria of consciousness filters, and ponder with some frankness how imposition of them on their own Source of reality conditions their experience thereof, and how the grand cultural amalgamation of personal filters, individual and collective, localized and global, are impelling that Source into the future.

ROBERT JAHN AND BRENDA DUNNE
Princeton, February 11, 2009

Sensors, Filters, and the Source of Reality*

ROBERT JAHN AND BRENDA DUNNE
PEAR/ICRL
Princeton, New Jersey

> *...Celestial light,*
> *Shine inward, and the mind through all her powers*
> *Irradiate; there plant eyes; all mist from thence*
> *Purge and disperse, that I may see and tell*
> *Of things invisible to mortal sight.*
> — JOHN MILTON[1]

Introduction

At birth, that tiny portion of the boundless, timeless spirit of all existence that defines our personal identity takes residence for one mortal span in a physical corpus we call the human body, which is given to us to experience, explore, and influence a sensible surround we call the world. That corpus, like the spacecraft and submersible vehicles with which we explore the physical environments of space and sea, has locomotive and manipulative capacities, and is equipped with an array of physiological sensors that can acquire specific forms of information about the environment in which it is functioning. It also possesses a neurological grid and control center, called the brain, which can be trained to interpret the signals generated by these sensors, and to activate therefrom appropriate responses. It is primarily *via* these channels of experience and response that we endeavor to infer, either intuitively or analytically, composite functional models of our world and of ourselves on which to base our subsequent behavior.

The biophysical architectures and the neurological and biochemical processes by which these sensors and channels execute their respective

---

* This article originally appeared in the *Journal of Scientific Exploration, 18*, No. 4 (2004), pp. 547–570, under the affiliation of Princeton Engineering Anomalies Research, Princeton University.

functions have been broadly and deeply studied, and are sufficiently well understood that their maintenance, protection, healing, and enhancement can be profitably practiced, but considerably less insight has been achieved regarding their roles in establishing the subjective qualities of life. It is well recognized that these physiological sensors have limited ranges of sensitivity, and thus ignore major segments of their corresponding stimulation spectra. Human eyes perceive only the narrow band of electromagnetic radiation from 400 to 700 nanometers in wavelength, and are oblivious to the much more extensive infrared and ultraviolet domains that border it. Our ears respond only to a similarly narrow range of acoustic frequencies, beyond which lie imperceptible infrasonic and ultrasonic realms of the same form of physical oscillations. Our taste, smell, and sense of touch likewise are sensitive only to tiny portions of their potential physical or chemical informants. Whereas we have become technically adept at artificially extending these ranges of information access *via* a host of optical, electrical, and mechanical devices, our brains must then translate their outputs into extrapolations of our physiological sensitivities to effectuate their utility. We also have developed an armamentarium of equipment to amplify and refine the incoming signals for both the natural and artificially extended sensory capacities: telescopes, microscopes, hearing aids, photographic facilities, radio and television technologies, seismographs, *etc.* While all serve to enhance our experience of the physical world, here again our brains must execute additional steps of recognition and logic if we are to benefit from them.

More salient to our thesis here, however, is the acknowledgment that other, more subtle mechanisms for acquisition of information, such as intuition, instinct, inspiration, and various other psychical modalities, also can enhance the flux of incoming information. Although commonly experienced, these channels involve less readily identifiable sensors and therefore are less susceptible to orderly reasoning, and they are correspondingly less respected and utilized in modern scientific practice, traditional education, and contemporary social activity. In the extreme materialistic view, this imbalance extends to total dismissal of these subtler capacities, thus restricting experience to the five primary sensory capabilities and their technological extensions alone. Consequently, the inferred models of reality are limited to those substances, processes, and sources of information that constitute conventional contemporary science.

In this paper we ally ourselves with the sharply contrary position that there exists a much deeper and more extensive source of reality, which is largely insulated from direct human experience, representation, or even comprehension. It is a domain that has long been posited and contemplated by metaphysicians and theologians, Jungian and Jamesian psychologists, philosophers of science, and a few contemporary progressive theoretical physicists, all struggling to grasp and to represent its essence and its function. A variety of provincial labels have been applied, such as "Tao," "Qi," "prana," "void," "Akashic record," "Unus Mundi," "unknowable substratum," "terra incognita," "archetypal field," "hidden order," "aboriginal sensible muchness," "implicate order," "zero-point vacuum," "ontic (or ontological) level," "undivided timeless primordial reality," among many others, none of which fully captures the sublimely

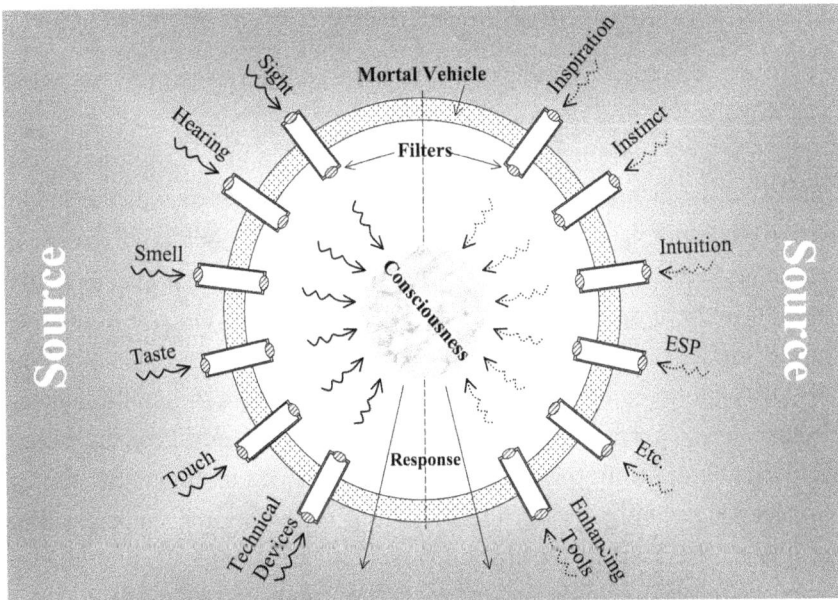

Figure 1. Schematic cartoon of information exchange between Consciousness and its Source: On the left, physiological sensory channels, conditioned by various physical, psychological, and cultural filters, acquire limited information from the Source, and transmit it to the Consciousness for organization into palpable experience and reaction thereto. On the right, other less well-comprehended subjective channels, also conditioned by pertinent attitudinal filters, supplement the information flux with an assortment of intuitive, instinctive, and inspirational sensations that may also influence the Consciousness response.

elusive nature of this domain. In earlier papers we called it the "subliminal seed regime,"[2,3] but for our present purposes we shall henceforth refer to it simply as the "Source."*

In similar spirit, we also reject the popular presumption that all modes of human information processing are completely executed within the physiological brain, and that all experiential sensations are epiphenomena of the biophysical and biochemical states thereof. Rather, we shall regard the brain as a neurologically localized utility that serves a much more extended "mind," or "psyche," or "consciousness" that far transcends the brain in its capacity, range, endurance, and subtlety of operation, and that is far more sophisticated than a mere antenna for information acquisition, or a silo for its storage. In fact, we shall contend that it is the ultimate organizing principle of the universe, creating reality through its ongoing dialogue with the unstructured potentiality of the Source. In short, we subscribe to the assertion of Arthur Eddington nearly a century ago:

> Not once in the dim past, but continuously, by conscious mind is the miracle of the Creation wrought.[4]

By whatever names we label these two primary poles of the information dialogue, it is our contention that the highly selective group of experiential channels based in our five physiological senses allows only very limited communication between them, so that *via* these narrow, cloudy windows in our Source-faring capsule consciousness can obtain only petty glimpses of the grand complexity and scope of its ultimate environment, and correspondingly petty reflections of itself. Like the fabled blind men examining the elephant, our experience of the world and of ourselves is severely circumscribed by our observational inadequacies, yet it is on the basis of these shallow specifications that we presume to construct correspondingly limited models of our environment and of our cogent minds. Worse yet, these impoverished models, their concepts and

---

* This assortment of contexts, labels, or models should not be regarded as mutually exclusive or hierarchical; nor are they isomorphic to one another. Rather, they represent different perspectives on the same basic search, and hence should be respected as collectively complementary. Where they reinforce one another, or display common features, this may indicate some degree of basic insight. Where they disagree on details, testable hypotheses may present themselves.

terminology, are then allowed to constrict further our channels of incoming information, by constraining our experiential data, their interpretations, and our responses, to conform to such authoritarian constructs of "reality" and the expectations they engender. This composite dilution of experience we shall henceforth refer to as "filters." (Figure 1 displays one of several possible geometrical representations of this conceptual situation.)

Beyond these major premises, we shall here offer three additional radical propositions, which if better understood and implemented, could bring us toward a more profound comprehension, representation, and utilization of this cosmic sea of existence in which our mortal Source-ship is traveling, and of its navigating consciousness:

1. The subjective "soft" channels of information acquisition mentioned above, severely neglected in contemporary science, should be elevated to comparable status with the more commonly trusted, objective, "hard" channels of sight, sound, touch, taste, and smell.

2. Both categories of channels have "two-way" capabilities, *i.e.*, they can pass information into the Source, as well as extract information from it. Thus, although the Source is heavily shrouded from consciousness, it nonetheless may be influenced by it. Indeed, it may engage in a dynamic dialogue with it.

3. The filters restricting both categories of channels and both directions of information flux are not necessarily static or passive. Some are "tunable," either autonomically or deliberately, to the extent that our prevailing expectations, attitudes, purposes, needs, desires, and reference contexts themselves can be altered, thereby yielding broader and deeper access to experiences and influences that are otherwise occluded.

In the following sections we shall explore each of these propositions a bit further.

Scientific Subjectivity

The elevation of subjective concepts and correlates to equivalent operational status with objectively definable properties in future scientific methodology has been proposed in several of our prior technical and philosophical publications, most notably throughout the text of *Margins of Reality*[5] and in the essay "Science of the Subjective,"[6] the abstract of which serves to summarize our position:

> Over the greater portion of its long scholarly history, the particular form of human observation, reasoning, and technical deployment we properly term 'science' has relied at least as much on subjective experience and inspiration as it has on objective experiments and theories. Only over the past few centuries has subjectivity been progressively excluded from the practice of science, leaving an essentially secular analytical paradigm. Quite recently, however, a compounding constellation of newly inexplicable physical evidence, coupled with a growing scholarly interest in the nature and capability of human consciousness, are beginning to suggest that this sterilization of science may have been excessive and could ultimately limit its epistemological reach and cultural relevance. In particular, an array of demonstrable consciousness-related anomalous physical phenomena, a persistent pattern of biological and medical anomalies, systematic studies of mind/brain relationships and the mechanics of human creativity, and a burgeoning catalogue of human factors effects within contemporary information processing technologies, all display empirical correlations with subjective aspects that greatly complicate, and in many cases preclude, their comprehension on strictly objective grounds. However, any disciplined re-admission of subjective elements into rigorous scientific methodology will hinge on the precision with which they can be defined, measured, and represented, and on the resilience of established scientific techniques to their inclusion. For example, any neo-subjective science, while retaining the logical rigor, empirical/theoretical dialogue, and cultural purpose of its rigidly objective predecessor, would have the following requirements: acknowledgment of a proactive role for human consciousness; more explicit and profound use of interdisciplinary metaphors; more generous interpretations of measurability, replicability, and resonance; a reduction of

ontological aspirations; and an overarching teleological causality. Most importantly, the subjective and objective aspects of this holistic science would have to stand in mutually respectful and constructive complementarity to one another if the composite discipline were to fulfill itself and its role in society.

Without repeating the detailed arguments presented in that essay, we would note only that this premise is essential to the invocation of the other propositions developed below. We also might note that despite their less secure catalogue of empirical evidence, access to these less tangible sources of information also has been abetted by a variety of man-made devices. Some of these have been carried forward from ancient mystical traditions, including, for example, dowsing rods, crystal balls, tarot cards, rune stones, I-Ching oracles, *etc.*, all purported to enable and enhance information access *via* these subtler channels. More contemporary technological versions, usually based on random physical processes, include the array of electronic, mechanical, optical, fluid dynamic, and nuclear random event generators (REGs) now commonly utilized in laboratory and field research to display and correlate consciousness-related physical anomalies.[7] As with the enhancers of the conventional sensory channels, however, all of these strategies also require a cognitive overlay to interpret and benefit from the additional information they provide.

Two-Way Channels

That the information derived from the Source by any of our limited sensory channels is utilized by our human consciousness and its physical corpus is beyond doubt. That there is also a reverse flow of information from our mind and body to this environment is a more complex and controversial issue. Clearly, when we decide to do something of a physical nature, *e.g.*, to clap our hands, drive a car, write a book, or compose a song, our physical, cultural, or social environment is affected in some way. How much of this influence is direct physical interaction and how much is achieved by subtler subjective means is debatable, but for either form it is even less clear to what extent the deeper Source underlying the perceived environment participates in, or is modified by, this outgoing direction of information flux.

Some insight into these questions might be derived by reflecting on the role of resonance in the more conventional sensory mechanics of incoming information acquisition. Taking hearing as perhaps the simplest example, we do not merely respond to the passage of sound waves traveling down our ear ducts. Rather, some portion of those incident waves is reflected by the eardrums, thereby establishing standing wave patterns in the ducts that stimulate the drum membranes to sympathetic mechanical vibrations. These, in turn, activate the auditory neurophysiology to transmit messages to the brain for its interpretation, *via* a corresponding pattern of standing electromagnetic waves in this segment of the channel. In other words, the ear canal, the eardrum, and the auditory neurophysiology comprise a complex acoustical/mechanical/electromagnetic resonator that is stimulated by the incoming sound signals from the environment.

In such a model, there is an inescapable byproduct that is usually ignored as negligible, namely those portions of the outgoing reflected oscillations that reemerge from the ear aperture back into the external environment. To be sure, this entails only a tiny fraction of the energy consumed in the ear stimulation, but therein lies a mechanism for informing the environment of what the ear canal, the ear drum, and the pursuant neurophysiology, including the brain, are doing, for they are all part of one composite resonant system, the oscillations of which are available for interpretation and use by both the brain on one end, and by the environment on the other.

Similar, albeit more elaborate resonant structures can be described for the eyes, mouth, nose, and tactile sensors that stimulate all manner of organic, neuronal, skeletal, and soft-tissue responses, some small portions of which are also reflected in the outgoing signals. For the eye, it is the retina that provides the two-way interface between the resonant optical cavity and the visual cortex of the brain. The resonating configurations attending the nose, mouth, and tactile skin are somewhat more subtle and complex, and utilize a broader selection of mechanical, electromagnetic, and chemical stimuli, but each of these also inherently provides re-emergent information fluxes that couple the environment and the sensing complexes into bonded resonant systems. In fact, these latter three present

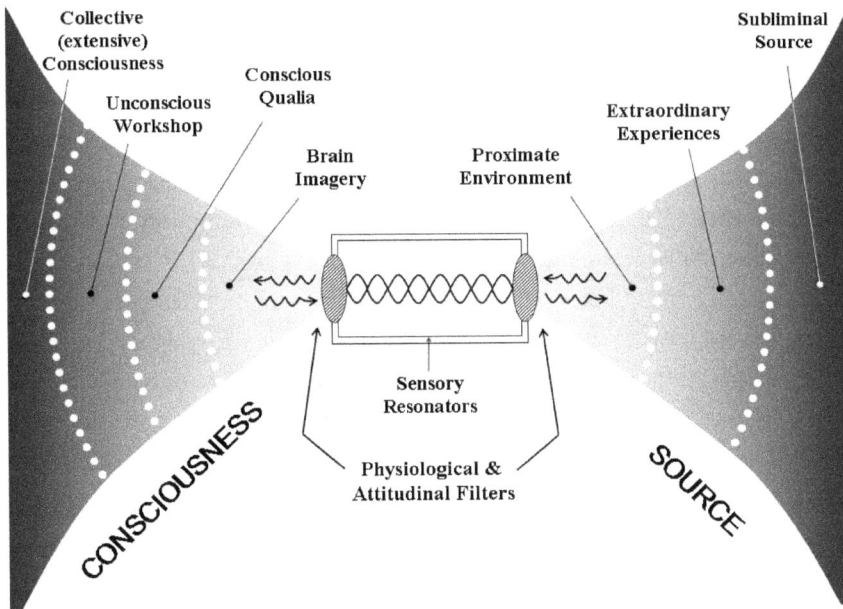

Figure 2. Schematic cartoon of the resonating sensory systems: Consciousness exchanges information with the Source *via* filtered sensory oscillators, each resonating within its particular physiological or psychical complex. From the information thus acquired, it assembles experiences, the subtlety and profundity of which depend on the depth and breadth of the information interpenetration. From relatively narrow and shallow penetrations it infers a model of its physical environment, but this is only a limited, emergent expression of the full potentiality of the ultimate Source. Deeper incursions, however achieved, can yield more profound and extraordinary experiences, probably first processed in the unconscious mind. The most extreme penetrations can precipitate extensive, collective psychical events, and may yield more ontological glimpses of the Source itself.

By the converse routes, consciousness also employs the sensory resonators to contribute information to the Source, thereby affecting it, and hence the palpable environment and all subtler experiences derived from it. Personal realities may thereby be responsive to individual and collective intentions, desires, and needs, to a degree determined by the intimacy of the consciousness/source coupling.

more explicit means of environmental influence *via* their normal respiratory, transpiratory, and thermal efflux cycles.*

So far, we have not yet invoked any of the subtler forms of information acquisition included in the previous section. The requisite system for

---

* Our list of physiological sensors does not extend to other proprioceptors, such as those associated with body orientation, movement, sensitivity to gravitational or magnetic fields, *etc.*, since their inclusion would add little to the essential bi-directional concept, and would needlessly complicate the specific illustrations. Nor have we attempted to specify the role of the brain/mind interface in such complex resonance systems.

two-way communication is already in place using only physical and physiological components and processes. But if we now expand our portfolio of communication channels beyond the primary materialistic modalities to include the various subtler passages of intuition, inspiration, instinct, or the array of consciousness-related anomalous information channels long researched in our laboratory and elsewhere, we may more broadly extend the same resonant holistic system metaphor. While the specific mechanics of these incoming and outgoing information carriers and the receptors thereof are less well understood, the role of resonance in such interactions, although less tangibly defined, is impressionistically quite evident, and may well be more significant than for the physical channels. Indeed, the establishment of such resonant states between the subjective experience of a living participant and its pertinent physical and emotional environment is one of the essential functions of all spiritual practices, creative enterprises, healing efforts, and, in our context, the scientific generation of such phenomena.

What then do such resonant channel models predicate? Clearly, the individual effect sizes are very tiny: a few phonons re-emerging from an ear or a few photons from an eye; some faint biophotonic mechanism[8] or chemical radiation from the body; or some microscopic flux of anomalous information riding on an unspecified subjective carrier, each attempting to inform the world about the information being processed in a small portion of the brain or psyche at the other end of that particular system. Ah, but how many ears, and eyes, and mouths, and brains, and psyches, of how many living creatures equipped with such capabilities are resonating their instruments, at their own particular frequencies, at any given moment? And what is the global concatenation of this grand cacophony of information radiations upon the world? And to what extent does that condition not only affect the proximate tangible environment, but also the ineffable Source from which it derives? Perhaps this imagery is akin to that William James had in mind when he referred to this mind/environment colloquy as "the blooming, buzzing confusion."[9] In any case, we now have in hand a conceptual model that can employ either hard physical or soft psychical elements not only to enable ongoing two-way communication and influence between mind and matter, but also to establish a subtle network of awareness and interdependence among all of the participating minds and substances, thereby elevating the consciousness component of the information dialogue from an individual to a collective level that may merit capitalization of that term, as well. Perhaps even more importantly, we may have the mechanism for individual and collective Consciousness to imprint itself on the universal Source. (Figure 2 offers one schematic representation of the Source/Consciousness resonant sensory system concept just proposed.)

At this point we might attempt to estimate quantitatively the amount of information of all physical and psychical forms currently permeating our environment that has been processed through the various resonant channels just proposed. We shall eschew that ambitious effort in favor of simply noting that any and all information that is actually extracted from the Source *via* the consciousness sensory systems is subject to such resonant reflections, and thereby couples these two ultimate entities to some small degree. What portion of this coupling is materialistically brain-based in character, what portion is psychically based in the subtler modalities, how these two genres complement and inform one another, and how the consciousness employs its brain utility in all of this, remain major issues. But direct physical processes for consciousness to influence the evolution of its Source of reality seem to exist.

We shall also pass over the multitude of possible secondary loops that connect our minds to the environment, other than to acknowledge that when we receive information through one or more of the sensory channels, mental processing may dictate a response that returns information to the environment in some other modality. When danger intrudes, I may run, resist, or perspire; when my dog nudges me, I may speak kindly to him, pat him affectionately, or take him for a walk; when I hear great music, I may smile, sigh, or even sing along. In all cases, my reactions are returning some information to the environment, and these indirect couplings, like the more direct resonances within the individual sensory channels, greatly proliferate the grand Consciousness/Source dialogue.

Filter Tuning

We have already noted the severe physiological restrictions imposed by our sensory equipment on the quality and quantity of information we can extract from the Source. Some of these can be improved by selective training or genetic aptitudes that favor particular modes of information acquisition, such as the enhanced sensitivities of accomplished or gifted musicians to particular tonalities; the capacities of great artists, designers, or organizers to grasp designs and patterns; or the abilities of superstar athletes to react to critical aspects of their games more rapidly and accurately than their competitors. Most of us will also concede that our prevailing subjective states of mind can color the way we perceive any events and respond to them; both are clearly conditioned by our purposes, expectations, moods, prejudices, and attitudes. Beyond these short-term sensitivities, various longer-lived cultural and psychological filters operate as well. As an extreme example, it has been reported that some pre-Columbian Native Americans literally could not see the large sailing vessels of the first European explorers to broach their shores because they had no cultural precedent for such an event or object, and no appropriate words in their vocabulary. Thus, in their context of reality, such things simply did not exist.

This blindness to items that are inconsistent with expectations has been demonstrated repeatedly under rigorous scientific conditions. A number of studies in perceptual psychology have established that people engaged in structured activities typically do not see unexpected, or even bizarre events that may intrude, even though these are clearly visible to uninvolved observers.[10] For example, in the classic Bruner and Postman experiments in perceptual psychology, subjects presented with pictures of playing cards at rapid intervals consistently misperceived incongruent cards having mismatched suits and colors.[11] The implausible, frequently symbolic or mystical imagery that characterizes dreams, meditations, hallucinations, and other altered or visionary states of awareness are probably attributable to the suspension or alteration of the sensory filters we have cultivated for use in our ordinary waking state. Outside the realm of human experience, it is evident that many other creatures, despite utilizing sensory equipment similar to our own, respond substantially differently to given environmental situations, depending on the behavioral heritages and enculturation that have tuned their own filters to particular functional purposes.

What we wish to pursue here, however, is a more proactive form of filter tuning wherein a particular physical perception, its inferred conceptualization, the patterns of conscious and unconscious response it stimulates, and the corresponding environmental reactions it induces may be altered more deliberately. This is the sort of process the celebrated Cherokee medicine man, Rolling Thunder, alluded to when he cryptically summarized his apparent ability to manipulate external events as "there's an attitude you can take."[12] We also confront it in the mystifying efficacy of the placebo, or in the demonstrable improvements in physical strength and control derivable from martial arts protocols. The deliberate use of hallucinogenic substances to alter patterns of awareness and allow access to alternative realities also has extensive cultural precedents throughout recorded history.

Our particular point here is that at whatever level and by whatever practice they may be invoked, such tuning techniques may condition both directions of the two-way information traffic discussed in the previous section, i.e., not only may they alter the quantity and quality of the information reaching the consciousness from its source environment, but also, via the resonant reflection processes or indirect response mechanisms just proposed, they may condition the information transmitted to the latter from the former as well. Thus, the holistic information loop of vital conversation between the two is to this extent responsive to the consciousness filters we choose to impose, and it is to these that we must turn to seek practical benefits from our composite model. The benefits we seek, of course, are better understanding of the Consciousness/Source dialogue, leading to its more effective utilization in our daily lives.

At this point the reader might reasonably anticipate some cookbook recipe for tuning the filters of consciousness to achieve more incisive penetration into its Source environment, thereby extracting from it an expanded range of information and experience and/or altering it in some observable way. Unfortunately, our 25 years of laboratory work have persuaded us that this aspiration is not so neatly obtainable, given the fundamentally unspecifiable natures of both the Consciousness and the Source. Although our minds acquire information in an inherently subjective fashion, in our Western culture they have been cultivated to conceptualize and express their experience and activity primarily via precise "this, not that" objective discriminations, largely neglecting the intangible subjective dimensions that can blur those distinctions. In contrast, the Source exists as a sea of ineffable, complexly intertwined potentialities that rooted in irreducible uncertainty that defies objective specification. Thus, the same impedance mismatch that limits our interactions with the Source also encumbers our efforts to devise and describe means for controlling the filtering process to enhance our access to it. Hence, rather than a step-by-step recipe, we can offer only an assortment of empirical insights and derived speculations that may seem to some of our precise scientific colleagues to be rather vague and esoteric, and to some of our more intuitive colleagues too mechanistic and constrained. A similar disclaimer must pertain to any effort to specify the subjective strategies actually employed by the participants in our experiments in generating the anomalous results that have stimulated these theoretical musings. These tactics are typically so intuitive and personal that they defy any attempts at generalization. We therefore must leave it to our readers to create their own recipes from these raw ingredients, with no assurances of effectiveness or replicability from one application to the next.

Within these caveats, five features strike us as being essential to any productive filter-tuning strategy:

1. The acceptance of the possibility of alternative realities;
2. The generous utilization of conceptual metaphors by which to access them;
3. The achievement of resonance, in both its objective and subjective senses;
4. The tolerance of uncertainty as a *sine qua non* in any creative interaction between Consciousness and the Source;
5. The replacement of conceptual duality by complementarity as the fundamental dynamic for the construction of reality.

In the remainder of this paper we shall strive to communicate our own sense of the essence of these ingredients, insofar as they can be linguistically represented.

1) *Alternative realities: The power of perspective*

It is the theory which decides what we can observe.
— ALBERT EINSTEIN[13]

The initial requisite for any proactive form of consciousness filter tuning is the recognition that the reality one is experiencing is only one possible expression of the multitude of potential realities available from the Source. Only with this conviction in place is it possible to suspend or deprioritize the particular perspective being deployed, to allow activation of other options. Under ordinary circumstances, however, we usually are so preoccupied with translating our experiences into objective descriptions that we fail to acknowledge at a conscious level the fundamentally subjective nature of those experiences and the accessibility of alternative representations of them. Rather, such alternatives are assigned relative probabilities *via* an unconscious mental algorithm that incorporates such factors as past experience, expectation, desire, or fear, along with the immediate purpose or intention. As these unconscious calculations converge on the interpretation that seems most likely within the prevailing perspective, an appropriate filter is thereby imposed. Typically, it is only at this point that the attribution of experiential meaning shifts to a conscious level.

Among the many unconscious factors that contribute to such mental sorting, the prevailing values of our culture play powerful, albeit subtle, roles. The primary objectives of most socialization and educational processes are the encouragement of individual beliefs and behavior that are consistent with the values and purposes of the collective, so that our personal worldviews align with the perspectives of the particular sociocultural milieux, peer groups, or professional hierarchies in which we are immersed. Each of these dispenses its own conceptual vocabulary and priorities to bias the weighting factors in our unconscious mental calculations toward those representations of experience that are most consistent with the established beliefs and goals of that system, thereby reinforcing the coherence of its collective structure. Any "thinking outside the box" undermines the system's control over individual experience and action and is discouraged *via* stern social sanctions of rejection or exclusion from group membership. For humans, as well as for other social animals, such treatment is usually sufficiently painful to enforce conformity to the "appropriate" information processing strategies and consequent behavior. Eventually, these constraints become so internalized and automated that most alternative perspectives, and their associated reactions, are not even recognized. In extreme cases, they can engender a variety of physical and emotional pathologies, including neuroses, psychoses, or muscular armoring[14] that can further limit or distort responses to stimuli. Given such cultural obedience training, the deployment of other interpretations, *i.e.*, other consciousness filters, requires a strong act of will, plus an acceptance of the psychological consequences of deviating from the security of the collective belief system. Only then are the rules governing the creation of reality recognized as mutable, rather than absolute, a realization that initially can be emotionally discomforting. But this is the inescapable price if we are to purchase the ability to extract from the potentiality of the Source a physical actuality that reacts to our conscious intentions.

In this processing, the organizing mind may apply a wide variety of conceptual filters to the boundless, undifferentiated potentiality that is the Source, whereby the emergence of countless corresponding realities are possible, perhaps reminiscent of the "many worlds" concept of some physical theorists. When the probing mind articulates an intention, *e.g.*, "Let there be X," that intention is automatically associated with a sense of its meaning within any given frame of reference. A sequence of discrimination is then initiated whereby X is successively distinguished from all associations that that mind regards as clearly not-X. Even with these eliminations, however, an assortment of potential associations with X still remains, each of which has some probability of pertinence in the prevailing reference frame, thereby constituting a kind of subjective probability distribution. As each of these possibilities is considered and rejected, the definition of X becomes more precise and the mind moves from a state of uncertainty, where its sense of control is tenuous, to one where it feels more comfortable, with an experience that seems more orderly and predictable. With the continued reduction in uncertainty, the residual interpretational possibilities that survive this elimination process take on increasingly higher likelihoods of being meaningful information, and the variance of the distribution of meanings narrows. One familiar example of this process might be the systematic solving of a crossword puzzle, where more than one word can fit a designated set of squares for which the clue is intentionally ambiguous.

Since most of the critical early distinctions that establish and maintain the frame of reference guiding the selection process take place at a non-conscious level, the conscious mind is rarely exposed to the less probable options. It makes its choices only among those alternatives that seem more likely within that frame of reference, where habitual, enculturated definitions of reality already have been well established. But if a different context of meaning is invoked, the distribution function of possibilities shifts to some degree, depending on how radically that alternative deviates from the conventional one. In a reference frame comprising a major change of perspective, the most likely outcome could well be out in the tails of the standard mind-set distribution; conversely, the most likely events in the latter context could be quite unlikely in the former. In other words, alteration of the prevailing context of meaning to one where an ostensibly lower probability option becomes dominant is essential for effecting significant change in one's reality.

As a particularly simple example of such an exchange of reality, consider the well-known Necker cube visual illusion. In this case, confronted by two equally likely perspectives, the mind finds itself in a superposition of states, shifting back and forth between the two available possibilities as it tries to determine which is the "correct" image. In such a delicately balanced situation, the slightest subjective bias toward one interpretation or the other can shift the equilibrium. Once this happens, the discriminatory function takes over and decides on "this, not that," and a "reality" is established. In this example, where the initial probabilities are essentially equal, the process could equally well have converged on the alternative reality. In more complex situations where the competing interpretations have very different probabilities, however, opting for the less likely interpretation requires a more substantial shift of perspective, which, when achieved, engenders a correspondingly larger change in the information patterns propagating between the mind and its environment. This may well be the controlling factor in limiting the scale of anomalous effects that characterize the laboratory-based studies, where for successful achievement the human participant must attempt from the outset to set aside the scientific "impossibility" of the assigned task and to invoke a reference frame in which the probability of the anomalous accomplishment is optimized.

It is interesting to note that, in contrast to our Judeo-Christian-scientific tradition, some cultures actually encourage the exploration of alternative interpretations of experience as a strategy for developing self-awareness and deeper understanding of the relationship between the individual and the environment. For example, certain Native American and East Asian traditions maintain that one cannot fully understand an experience until it has been considered from at least seven different points of view.[15] In this sense, the terminology "alternative reality" might better be replaced by "multiple reality," which also befits our particular application of this concept. While we shall not attempt to describe here the various strategies deployed by such societies in this process, nor to provide an anthropological/sociological critique of their effectiveness, their applications within their own cultural contexts confirm that our narrower Western approach to the interpretation of experience is not the only option.

2) The magic of metaphor

> *I will open my mouth in parables,*
> *I will utter things hidden since the creation of the world.*
> — PSALMS 78:21[16]

Note that throughout this paper we have resorted to metaphor several times, invoking the familiar properties of "space capsules," "distribution functions," "crossword puzzles" "Necker cubes," *etc.*, in an attempt to clarify the intended meanings of potentially unclear abstract concepts. Metaphor is, in fact, a powerful technique for resolving or utilizing ambiguity in order to convey subtle nuances of meaning or to express otherwise ineffable experience. It stimulates the associative capabilities of the mind, *vis-à-vis* its discriminatory techniques that attempt to minimize uncertainty by assigning names, categories, and functions to subjective experience in order to reduce it to more precise objective description. Discrimination, the tool of logic, presents the consciousness with sequences of "either/or" decisions that inevitably lead to a dualistic view of reality; association, the tool of creativity, raises awareness of possible connections between apparently disparate interpretations and allows the consciousness to move beyond duality in representing its experience. Metaphor thus encourages the mind to pay more attention to the similarities among various interpretational options than to their differences, and thereby empowers rather than reduces the uncertainty, as discussed more fully below. (This is the essence of the so-called Law of Similarity that played a central role in the ancient practice of alchemy.)

In this spirit, let us return to a quantum mechanical metaphor we introduced in previous publications,[5,17] wherein we spoke of reality as the product of the interaction of consciousness with its environment. In that representation we intentionally defined consciousness very loosely, "to subsume all categories of human experience ... including those commonly termed 'conscious,' 'subconscious,' 'superconscious,' or 'unconscious,' without presumption of specific psychological or physiological mechanisms." Our similarly comprehensive definition of environment included "all circumstances and influences affecting the consciousness that it perceives to be separate from itself, including, as appropriate, its own physical corpus and its physical habitat, as well as all intangible psychological, social, and historical influences that bear upon it." Thus, reality was regarded as the product of a consciousness/environment interface that was intrinsically subjective and situation-specific, so that the Source could only be perceived through the prevailing filters of consciousness, much like the shadows in Plato's cave.[18]

In applying this quantum mechanical metaphor, we also had occasion to define a "consciousness atom," using a set of spherical "consciousness coordinates" labeled "range," "attitude," and "orientation," which proved useful in representing various states of consciousness. For our purposes here, we can identify "range" with the emotional intensity, "attitude" with the point of view, and "orientation" with the context prevailing in a given interaction of consciousness with the extended environment of its Source. Alteration of these subjective coordinates of the mind can affect the quality of the experience by fine-tuning the resonant channels of the physical and psychical senses through which the consciousness observes and interprets the stimuli imposing on it.

As an exercise in exploring this tactic, consider the word "green" (since cognitive scientists, philosophers of science, and theoretical physicists are fond of using color as an example of a quale). Note how the consciousness coordinates adjust to the following associations: green light; green thumb; greenhouse; greenhorn; Greenpeace; green about the gills; Green Man; green with envy; greenbacks; Green Bay Packers; wearin' o' the green; *etc.* The concept of "greenness" thus extends over a range of metaphorical implications and associated subjective meanings that goes well beyond the standard physical definition of light with a wavelength of approximately 520 nanometers. There is no single "correct" meaning, nor is there anything that precludes conscious deployment of any of the many possible meanings to color one's desired reality.

This multivalent ambiguity is the essence of art, of poetry, and perhaps most ubiquitously, of humor. Virtually all jokes, cartoons, and whimsy utilize metaphor in some form, to poke fun at our foibles, fads, and follies in a friendly, unthreatening fashion that encourages fresh attention and releases creativity. Consciousness invokes such attitudinal lubricant to facilitate adjustment of its contextual filters, thus enhancing the propagation of the incoming information from the environment. In so doing, the reflection of information back into the environment is also enhanced, and in this way the mind's intention, or any other of its subjective priorities, can be imposed on the Source, and hence on the reality constructed from it.

While our Princeton Engineering Anomalies Research (PEAR) program has never pursued any systematic study of the subjective strategies employed by its experimental operators, it has been evident from personal communications and casual observations that metaphorical techniques are commonly deployed. These have included frank anthropomorphism, *i.e.*, attributing living qualities to the experimental devices; linguistic association, *via* creation of lists of words free-associated with the intentions currently being asserted; or visual association of the feedback displays with images of living processes, such as perceiving a high-intention cumulative deviation trace as a bird or plane taking off into the air, or a low-intention trace as that of a fish diving into the depths. Remote perception percipients have described their tactics in metaphors as well, such as staring at a blank screen waiting for a movie to begin, or opening a window onto a desired scene. In both classes of experiment, metaphor appears to be an effective technique for shifting the perceived context of the task at hand from one that seems impossible to one where it is an attainable, even if unlikely, possibility.

3) *The role of resonance*

> *It's Love that makes the world go round.*
> — W.S. GILBERT, *IOLANTHE*, ACT II[19]

One of the most powerful and commonly employed metaphors to link the world of objective, physical events with the world of subjective, emotional experience is that of "resonance." Examples of resonant oscillatory interactions abound in all manner of mechanical, electrical, optical, and chemical systems, and characteristically entail substantial departures in behavior from those of their separate components. The signal-to-noise ratio and sharp selectivities of conventional communications systems, musical instruments, and lasers of all types; the destructive oscillations of aerospace vehicles and of the Tacoma Narrows bridge; the microscale interactions that bind atoms into molecules; and the pulsations of stars and galaxies are all critically dependent on various forms of internal and external resonance. But the conceptual nomenclature is equally apt in capturing the subjective essence of interpersonal bonds between lovers, siblings, parents and children, and friends; of hyper-productive relationships between individuals and their household, computational, artistic, athletic, or automotive equipment; or even of the intensive personal associations with particular social purposes, projects, or missions. In all these contexts, the emergent resonant experiences, products, or performances can significantly exceed those achieved by the individual partners acting alone.

It is not unreasonable, therefore, that our attempts to represent and to enhance the interactions of Consciousness with its environmental Source would similarly benefit from the establishment of some form of resonance between them. The problem, of course, is the identification of some common conceptual platform on which these two apparently disparate entities may join effectively in a resonant dialogue. Our suggestion is that the requisite exchange may draw on the wealth of potential information resident in the complex, chaotic uncertainty of the Source, in concert with the extensive repertoire of potential interpretations or meanings which the mind may contribute.

Resorting again to our quantum mechanical metaphor, it was there suggested that just as the binding energy of a physical molecule derives from the indistinguishability of the two participating valence electrons, in a similar fashion the anomalous experiences that can occur among people who are "on the same wavelength," or who are engaged in resonant human/machine interactions, also may derive from the surrender of distinct individual identities in favor of a more complex "molecular" composite. For our purposes here, we propose further extension of this analogy to the establishment of resonant oscillations of experience between the potential information chambers of the mind and of the Source.

To develop this proposition a bit further, we might note that any experience of emotional resonance is closely associated with the perceived meaningfulness or importance of the interaction. It is the visceral feeling that shifts the filters of consciousness from those of passive, objective observation to ones of proactive, subjective participation, and this participatory immersion in the experience modifies its perceived reality. This immersion may be enhanced by progressive elimination of the specific discriminations that distinguish Self from not-Self, until the Consciousness approaches pure experience, a state the Zen masters refer to as "samadhi." Such a state is ineffable by definition, but those who have known it, and the traditions that have cultivated it, maintain that it is the ultimate reality. Some have described it as the sense of being immersed in the unmanifest potential of the universe where everything and anything is possible. Clearly, this is a very different perspective of reality than that experienced through the usual filters of perception, and its achievement may elude most of us. But many of us have experienced more modest forms of subjective resonance, such as being in love, or Buber's "I and Thou" relationship,[20] where two previously independent "I's" comprise a shared "We" that can change the perception and interpretation of reality. In essence, in altering its definition of Self, consciousness attains propitious reference frames for modifying the information dialogue with its environment, and thereby enhances its ability to alter the probabilities of physical events.

This "I/Thou" connection is frequently mentioned by PEAR's successful operators, many of whom seem to develop intimate emotional relationships with the experimental devices, akin to those felt in other forms of intense human/machine interactions, *e.g.*, with a musical instrument, an automobile, or a piece of athletic equipment. One particularly touching expression of this occurred when the random mechanical cascade apparatus, known to its friends and operators as "Murphy," had to be shut down for repairs and one of the operators sent it a personal get-well card. Such resonance effects also manifest in the remote perception experiments in instances where the assigned target holds a strong personal attraction for the participants, or where the percipient and agent are personally involved with one another, and our methods of analysis have taken explicit precautions to preclude illegitimate information leakage from such causes.

4) The use of uncertainty

The more alternatives there are, the more uncertain the outcome.
The more uncertainty, the greater the potential for information
transmission.
— LACHMAN *ET AL.*[21]

It is the ethic of virtually all scientific investigation to strive for precision: precision of measurement; precision of analysis; sharpness of conceptualization and interpretation; maximization of the "signal-to-noise" ratio. Yet, in the particular scientific context we are addressing here, this otherwise commendable zeal for precision of technique and its corresponding refinement of interpretation and prediction paradoxically can become a double-edged scholarly sword. Not only have we accumulated extensive empirical evidence testifying that excessive rigor in experimental design and analysis tends to reduce rather than to enhance consciousness-related anomalous effects, but there are also some indications that the uncertainty itself may be an essential ingredient for the generation of the anomalous phenomena. We attempted to demonstrate a particular example of this empirical enigma in considerable detail, and to explore its broader implications for anomalies experiments in the article entitled "Information and Uncertainty in Remote Perception Research."[22] There we concluded that in anomalies research, as in any expression of human creativity, it is essential to establish a balance between rigor and flexibility, discipline and innovation, precision and ambiguity, if one is to navigate between the Scylla of sterility and the Charybdis of chaos.

It appears that the narrow channel that separates these complementary extremes follows an epistemological uncertainty principle similar to that which Heisenberg introduced as limiting the precision of observation of conjugate physical properties, such as momentum and position or energy and time. It is also relevant to note that one technical representation of the Source domain, namely the "zero-point field" that is postulated to permeate the universe with vast energetic potentiality, ultimately derives from the imposition of this same uncertainty principle on atomic-scale harmonic oscillators. In other words, both the objective physical world and the subjective creative processes of consciousness seem to be constrained, and enabled, by the same intrinsic ambiguity.

Uncertainty inescapably characterizes the interface where the two complementary coordinate systems of mind and matter overlap, creating the interpenetration from which reality emerges. In any given interaction, each of these partners enters in a state where information is still only potential, waiting for consciousness to select a frame of reference within which to address the Source, impose appropriate subjective and objective filters, and thereby actualize it as an experience. This done, the event can be labeled and communicated, but in so doing any alternative perspective is dismissed, and with it any information that perspective might have conveyed. It is only in the prior phase of unresolved uncertainty, at the margins of reality, that consciousness has provisional access not only to those realities with which it is familiar, but also to the vaster uncertainty that constitutes the ultimate Source. Progressive modification of these filters with each new application further complicates the task and, given the intrinsic uncertainty that attends any chosen frame of reference, it is inevitable that all determinations of reality are inherently probabilistic. It is not surprising, therefore, that replicable results in anomalies research remain so elusive.

Notwithstanding, many experienced PEAR operators have come not only to recognize and accept this inherent uncertainty, but also to utilize it in their data-generating tactics. They speak of avoiding personal attachment to the outcome of any particular trial or run, preferring instead to "flow" with the indeterminacy itself. Or as one operator expressed it, "... when it goes where I want, I flow with it. When it doesn't, I try to break the flow and give it a chance to get back in resonance with me." Successful percipients in the remote perception experiments likewise recognize that any valid information they may acquire about their targets is convected on a background of uncertainty and possible misinformation, to which they should maintain an attitude of "high indifference."

5) *The case for conceptual complementarity*

> *Contraria sunt complementa.*
> — Coat of Arms of Niels Bohr[23]

Niels Bohr first proposed that the celebrated and perplexing wave/particle dualities appearing in atomic-scale physical interactions could be rationalized only by regarding these two modes of behavior not as contradictory but as "complementary," in the sense that each displayed a legitimate aspect of the interaction, and both were necessary to specify it completely. And it was Bohr himself who subsequently offered a sweeping generalization of this physical complementarity principle into much broader philosophical and cultural dimensions: "... the nature of our consciousness," he asserted, "brings about a complementary relationship, in all domains of knowledge, between the analysis of a concept and its immediate application."[24] This huge extrapolation was fully supported by Bohr's colleagues Heisenberg and Pauli, and in their philosophical writings all three of them invoked numerous metaphors to illustrate this generic relationship.[25]

The magnitude of revision in conceptual and operational perspective predicated by this radical proposition should not be undervalued. Until that time, virtually all Western thought, including physics and metaphysics, had been dominated by Cartesian duality and was largely content with absolute and polar measures. Classical philosophy spoke of the dialectic tension between thesis and antithesis; theological discourse divided the world into domains of good and evil, spirit and matter; and this polarization of reality was reflected in most common conceptualizations as well. In this cultural mindset, the "mind/body problem" remained at least as intractable as the "wave/particle duality." Then, from the world of hard scientific formalism, came this radical proposition that some of

these sharp dichotomies should be replaced by more subtle and sophisticated complementarities, wherein arbitrary proportions of superficially
disparate properties might profitably be combined to deal with given situations. Despite its counterintuitive character, considerable theoretical el-
egance, as well as pragmatic benefit, in modeling both the physical world
and cultural attitudes was obtained thereby. We suggest that extension of
this principle into the yet more challenging domain of consciousness mechanics can prove to be similarly beneficial.

Following this lead, we extend our metaphorical license to propose
that many of the filters of consciousness that we have been addressing here
also may be complementary to one another in this more general sense.
Grouped in appropriate pairs, such attitudes and perspectives entail the
same orthogonal irreducibility, yet can provide the same conceptual re-
inforcement as the conjugate physical quantities, and can serve similarly
to define the operational spaces of consciousness. It may well be that this
relationship also pertains to the essence of the mind/matter interface itself,
and to all of the modes of interaction between consciousness and its environment. The primary benefit of a complementary approach to the filter-
tuning process is that the consciousness conjugates need not be competi-
tive characteristics, but can be combined in arbitrary proportions as befits
a given situation. Participation in an experience does not preclude observation of it, nor do subjectivity and objectivity stand in contradiction to
one another. In fact, once the uncertainty injunction that rules out precise
simultaneous specification is accepted, it may actually help define the op-
timal balance between any pair of consciousness conjugates. Our research
strategy has attempted to exploit this complementarity by encouraging all
PEAR staff members to serve as operators and by treating all operators as
coexperimenters, thus blending the perspectives of objective assessment
and subjective immersion in a hands-on experience of how the filters of
perception can alter the reality being experienced.

Given our extensive musings elsewhere about the complementarity of consciousness in a variety of contexts,[5,12,26] we shall here add only
two other examples that are particularly pertinent to the purpose of this
paper: the complementarity of intentionality and resonance, and that of
Consciousness and Source themselves. Intentionality and resonance both
are essential for determining the nature of an experience, although the

former is explicitly proactive and the latter intrinsically responsive. Intention imposes the filter through which the experience will be interpreted; resonance enhances the consciousness participation in the experience. Asserting an intention is essential for limiting the potential information to a given context, but it is the subjective immersion in the interaction that modifies the consciousness coordinates and thereby the meaning of the resultant information. By establishing an appropriate balance between these two conjugate states of mind, the corresponding uncertainty becomes available as a medium wherein the probabilities of possible interpretations may be altered to manifest the desired reality.

But the ultimate pair of complementary conjugates, of course, is that of Consciousness itself and the ineffable Source in which it is immersed, and with which it intersects to generate all manner of experience. Despite their vast disparity of character and function, it is they who comprise the universe of life, and they who are the parents of all reality.

Summary

On the basis of a quarter century of laboratory and field experimentation on consciousness-correlated physical anomalies, extensive informal personal discussions with our operators and other colleagues, and a number of previous attempts to pose conceptual models consistent with the empirical results, we have offered here another metaphorical perspective on those aspects of the mind/matter dialogue that may underlie its anomalous manifestations. Like its predecessors, this model deviates from causal physical logic, which may actually be the culprit in the anomalous appearance of such phenomena, in favor of a more generic comprehensive approach to the creation of tangible reality. More specifically, we have proposed that the normal physiological sensory channels that provide our material brains with information about our physical environment are routinely supplemented by various subjective modalities that inform a more extended, less physicalistic consciousness. Both of these categories are posited to have two-way capabilities, *i.e.*, they comprise direct resonant couplings between the mind and its environment, as well as stimulate a variety of indirect responses, all of which are capable of transmitting information in either direction. We also have proposed that our palpable physical surround is an emergent property of a much vaster intangible reservoir of potential information, which we have labeled the Source, and that the emergence is enabled by the resonant coupling of this Source with its cosmic complement, the organizing Consciousness. Finally, we have suggested that the intensity of that resonance is limited by the physiological and mental filters imposed upon our objective and subjective sensory channels by various physical, cultural, and emotional factors.

We then turned to explore possible means of relaxing or tuning of those filters to enhance the resonant dialogue between Consciousness and the Source, thereby allowing richer experiences to unfold, and providing some insight into the nature of the Source itself and of the extensive Consciousness. Possible strategies for such pro-active filter tuning, while inherently difficult to specify and communicate, were suggested to entail a constellation of counter-conventional attitudes and beliefs. These include openness to alternative interpretations of experience; invocation of interdisciplinary metaphors by which to express and reify those alternatives; surrender to resonance with those realities and thereby to their Source; recognition and acceptance of uncertainty as an intrinsic characteristic of both the Source and the Consciousness, and thus as an essential ingredient in the creation of any reality; and relinquishment of "either/or" mental duality in favor of creative complementarity of concepts, especially those of intention and resonance, and of Consciousness and the Source themselves.

These are not trivial alterations of our attitude toward the establishment of reality, and collectively they appear to be at fundamental odds with the conventional scientific tenets of objectivity, replicability, falsifiability, quantifiability, causality, and determinism. Certainly, they are not the usual attributes drilled into young scholars aspiring to standard scientific careers. But they are consistent with, indeed impelled by, the accumulated research evidence that has repeatedly verified the existence of mind/matter phenomena that refuse to be accommodated by the traditional assumptions, and they have proven to be productive, indeed necessary, expansions of scientific attitude for their systematic study. Most especially, as it becomes increasingly apparent that physical reality can be objectively affected by subjective factors that usually are disregarded in the prevailing scientific paradigm, it becomes correspondingly imperative that these be acknowledged and formalized if the study of such anomalies, and indeed of Consciousness itself, is to be brought to both rigorous and productive research. The most direct means for such acknowledgment would seem to be the generalization of what heretofore have been regarded as the objective scientific principles to more comprehensive forms that explicitly include attitudinal factors, and thus can apply to these elusive, subjectively correlated, but nonetheless profound and powerful phenomena.[6]

In pursuing this transition, it may be reassuring to recall that while the prevailing secular premises of contemporary Western science are relatively recent in the history of human thought, they nonetheless have their roots in medieval alchemy wherein the consciousness of the practitioner was accepted as a proactive agent in the study of nature. Indeed, Francis Bacon, Isaac Newton, and most of the other original architects of the scientific method all were practicing alchemists who clearly respected the role of consciousness in the generation of physical and chemical phenomena.[5] The subsequent gradual rejection of subjectivity in science was driven by an increasing desire for predictive certainty, but it came at the cost of excluding the observing mind from the process under observation. Now, in much the same fashion that the augmentation of our observational capabilities through more sensitive instrumentation forced extensions of the classical view of a mechanistic universe into relativistic and quantum formulations, major refinements of our contemporary information-processing tools are forcing us to re-invite the subjective aspects of information into the workshop of science, and thereby to recover the baby we threw out with the bath water more than three centuries ago.

Acknowledgments

The authors here record their appreciation to a number of colleagues who have contributed their thoughts to the evolution of this essay, most notably the members of the International Consciousness Research Laboratories (ICRL) consortium and its PEARtree affiliate; Prof. Henry Bauer, Mr. Ray Buckman, and Ms. Gina Leone; and, of course, all the members of the PEAR laboratory staff.

The research programs of the PEAR laboratory have been supported in part by gifts from Mr. Laurance Rockefeller, Mr. Richard Adams, The Lifebridge Foundation, the Institut für Grenzgebiete der Psychologie und Psychohygiene, the Izunome Association, and other donors who prefer to remain anonymous.

References

1. John Milton. *Paradise Lost: The Third Book*. The Harvard Classics, 1909–14.
2. Robert G. Jahn and Brenda J. Dunne. "A modular model of mind/matter manifestations (M^5)." *Journal of Scientific Exploration, 15*, No. 3 (2001). pp. 299–329.
3. Robert G. Jahn. "M*: Vector representation of the subliminal seed regime of M^5." *Journal of Scientific Exploration, 16*, No. 3 (2002). pp. 341–357.
4. Arthur Eddington. *The Nature of the Physical World*. The University of Michigan Press, 1978.
5. Robert G. Jahn and Brenda J. Dunne. *Margins of Reality: The Role of Consciousness in the Physical World*. New York: Harcourt Brace Jovanovich, 1988, and many references therein.
6. Robert G. Jahn and Brenda J. Dunne. "Science of the subjective." *Journal of Scientific Exploration, 11*, No. 2 (1997). pp. 201–224.
7. Robert G. Jahn, Brenda J. Dunne, Roger D. Nelson, York H. Dobyns, and G. Johnston Bradish. "Correlations of random binary sequences with pre-stated operator intention: A review of a 12-year program." *Journal of Scientific Exploration, 11*, No. 3 (1997). pp. 345–367.
8. Fritz-Albert Popp and Lev Beloussov. *Integrative Biophysics*. Dordrecht — London: Kluwer Academic Publishers, 2002.
9. William James. *Some Problems of Philosophy: A Beginning of an Introduction to Philosophy*. New York: Longmans, Green, 1911.
10. Daniel J. Simons and Christopher F. Chabris. "Gorillas in our midst: Sustained inattentional blindness for dynamic events." *Perception, 28*, No. 9 (1999). pp. 1059–1074.
11. Jerome S. Bruner and Leo J. Postman. "On the perception of incongruity: A paradigm." *Journal of Personality, 18*, No. 2 (1949). pp. 206–223.
12. Doug Boyd. *Rolling Thunder*. Dell Publishing, 1976.
13. Albert Einstein. In Werner Heisenberg, *Physics and Beyond*. New York: Harper & Row, 1971. p. 63.
14. Wilhelm Reich. *Character Analysis*. New York: Orgone Institute Press, 1949.
15. Standing Bear Wilkes. Personal communication, 2004.
16. The Bible (New International Version). *Psalms* 78:21.
17. Robert G. Jahn and Brenda J. Dunne. "On the quantum mechanics of consciousness, with application to anomalous phenomena." *Foundations of Physics, 16*, No. 8 (1985). pp. 721–772.
18. Plato. *The Republic*, Book 6.
19. William S. Gilbert. *Iolanthe*, Act II.
20. Martin Buber. *I and Thou*. Charles Scribner's Sons, 1970.

21. Roy Lachman, Janet L. Lachman, and Earl C. Butterfield. *Cognitive Psychology and Information Processing: An Introduction.* Hillsdale, NJ: Lawrence Erlbaum Associates, 1979. Chapter 5, p. 137.

22. Brenda J. Dunne and Robert G. Jahn. "Information and uncertainty in remote perception research." *Journal of Scientific Exploration, 17,* No. 2 (2003). pp. 207–241.

23. Coat of Arms of Niels Bohr; A. I. P. Niels Bohr Library/Margrethe Bohr Collection, p. 269.

24. Niels Bohr. *Atomic Theory and the Description of Nature.* Cambridge: The University Press, 1961. p. 20.

25. Robert G. Jahn and Brenda J. Dunne. "On the Quantum Mechanics of Consciousness with Application to Anomalous Phenomena: Appendix B: Collected Thoughts on the Role of Consciousness in the Physical Representation of Reality." Technical Report PEAR 83005. Princeton Engineering Anomalies Research, Princeton University, Princeton, NJ, June 1984.

26. Robert G. Jahn. "The Complementarity of Consciousness." Technical Note PEAR 91006. Princeton Engineering Anomalies Research, Princeton University, Princeton, NJ, December 1991.

Four Essays*

William Eddy, Jr.
Adjunct Professor Emeritus, University of Vermont
West Burke, Vermont

Indoors and Outdoors

Some years ago there was a popular cartoonist by the name of Walt Kelly. Readers may recall his character Pogo, a small, furry, 'possum-like figure from the Okefenokee Swamp, who shared with his friends Albert the alligator and a turtle named Churchy LaFemme a variety of adventures that mirrored the human condition in America during some difficult times in the '50s and '60s.

Like many humorists and satirists, Walt Kelly was a serious and thoughtful person. Before he became well known, I recall hearing him give a talk on the freshness of perception of the very young. He felt that little children had not yet learned to project already predetermined meanings onto their experiences, as we adults tend to do. By way of illustration, he described how one day his young son had come up to him and asked, "Daddy, why is it that people always build their houses outdoors?"

It is a lovely question, and it has many implications.

In our culture, that doorway represents a kind of illusory dividing line. Inside is our world; outside is what we have learned to call nature. So ingrained is this dividing line created by the doorway that we refer to someone who likes to climb mountains and hunt, to canoe and fish, as an "outdoorsman." We even have magazines called *Outdoors* and

---

• Editor's Note: The following brief essays were originally published in *The Other Side of the World: Essays and Stories on Mind and Nature* (Mind-Nature.com, 2002),[1] a collection of discourses that illuminate the landscapes of the mind. The author has kindly given his permission to reprint four of these in this volume, each of which illustrates how verbal metaphors shape human thought and challenges us to reconsider our relationship to the natural environment. They provide provocative examples of how profoundly the filters of culture and language can influence our perceptions of the world.

Outdoor Life. Thus, for us, that doorway has become an important frame of reference, but for the most part an unconscious one.

I tell the story of Walt Kelly's son and his delightful question because in that strange dualism of "outdoors" and "indoors" we have the opportunity to see clearly two elements, each of which provides the environment from which the other may be seen. In fact, oddly enough, neither one can exist without the other. If you attempt to remove one part, the other disappears as well.

A similar relationship exists between other pairs of concepts like "front" and "back" or "up" and "down." And is it possible that the idea of something being "infinite" really has no meaning except as it starts at a particular point in space and time called the "finite?" Could a similar relation be said to exist between "consciousness" and "unconsciousness," or between "maleness" and "femaleness?"

My point might be better expressed as a corollary applicable to all perception: it is impossible to perceive any environment except from the context of another one. We can find any number of proverbs that illustrate this. "You never miss the water 'til the well runs dry," or "only the blind know what it really means to see."

In a slightly different way, we see this corollary at work when we hear of the Peace Corps volunteer from Akron, Ohio, who has spent two years in Kenya. She can never return to Akron and see it as she did before she left. She has an entirely different environment of experience from which to measure everything American.

So this corollary functions across time as well as space. Wasn't this what St. Paul was expressing when he wrote in his first letter to the Corinthians, "When I was a child I spake as a child, I understood as a child, I thought as a child"? Certainly this isn't a statement that a child would make. It is only meaningful from another perspective in time.

Different historic periods, then, represent different environments of thought from which people may become aware of different ways of looking at the world at other times. Youth or old age might be considered such environments, but so too are the Middle Ages or the Renaissance. Neither of those familiar labels was applied historically much before the 17th or 18th centuries.

So we might say that it is only from a different environment in time that any era can be encompassed by the mind and even given a name.

It makes one wonder how our own time will be described by future historians. If they were to label us, say, as the "objectivists", as the people who believed that objects could exist independently of subjects, we might feel surprised, perhaps, and even a bit defensive. For their description of us would suggest that our way of seeing is only a subjective perspective — not unlike the way we look upon the "superstitious" beliefs of the Middle Ages. We are convinced that our view of the world is based on the hard facts of both sense experience and objective analysis. So we might say to them, "Of course we believe in the nuts and bolts reality of the physical world. After all that's just common sense."

The question is whether 500 hundred years from now that "sense" will still be commonly shared, or will people by then have come to understand that the objective world and the subjective world have no meaning except in terms of each other — a relationship that seems very similar indeed to the one we discovered earlier between "indoors" and "outdoors".

Metaphor

In another essay I used the word metaphor to describe the way in which new meaning is introduced to language. It is a process in which a relationship is made in a speaker's mind between two apparently separate sense experiences, as when someone says, "The ship plowed the waves."

Most often we think of metaphor in connection with poetry — as when Shakespeare in the opening lines of one of his sonnets compares the succession of waves on a beach with the passage of time in human life. "Like as the waves make toward the pebbled shore / so do our minutes hasten to their end." But while such metaphors are simple and clear, we tend to remain unaware of how metaphor pervades all of language, and, more importantly, of its tremendous power to influence how we think.

The word metaphor, itself, can be traced back to two Greek terms: "*meta*" meaning across or beyond; and a second term "*pherein*", which was the Greek verb "to carry" or "bear". The "ph" sound in Greek became an "f" in Latin and later showed up in English in a word like "ferry". A ferry boat is one designed to "carry or bear" passengers. This same idea occurs in the "fer" of an English word like "transfer", which means to carry something across. A metaphor, then, carries across or transfers meaning from one sense experience to another. "He ran like the wind." Thus it makes possible entirely new ways of seeing and interpreting experience — something that poets have been especially good at for a long time. It is a peculiarly human capacity of which most of us remain completely unconscious.

Imagine, if you will, that you had lived in the country outside ancient Rome. There, a road from the south intersected one from the west and another from the east. Over time, at this intersection of three roads, you saw a small market grow up — a few stalls that sold cloth or spices, various foods, cooking utensils, or cheap jewelry. Thus the intersection became a stopping place for people traveling through, and in time a small village may even have appeared. Then, as more time passed, you began hearing a new word — one that was used to sum up the characteristics of such intersections, all of which seemed to involve a similar kind of activity — one that wasn't world shaking, one that didn't shape the events of the empire as great battles or as decisions of the Roman senate did. It was a special kind of activity that required a human mind to identify and to name. The new word was made up from the Latin for "three roads". The first syllable was "tri" — meaning three — as in English "triangle" or "tricycle." And the second syllable was the Latin for roads — "via." Together they entered our language as the familiar English word "trivia."

Thus a new meaning had been created in which the three roads of the intersection had become a metaphor for the most common and daily of human experiences, those which we speak of today as being "trivial."

Many other metaphors are much more difficult to see. In English, for instance, we attribute to many abstract concepts specific dimensions of physical space — as when we say we are feeling *down* or that things are looking *up*. When something is unresolved or unknown, we also often associate it with being *up*. That's perhaps why we go to look something *up* in the dictionary — because we aren't sure what a word means. Or we say, "Why don't you *raise* that question at the meeting?" Or "Bring that idea *up* on Wednesday."

And when something is resolved we move in the opposite direction. "Well, that *settles* it." Or, "We finally got to the *bottom* of this." Or, "What it really comes *down* to is ..."

And, again, although we use these words every day, we aren't aware that we have almost no choice but to speak in their terms.

And finally we might consider the spatial dimensions of a word we use every day but seldom think of as spatial. I'm thinking of the word "understand." What a strange word when looked at spatially. What kind of a relationship do we have with someone whom we "understand"?

So words themselves might be described as metaphors for nonverbal sense experience.

In this light, then, it is interesting to realize that the sensory stimuli that arrive from the world around us are, and have been, the same for all humans everywhere. It is the interpretation of those data that has given us such widely differing views of reality — interpretations shaped by the metaphors of the particular language inside our minds to create the very different worlds outside.

It would almost seem as though we might posit a law of human perception: Sensory data do not become information until they have passed through mind and been filtered by language.

Let's Change the Subject

In a previous essay, I wrote that it was in the year 1623 that Galileo published a scathing attack on a prominent Jesuit astronomer who had had the temerity to suggest an explanation for comets that was different from Galileo's. And there, buried amidst all his anger and vituperation, Galileo quietly introduced one of the most important ideas in modern thought. He described, for the first time that I am aware of, the distinction between those qualities that are inherently part of an object and those that are contributed by the mind and senses of an observer.

Let's take the example of a brown leather briefcase.

Now Galileo would have said that our experience of the briefcase involved two sets of qualities. What he called primary qualities were those he believed to be inherent in the briefcase itself — ones that existed independently of us as observers. They would have included the briefcase's shape, solidity, position in space, and its number — in this case, one — and its motion, if any.

What he called the secondary qualities were colors, odors, tastes, and sounds. For these existed, he said, only when a human observer was present.

He wrote of the distinction this way, "I think if ears, tongues and noses were removed, shapes and numbers and motions would remain but not odors or tastes or sounds. The latter are nothing more than names when separated from living beings."

What Galileo was describing were the early stages of that remarkable separation that was beginning to take place in the 17th century between the human as subject and the world as object — a separation that was to grow rapidly over the next 300 years.

One of the most interesting ways to trace such revolutions in thought is to consider how the meaning of words like "subject" and "subjective" have changed over that same period of time. That great record of the history of Western thought, *The Oxford English Dictionary*, tells us that prior to the 17th century the word "subject" meant "the essence or reality of a thing," and "subjective" meant "real or essential." This meaning still lingers today when we speak of students taking different "subjects" in college, or when we speak of the "subject" of a sentence.

But within a hundred years of Galileo the word "subject" had begun to reveal a subtle change in meaning. By the mid-18th century, the *O.E.D.* describes it as that which is "peculiar to an individual subject or his mental operations" — that which is "personal" or "individual." And by the late 19th century, the change was complete. By then, "subjective" had come to mean "existing in the mind only, without anything real to correspond with it — illusory or fanciful."

But soon after this gulf had been opened between the imaginary and the real, between the subjective and the objective, then another extraordinary change began to take place.

Early 20th-century physicists had inherited from such thinkers as Galileo, Newton, Descartes, Bacon, and many others, a "real" world of solid objects that existed whether or not an observer was present. But it wasn't long before discoveries in relativity and particle physics led scientists to consider that the position, motion, and solidity of things were, in fact, qualities that had meaning *only* if an observer were present.

It is interesting to note how tenaciously our belief persists in the existence of an external world that is solid, shaped, and in motion independently of us. Entire sciences have been created based on that perception — geology for one and evolution for another — sciences that depict the world as it was for millions and even billions of years before humans appeared, but whose description, we can now perhaps begin to understand, is meaningless except in terms of human sense experience as interpreted by a Western-educated observer from the 21st century.

So in our time, Galileo's careful division between the properties of objects and the properties of mind has indeed become blurred. Today it appears that the only remaining property attributable to objects themselves is number. The rest of reality seems to be up to us.

Perhaps we might conclude from this that the only way to really change the world is to change the subject.

Thou and It

The name of Henri Frankfort is not exactly a household word. Nor is the title of the book that he co-authored in the early 1940s called *The Intellectual Adventure of Ancient Man.* Frankfort was from Holland and in the 1920s he became director of the Egypt exploration society from London. Later, at the University of Chicago he directed archaeological studies in Iraq for the famous Oriental Institute.

Frankfort was particularly interested in how early people saw their world in comparison to how we in the Western cultures today see ours. He didn't fall prey to the assumption that the words "early" or "primitive" are synonyms for "backward" and "ignorant."

Frankfort wrote:

> The fundamental difference between the attitudes of modern and ancient man as regards the surrounding world is this: for modern, scientific man, the phenomenal world is primarily an "it"; for ancient — and for primitive man — it is a "thou." This does not mean that primitive man, in order to explain natural phenomena, imparts human characteristics to an inanimate world. Primitive man simply does not know an inanimate world. Every phenomenon which confronts him — the thunderclap, the sudden shadow, the eerie and unknown clearing in the wood — the stone that hurts him while on a hunting trip — any phenomenon may face him at any time not as "it" but as "thou".[2]

The vast difference between the view of nature as "thou" and as "it" reveals something of the way that the human mind itself has evolved. It speaks not so much of growing intelligence in humans over time but of a substantive change in the way that humans have come to perceive their world.

In its earliest stages, human consciousness as revealed in the ritual and art of so-called primitive peoples perceived nature and "being" as inseparable. There was no self-awareness of the kind that we take for granted today, and what we now call the psyche was seen by early humans to be reflected in the phenomena of nature. Then gradually over time, and

I would suggest paralleling the development of language, "thou" or "be-ing" became separated from nature and internalized in us as the human psyche or self-consciousness — that sense of "me." It was through this process that nature became an "it" and today has come to appear to us as a collection of physical objects ranging from atoms to galaxies that are exclusively physical, chemical, and biological, and governed by that we describe as the "laws of nature." And so complete today is this apparent separation of the "me" from the "it" that the laws of nature themselves are seen purely as properties of an external physical world rather than as metaphors created by the human mind.

Thus, the evolution of human perception from the experiencing na-ture as "thou" to the objective exploitation of nature as "it" has led us into a world that we are able to manipulate with increasing and even frighten-ing skill, but which is also, for many, increasingly devoid of meaning. It seems to me that the environmental movement of recent decades, at least in part and wearing many different guises, represents an unconscious ef-fort to reestablish "being" in nature. Whether it be saving the whales, or creating rights for animals, or protecting the northern spotted owl, these seem to me as an indication of a need at least for some, for a psychic "other" than ourselves and the need to recreate a nature whose "being" is in some way an extension of our own.

In a sense, all of us have been through this before in that early dis-covery of our bodies as being. Joseph Church in his interesting book, *Language and the Discovery of Reality*, describes this process. Speaking of the very young child, he says:

When shortly before six months, he discovers his hands explicitly and visually, it is as external objects. More striking still, is the baby's discovery of his or her feet, which are treated as alien entities — and which his now active hands capture and bring to his mouth for tasting. When he bites on his toes, he seems surprised that it hurts.[3]

Doesn't this sound surprisingly like our recent growing awareness that nature may, in fact, be an extension of us — that when we "bite" her, as it were, it is we who are hurt? To understand that those external objects that we call nature may be an extension of our own being, much as our bodies are, much as an unfamiliar perspective is. It requires a redefining of the meaning of self that transcends both individual mind and body.

Is it possible, then, that our present capacity for self-awareness, so recently developed and yet assumed to be so permanent, is but a stage in the evolution of human consciousness on its way to an entirely new understanding of the meaning of being? Humankind, in the process of coming to observe nature as object, created the only environment from which the observer could also become aware of the self as distinguishable from nature. And thus the separation of "thou" for "it" was complete. Clearly the next step in this evolution would see to lie in our conscious recognition that, although we can distinguish between the outer and the inner worlds, their apparent separation is, in fact, an illusion. Isn't this the real meaning of "at-one-ment"?

References

1. William H. Eddy, Jr. *The Other Side of the World: Essays and Stories on Mind and Nature.* Lunenburg, VT: The Stinehour Press, 2001.
2. Henri Frankfort, Henriette Antonia Groenewegen-Frankfort, John Albert Wilson, Thorkild Jacobsen, and William Andrew Irwin. *The Intellectual Adventure of Ancient Man; an Essay on Speculative Thought in the Ancient Near East.* Chicago: The University of Chicago Press, 1946.
3. Joseph Church. *Language and the Discovery of Reality; a Developmental Psychology of Cognition.* With a foreword by Robert B. MacLeod. New York: Random House, 1961.

Primordial Wholeness:
Hints of Its Non-Local and Non-Temporal Role in the Co-Evolution of Matter, Consciousness, and Civilization

EMILIOS BOURATINOS
International Society for Greek Philosophy
Ekali, Greece

Only when the one is completely the many can it be called the one; and only when the many is completely the one can it be called the many.
— FA-TSANG

To [properly] look at an object is to inhabit it.
— MAURICE MERLEAU-PONTY

It will be seen as remarkable ... that the very study of the external world led to the conclusion that consciousness is an ultimate reality.
— EUGENE WIGNER

The following text is based on a notion of consciousness that differs from most of those currently in vogue. On the one hand, this notion is inspired by insights from modern physics, neurophysiology, fuzzy logic, and chaos theory, with their predominantly factual approach. On the other hand, it is inspired by insights from the ancient quest for deeper understanding, with its distinctly intuitive approach.

This interpenetration of factual and intuitive information[1] may appear strange to a reader who has been raised in the belief that the two approaches do not mix. But the history of science is packed with examples to the contrary. Not only can factual analysis and direct intuition co-exist. There is no fact where previous intuition has not prompted one to point

---

1. Among these schools of thought in philosophy and science can be counted Parmenides' conception of motion as illusory; Socrates' secret war on reason; Advaita; Zen; A.N. Whitehead's process philosophy; David Bohm's holomovement; Kurt Gödel's fundamental distinction between truth and provability; the 'strange attractors' developing out of infinite sensitivity to initial causes in chaos theory; Hua-Yen Buddhism; and Bernard Baars' global workshop theory of consciousness.

to its existence, just as there is no intuition where previous fact has not directed one to look.

It follows that consciousness is not viewed here as a mere synonym for mind or awareness. Still less is it viewed as coming into being only with the appearance of humans, the birth of the critical faculty, the 'invention' of language, or even the appearance of life. Consciousness is viewed as playing the key role in the creation of physical reality itself. If it relates to any other concept at all, it is to that of qualitative wholeness. The further from it one moves, the less conscious one becomes — and the more conscious one becomes, the more easily does one sense the qualitative whole informing the fragments one is dealing with.

Consciousness As Wholeness in Action on Its Parts

Let us examine some of the implications of this conception of consciousness. Their discussion necessarily will be far from exhaustive. Anything more than brief hints at what consciousness is, does, or implies would turn the next pages into an unwieldy exercise.

We will start from Descartes. Ever since his time, consciousness has been seen as an entity, a force, or a state separate from the material it manifests in. This reflects a misconception derived from a too-object-mediated, mechanistic, and exclusive way of thinking. Another more general, functional, and feeling way yields a different understanding. Consciousness in this sense represents the process whereby physical reality wraps itself into form. It doesn't represent a definable commodity. It represents what triggers the constant reconfiguration of reality in all its manifestations.[2] Without it ontogenesis is impossible. Being literally thinks itself into existence.[3]

In this sense consciousness has its roots in what J. Scott Jordan and Marcello Ghin call "proto-consciousness." However, there is a difference.

---

2. Form is what keeps matter together. But just as matter without form disintegrates into disjointed existence, so form without recurring reconfiguration disintegrates into ineffectiveness. In last analysis change preserves — and re-enforces — structured matter. Since form is no-thing, things are supported by no-things.

3. In no way does this imply idealism. It implies that our ways of perceiving and thinking make us choose particular instruments which deal only with particular elements and interactions from the many on offer by physical reality. In the words of Parmenides: "For to be and to understand are one and the same." (Fr. 3.)

Proto-consciousness doesn't come into existence with the unfolding of organic matter, as the two researchers believe. It comes into existence with the first combination of particles after the sudden appearance of space-time. Primordial compactness transforms itself into an ontogenetic force. It re-arranges particles into ever more complex patterns of interaction.

Consciousness becomes, as it were, "a contextually emergent property"[4] of the great self-organizing system that keeps the universe evolving in and through time and space. It extracts quality from quantity and order from chaos. It acts out what the etymology of the ancient Greek word for intelligence (euphyia) suggests — 'good growth'. The end-product of the long process is *homo sapiens sapiens.*

From Compactness to Complexification

Two conclusions follow. First, in this protean sense, consciousness resembles energy. Though pushing electrons in a specific direction, energy itself cannot be isolated as an observable commodity. One can only detect it in (and because of) the fundamental particles it pushes around.

Something similar happens with consciousness. Whereas energy pushes particles in a specific direction, consciousness binds them into a sustainable pattern. The one type of action is impossible without the other. Consciousness and energy are the two mutually dependant intangibles underlying all tangibles. They undermine the classical epistemological principle according to which the only validation system worth the name is that which reduces all entities to observable or computable initial causes. Chaos theory tells us that such initial causes can *never* be actually perceived. The deeper one digs into the structure of things, the more of this structure is revealed to dig into.

Second, consciousness catalyzes a new order of existence in relation to what held sway before creation. Particles, which had earlier been literally on top of each other because of the absence of time and space, suddenly become separate and distinct. In the beginning they fly all over

4. J. Scott Jordan and Marcello Ghin. "(Proto-)consciousness as a contextually emergent property of self-sustaining systems." *Mind and Matter, An International Interdisciplinary Journal of Mind-Matter Research, 4,* No. 1 (2006). pp. 45–68.

the place in chaotic disarray.[5] Later, in the guise of negentropy, gravity, or of what chaos theory calls 'strange attractors', consciousness gradually promotes coherent interaction among them.

In this way, compactness before the big bang transforms into ever tighter complexification after it. Consciousness counteracts the disorder initially sowed by the sudden appearance of space-time. It sees to it that differentiation replaces similarity and organization supplants compactness.

The ancient Greeks, who first coined the term for 'consciousness' in the West, realized that it plays a unifying — and therefore sustaining — role. Their word for it, 'syneidesis,' is composed of the prefix 'syn' ('bringing together') and the noun 'eidesis' ('thing, plus the information concerning it'). So 'syneidesis' originally implied for the Greeks 'the bringing together of objects known to be as they are.' For them consciousness didn't come into being as some end-product of evolution. It was what brought evolution about to begin with.

Qualitative Differentiations

We come now to how consciousness organized physical existence after the sudden appearance of space-time 13.7 billion years ago.

Though continuous, consciousness developed in two phases. The first began with the initial steps of inorganic matter — whenever and however this may have happened. During that phase, the interaction among physical units mutually attracting one another was relatively slow. But once the momentum grew and a certain threshold of complexity was reached, patterns of interaction (and later patterns of such patterns) began to form more easily and quickly.

At the end organic matter emerged. Having its roots deep in qualitative wholeness, consciousness eventually pushed for something more than mere ordered existence. The way by which physical units operated changed. Whereas during the initial phase consciousness brought physical units together through interactions applicable to *all* matter of identical make-up,

---

5. From a relativity point of view, one can claim that the particles actually created the 'place' by flying into it. Space leads into time, time into space. They represent the two sides of the same coin. When one objectifies action, one gets time. When one objectifies its effects, one gets space.

during the later phase it brought them together through patterns applicable only to particular units for their particular activities. Structure was enriched by process, repetition by differentiation, certainty by potentiality.

This is when (and why) the brain came into being. It developed to restore the ability of physical units to commune with at least some local manifestations of wholeness.

Of course, communion had been possible earlier too, when physical units owed their very existence to a general state in which they all participated. But as evolution moved toward ever increasing complexification, physical units were able to re-direct themselves toward wholeness in a different way.

This was achieved by developing an ability for ever more sensibilities. Existence began articulating itself through things rather than in them, as had been the case up until then. Non-temporal and non-local oneness, which had been shattered by the introduction of space-time, began to re-articulate itself through inter-temporal and inter-spatial activity. From suffocating mutual embrace nature moved to creative interpenetration; from absolute streamlining to unity in variation.

Humans represent the most advanced stage of this movement toward qualitative re-wholification. They pursued a different class of choices altogether — composite strategic choices. Through these they develop not just a sense of and taste for wholeness. They develop a vision of it in the form of gods and/or teachers of one kind or another. The two extremes, uniqueness and generality, began to interpenetrate.

Man as a Tool for Evolution toward Re-Wholification

This increased ability for joining opposites became manifest through two uniquely human types of yearning. The first was for what exceeds our grasp. The second was for getting to know what knows — and what is there for the knowing to begin with. Mere awareness no longer suffices. It needs to be turned on itself. Humans want to know if they can improve it, or free it from at least some of the objectifications now obstructing their communion with wholeness.

This is why ever since the Greeks, two sets of questions have become dominant. The first touches on how people apprehend the world.

Do they focus on specifics exclusively or inclusively? Do they apprehend new entities, states, or relationships independently, or at least semi-independently, of previous perceptions? In conceiving such entities, states, or relationships does the mind inform the feelings, do the feelings inform the mind, or do the two mutually inform (and enhance) one another?

The second set of questions touches on what the human being thinks of himself. Does he extend ontologically into the world, or is the world separate from him? To what degree do his immediate whims overshadow his long-term requirements — and for what purpose?

In principal, ancient cultures realize that whereas events and entities appear self-circumscribed on the local/temporal/causal level, they also interpenetrate with their ontological frameworks and with other events or entities outside their immediate locus and time-frame. For example, Minoans perceived events or entities as depending on their innate link to wholeness, which took the form of a goddess. By developing a feel for what exists and what happens across time, space, and form they were better equipped to handle what lies within time, space, and form.[6]

Today we have mostly lost the ability to develop such a sensibility toward interpenetration and the sense of measure it gives rise to. Of course the know-how for acting in measured ways still survives. At the same time we have developed a counterproductive habit. We use our ontological filters — the purpose of which had originally been to weed out irrelevant information to our species — for an additional task:[7] to lock into those objectifications alone which are in tune with our cultural, informational, and individual predilections.

---

6. To explain the dialectic between temporality and non-temporality, ancient India developed the notion of a 'library' containing all the information about the entire universe across time, space, and levels of description. Interestingly, Albert Einstein's and Kurt Gödel's conception of a 'block universe,' where time and space are non-existent, lends support to this idea. However, we ordinary humans of the 21st century are completely dominated by the notions of time and space. Thus we cannot grasp how reality may work without them. Just like we cannot understand infinity in finite terms or non-linearity in linear terms, we cannot understand non-temporality in temporal terms, non-locality in local terms, and non-causality in causal terms. The best we can come up with on the conceptual level is the 'anthropic principle,' the fractal structure of matter, and the correspondence between the mathematical descriptions of reality and reality itself.
7. Our body is bombarded by two million bits of information every minute. If we were unable to filter out the vast majority of these bits, we would go mad in one second. Remembering more than one needs is a mental disease.

Unquestionably we need some sort of filters to pick out those events, forces, entities, fields, interactions, or relationships that we want or need to focus on. This doesn't mean we should keep such filters in place at all times, or use them for other purposes than those they were originally intended for. If properly handled, filters can both isolate the objects we need to interpenetrate with and reveal their relationship with other objects and the whole. They needn't switch from an ontological to a conceptual mode. They can be both — like two sides of the same coin.

Where Did Consciousness Filters Come From — and Why?

Two further questions now become pertinent. The first touches on how conceptual filters connect with the brain. Two stages seem to be involved here. The first appears in conjunction with brain growth. As we acquire more and more neurons, we abandon our earlier habit of flowing with things as they come. The result is that nature, from the tight embrace of which we have now gradually disengaged ourselves, starts to fascinate us! We are inspired to develop a new habit — plus lock into our objectifications of it. The latter filter our perceptions, colour our emotions, and mould our actions.

The second stage in the emergence of conceptual filters appears in conjunction with a new notion. Starting from the premises of our now well-established mental habit of self-locking objectification, we think that communion with wholeness can be concretised. This signals a dangerous derailment of our thinking.

Wholeness cannot be conceived as a quantity. It can be conceived only as a quality. When we apprehend wholeness as a quantity, our return path to it increasingly twists and turns until it becomes labyrinthine. We forget not just how to experience reality without locking into some objectification of it. We forget how it feels to entertain a notion without identifying with it. Wholeness now represents for us a state to *describe* or to *reach*. It doesn't represent a state in which to be — much less to act from.

It is this type of intellectualized approach that feeds belief-based religion and ideology-inspired philosophy. The wholeness we occasionally succeed in re-immersing ourselves in no longer reflects the wholeness we once communed with. It reflects a theological construct, which blocks the natural flow toward dynamic wholeness. Only certain highly evolved mystical states and practices can insure immersion in such a profound state. If anyone secures it by accident, he fails to understand what has happened to him — and cannot sustain it for long.

From Implicit Information to Representational Description

We come now to the second additional question. When did human communion with the whole begin to slacken?

It looks as though the slackening commenced after we fully developed our inclination[8] to make artifacts of one sort or another around 42,000 years ago. This goes hand-in-hand with our need to objectify more and more entities, states, fields, and relationships in order better to understand the world we were beginning to abstract — and therefore to get estranged from.

Of course we still retained the older ability to handle some of our particular requirements through interpenetration with wholeness. But we also started locking into at least some of our objectifications. This is when the now fully operational conceptual filters came to be used systematically. Implicit information transmogrified into explicit "representational re-description" — as consciousness researcher Karmiloff-Smith puts it.[9]

The repercussions of this shift were not felt immediately. To the extent we still managed to release some of our objectifications, we were able to continue handling our affairs in a more or less satisfactory manner. But to the extent we locked into them, we began having problems. Just local and

---

8.   There is here a misunderstanding among neurophysiologists. Brain uses don't depend on brain capabilities. They depend on the *wish* of an individual or group to engage in a particular new type of action, or to obtain particular new results. This wish, if persistent, will eventually develop the brain capability necessary for fulfilling it. If the individual or group is fully satisfied with the way life is going, there will be no wish to change something — and no brain capabilities to serve the change. Mind comes first; brain follows.

9.   Annette Karmiloff-Smith. *Beyond Modularity: A Developmental Perspective on Cognitive Science*. Cambridge, MA: MIT Press, 1992. [As quoted in: John Stewart. "The future evolution of consciousness." *Journal of Consciousness Studies, 14*, No. 8 (2007). pp. 58–92.]

provisional elements now claimed our attention. The sense of measure —
so dependent on a feeling for and an experience of wholeness — began
to wane. The more we stuck to our objectifications, the more we lost our
ability to handle objects. Our increasing ontological isolation overshadowed what John Stewart calls "the massive parallel processing" system in
our brain.[10]

In this way, both the positive and the negative effects of particular
objectifications eventually came to be attributed to their *semantic content*. The pitfalls in discussing the latter were not considered. When we
experienced the positive or negative effects from a particular self-locking
perspective,[11] we either elevated them to the heights of absolute truth, or
rejected them as the lowest expression of deplorable falsehood.

Culture and Self-Locking Objectification

It is sad that ever since Aristotle, the Western mind failed to realize the
qualitative nature of wholeness. On the one hand we tried to re-establish
communion with it. On the other hand we locked into wholeness conceptually and psychologically. Western scholars and thinkers didn't realize
that their philosophical opposition to generalized thinking occurred in
the same conceptual milieu and on the same level of abstraction as generalized thinking itself. Thus object-mediated understanding, which lies at
the heart of generalized thinking, spread throughout the West. Everybody
became convinced that this was the way to promote — and sustain — a
wholesome outlook.

They were encouraged to do so because many of their most important
insights were actually the product of a profound experience of wholeness.
People didn't realize that, unless they practiced some effective mental exercise, the profound sense of wholeness would eventually be transformed
into an absolutist generality by the very individuals who had it. If there
was any personal sentiment still involved, it would be inspired by the

---

10. John Stewart, *ibid.* The one system deals with the particulars as such, the other with the
particulars as embedded in and dependant on a larger framework.

11. Such perceptions are, for example, that of the distortion of the notion of sacrifice after the
invention of farming around 10,000 B.C.E.; that of the conceptual inconsistencies contained in
Aristotelian logic; or more recently, that of the possible dangers inherent in genetically modified
foods.

words in which the sentiment was now presented. It would not be inspired by what goes *beyond* the words *in* the words themselves, as happened when people originally lived in the embrace of wholeness.

In this manner the ground was prepared for either accepting or rejecting the now fossilized version of these original experiences. Focusing on the qualitative dimension of these experiences, without locking into their objectifiable content, no longer represented an option. Quality could not be extracted from its descriptions; meaningfulness could not depend on meaning; experiencing could not arise from conceiving the experience.

This explains why Western philosophy grew like a self-perpetuating succession in semantic misunderstandings of and conceptual reactions to, earlier absolutist or prescriptive theories. The latter may have originally been triggered by some profound realization of wholeness in relation to preexisting fragmented ideas and notions. But they were later systematically abstracted into absolutist pronouncements themselves.

In this way, each successive generation discovered different points of agreement or disagreement with them *on a purely semantic level.* Why such formulations occurred to begin with seems not to have preoccupied either their upholders, or their detractors.[12] Identification with abstract statements — religious or secular — now reigned supreme.

In the case of Christianity the point is that it too had started as a healthy reaction to earlier self-locking objectifications. The teachings of Jesus of Nazareth were turned into a religion when people in the Roman eastern Mediterranean began realizing the sorry state to which their paganism had degenerated.

For one thing, the pagan gods had stopped evoking a sense of wholeness among their worshippers, as they had in earlier times. By the second century B.C.E., the old religions of the eastern Mediterranean had degenerated into empty rituals, superficial syncretism, and cheap magic. For another, the old religions had become grossly indifferent to the individual's personal plight — his life, his soul, his welfare.

Christianity cashed in on these shortcomings. It instilled among its followers a sense that they are part of a larger scheme, with which they

---

12. Many current attitudes, such as fundamentalism, secularism, scientism, political correctness, meaningless art, and reductionism are the product of such misunderstood experiences.

could identify. Wholeness was recast in the garb of a benign and powerful supreme God, who loved all and cared for each. No pagan religion in the Middle East had emphasized the quality of love and the value of the individual to the extent Christianity had.

Qualitative Reactions to Self-Locking Objectification

Of course, after Christianity became the established religion of the Roman Empire, it too began locking into its objectifications and imposing them in the form of doctrines. Thus the new religion mostly lost its ability to put believers in touch with qualitative wholeness. The reactions to this were of many types and on many levels.

One type came from individuals who had both the ability and the inclination to experience what both Sufism and Orthodox Christianity describe as 'the essence of God' and Meister Eckhart calls 'the Godhead.' Individuals so inclined developed an ability to immerse themselves in the total stillness of mere being — without losing their ability to act on the practical or the intellectual level. Among them can be found such towering figures as LaoTse, St. Maximus the Confessor, St. Gregory of Nyssa, Shankara, Isaac of Nineveh, Milarepa, Nicholas of Cusa, Francis of Assisi, Paracelsus, St. John of the Cross and in recent times, Thomas Merton and Pierre Teilhard de Chardin.

In some cases (for example in the Arthurian tales, in Dante's *Divine Comedy*, or in Giordano Bruno's writings), the reaction to self-locking objectifications led to the adoption of patterns of thought that had a mythical, as well as a mystical, component. Even so, Christianity continued to be gently present in these texts.

A second type of reaction was indirect and came from the individuals who had developed a philosophical inquisitiveness more or less unrelated to what the Church taught. Here were thinkers like Roger and Francis Bacon, Marsilio Ficino, Galileo, Kepler, Descartes, Newton, Leibniz, and others.

Unwitting Reactions

A third type of reaction came in the form of movements which, totally disillusioned with the shortcomings of doctrinal religion, proclaimed an entirely materialistic message. Atheism, nihilism, existentialism, anarchy, logical positivism, and scientism are some of the schools of thought that sprang up from this type of self-locking reaction.

The most significant of these schools of thought was 18th-century Enlightenment, which disregarded Church doctrine only to set up its own. It pushed its mechanistic/reductionist approach so far that science eventually realized its findings didn't correspond to what happens in the actual world. Thus, ever since relativity and quantum mechanics, we have been witnessing a progressive movement away from the compartmentalization of our understanding of physical reality and the self-locking practices it caused. A good part of 20th-century thinking does away with mind-matter dualism and encourages investigation of the structural connection between science and consciousness.

One further point. All philosophical and religious reactions to other philosophical and religious positions have their roots in the primal longing for wholeness. Under the sway of this unconscious desire, people may experience some inspired revelation. Or they may sublimate their longing for wholeness into some form of public action. In either case, what they experience is interpreted by them in the light of the cultural, psychological, and conceptual baggage they carry.

The longing for wholeness also manifests among dedicated proponents of self-locking thought-systems. A striking example is the current fascination of scientists with unification. It articulates itself in two ways. The first is to base all understanding on Hilbert-like mathematics and on Carnap-like logic. The second is to search for 'a theory of everything.' The object-mediated manner in which scientists go about these two enterprises differs but little from the equally object-mediated manner in which monotheism extends its insights to engulf all reality. The urge for unification is as powerfully ingrained in believers as it is among non-believers.

The lesson is that we need to promote both intellectual comprehension and contemplative experience simultaneously. We can then start again to make sense of things in terms of sensing the qualitative wholeness sustaining them. More importantly, we can use conceptual filters both for what they allow us to focus on and for making us aware of what our focus leaves out.

Such an attitude will express the essence of our humanity in both its rational and intuitive aspects. It will, furthermore, do so in a balanced way. Through intuition we will penetrate to the whole informing the phenomena from *within their formal expression*. Through reason we will discover the best way of handling the phenomena in the light of their rootedness in the whole.

Moving to Self-Releasing Objectifications

A scientist, who thinks unencumbered by his objectifications, will be using these as much as an encumbered one. But the former will be aware of the limitations of the conceptual filters he introduces as he objectifies reality. He will not allow these to write off non-objects like long-term interactions, resonances, or overarching links. He will sense what can never be an object to begin with and he will know what falls in between rigid categories.

Such mental reversal will have a significant effect equally on ourselves and on those around us. The drive to objectify ever more different states, modes of being, hunches, things, sensibilities, fields, interactions, and levels of organization or abstraction, is fundamental to the unfolding of consciousness. However, since the dawn of civilization as we know it, we have failed to form such objectifications without eventually locking into them. The moment has come to reverse this trend. We must learn to focus our understanding without isolating its subjects conceptually or emotionally.

The fewer objectifications we lock into, the better equipped we are to use them without distorting reality. The less we distort *reality*, the more real entities, states, and relationships we become aware of. The more states and aspects of reality we become aware of, the better can we handle things. And the better we can handle things, the more easily are we able to savor the wholeness sustaining them.

This reintegration of objectification with what informs it — this relinking of the specific to what makes it possible to begin with — represents what the world today needs. We must pursue it with perseverance, ingenuity, and wisdom.

Semiotic Filters: The Mediate Nature of Signs

SHANNON FOSKETT
Committee on Cinema and Media Studies
The University of Chicago

*There will be no unique name, even if it were the name of Being.
And we must think this without nostalgia, that is, outside of the myth
of a purely maternal or paternal language, a lost native country of
thought. On the contrary, we must* affirm *this [...] such is the
question inscribed in the simulated affirmation of* différance. *It bears
(on) each member of this sentence: "Being/ speaks/ always and
everywhere/ throughout/ language."*
— DERRIDA[1]

Language is the house man lives in.
— JULIETTE JANSON, *DEUX OU TROIS CHOSES QUE JE SAIS D'ELLE*
(JEAN-LUC GODARD, 1965)

The rise in semiotic consciousness in the early twentieth century — exemplified, among other movements, by analytic philosophy, linguistic structuralism, psychoanalysis, and developments in the visual arts — gave way to a self-reflective critique of signs and textual systems in their relationship to the world. This paper will discuss Jahn and Dunne's notion of filters from a semiotic and poststructuralist perspective. Following Charles Peirce's (1839–1914) semiotic metaphysics, the point will be developed that signs, in their mediate nature, can be considered equivalent to filters, and that this ontology of signs, or, "semiotic filters," is the basis for the "filtering process," from sensory perception, through cognitive and cultural formations, towards the psychic. The question of the difference between the Peircean sign and (the notion of) the Real, will also be addressed, asking to what extent semiotic filters keep us at a distance from reality, or actually comprise the fabric of reality itself.

Semiotics has often been defined as "the science of signs." This is completely accurate, but a fuller picture might be gleaned — at least, in

---

1. Jacques Derrida, pp. 79–153.

the human, knowledge-seeking context — by calling it "the science of meaning," or "the science of significance." This is also completely accurate, since the nature of a sign and the condition for its existence is to hold significance for another semiotic agent. Before further discussing these terms, I will briefly outline what I see as the relevance of semiotics for the notion of experiential filters developed by Robert Jahn and Brenda Dunne.

Jahn and Dunne refer to the total effect of all sensory, cognitive, and psychic filters as a "composite dilution of experience,"[2] akin to listening to a live concert wearing earplugs, or never having left the town of one's birth — as happens to the protagonists of *The Truman Show* (1998), *Pleasantville* (1998), and other Hollywood films where characters begin to question what otherwise constitutes the boundaries of their world. When Neo, awakening after having been "unplugged" from the Matrix, asks "why do my eyes hurt?" Morpheus replies, "because you've never used them before" — referring to the experience of the absence of a second-level sensory filter on "the real world."

The resonance of this familiar "inside/outside" trope has been a serious point of questioning throughout the history of philosophy. The Platonic ideal Forms of Beauty, Truth, and the Good were impossible for mortals to know directly; all the Ancient Greeks had was a world of inferior "copies." For Immanuel Kant (1724–1804), it was the noumenal level of reality that was beyond the reach of humans, who necessarily only experience the phenomenal world through their own aesthetic and cognitive categories.

The epistemological divide becomes especially pernicious in sociological perspectives on science, where it cuts to the heart of the realist/anti-realist debate on the nature of objectivity and the possibility of true knowledge. Philosopher of science Robert Klee even refers to Kantian epistemology as "The Great Filtration:"[3] the boundaries of human (scientific) knowledge may continually expand, but the nature of our own cognitive composition, like a piece of translucent plastic that stretches out ahead of us, keeps us from ever directly, *immediately* meeting with what

---

2. Robert G. Jahn and Brenda J. Dunne, pp. 549–550.
3. Robert Klee, pp. 171–72.

is on the other side of the plastic, even if we may come to see what it all is, more or less.

Likewise, Jahn and Dunne argue that "there exists a much deeper and more extensive source of reality, which is largely insulated from direct human experience, representation, or even comprehension."[4] But the authors argue that we can, with practice, come to deliberately "tune" our sensory, cognitive, and psychic filters so that it would become possible to have a clearer understanding of the relationship of consciousness to this great "Outside" — what they have previously called the "subliminal seed regime."[5]

In what follows, I would like to propose semiotics — the study of signs — as a method and tool for analysis of the filters placed on our consciousness and for obtaining feedback concerning how well we may be "tuning" our filters. Semiotics is especially pertinent in this regard for a few reasons. As I will suggest:

1. signs themselves are filters;
2. signs are co-extensive with thought, and arguably everything else in the universe;
3. it is more economical and pragmatic to regard all classes of filters in terms of signs;
4. sign analysis would be useful for referring to all types of filters, but the body of accumulated research into cultural, communicative, and ideological sign analysis would be particularly powerful in targeting the class of all cultural filters (status quo, dogma, hegemony, herd instinct, superstructure, dominant paradigms, conventions) — arguably the most pernicious of all to dismantle.

---

4. Robert G. Jahn and Brenda J. Dunne, p. 553.
5. Although this has been referred to by many names — the Implicate Order, the Akashic Record, Tao, the Source, *etc.* — I will refer to it in this paper as "the subliminal seed regime." Although "the Source" is a more economical choice, it implies a transcendent directionality, originality, and hierarchy. The "subliminal seed regime" is desirable not only for the process of defamiliarization it creates in the reader, but seems to better evoke the role that individual/ collective choice and participation play in the co-creation of reality. It also subverts a simplistic inside/outside dichotomy and preserves a connotative connection to the myriad of developing post-quantum cosmologies, *e.g.*, holographic and superstring theory.

The semiotics of communication is even more relevant insofar as much of humanity's major goal appears to be an improved dialogue or communication with the subliminal seed regime — the increased attention to symbol systems in the past century or so provides a fertile horizon upon which to implement further systematic study of signs in fields of inquiry that have not yet done so.

Thus, the primary aim of this paper is to suggest semiotics as an analytic tool for improving our understanding of our relationship to the subliminal seed regime. After providing some background, I will briefly introduce sign theory and give further suggestions as to its analytic utility. A secondary, much smaller, aim of this paper is to raise the implications of Peircean sign ontology for thinking about the subliminal seed regime in relation to human consciousness.

Symbolic Consciousness

Among other things, the twentieth century may be known for the steep rise in consciousness of the nature of symbols and symbolic processes that occurred in many neighborhoods of the global intellectual community. A good deal of this symbolic awakening was a deliberately anti-metaphysical move. The positivist doctrines of French philosopher Auguste Comte (1798–1857), and later Austrian physicist Ernst Mach (1838–1916), made a sharp distinction between the questions that metaphysics could ask and the ones that experimental science should ask — going so far as to equate metaphysics with superstition. Comte maintained that science should not attempt to "go beyond" phenomena in search of "deeper" causes and explanations. Together with the work of German mathematician Gottlob Frege (1848–1925), the influence of these thinkers generated a body of thought that came to be known around 1930 as *logical positivism* (or logical empiricism). Proponents of this philosophy, which included British philosopher Bertrand Russell (1872–1970), along with Rudolf Carnap (1891–1970) of the Vienna Circle, were equally influenced by the *logical atomism* developed by G. E. Moore (1873–1958), Bertrand Russell, and his student Ludwig Wittgenstein (1889–1951). Symbolic logic developed out of the logical atomist method, for which the "analytic" school of philosophy got its name.

The "other culture" of twentieth-century philosophy is continental philosophy, which grew from German Idealism in the wake of Kant on the one hand, and from Brentano (1838–1917), through Husserl (1859–1938) and Heidegger (1889–1976), on the other. Neo-Kantian Ernst Cassirer (1874–1945), known for his philosophy of symbolic forms, is often considered somewhat of a bridge between these two approaches to philosophy. Although he was not explicitly a semiotician, Cassirer arrived at important semiotic insights into human culture. In *An Essay on Man*, he equates the ontological and semiotic status of the physical world with the world of human cultural production, a move that parallels Peirce's theory of signs.

> No longer in a merely physical universe, man lives in a symbolic universe. Language, myth, art, and religion are parts of this universe. They are the varied threads which weave the symbolic net, the tangled web of human experience. All human progress in thought and experience refines upon and strengthens this net. *No longer can man confront reality immediately; he cannot see it, as it were, face to face. Physical reality seems to recede in proportion as man's symbolic activity advances.* Instead of dealing with the things themselves man is in a sense constantly conversing with himself.[6]

Cassirer's is an admirable description of the mediate nature of signs and sign networks that are present in all scientific and philosophical investigation and communication. Pure mathematics and the philosophical study of mathematical foundations are excellent examples of the use of signs to study signs, and of Cassirer's observation that "physical reality seems to recede in proportion as man's symbolic activity advances."

Increased attention to the formal aspects of systems has also occurred in the visual arts — from the Dadaists, Kandinsky and Malevich, to Pollock in 1949, in the films of Warhol, Brakhage, and Snow in the '60s, and in the contemporary work of Cindy Sherman and others. In fact, one of the hallmarks of the postmodern era (generally speaking, life in

---

6. Ernst Cassirer, p. 43. Emphasis mine.

the developed world since the late 1960s) is considered to be the mass recycling of the forms of the past (think of any remake, sequel, cover, or sample; or recall any use of Michelangelo's *David* to advertise soda pop or deodorant). Cultural theorist Jean Baudrillard (1929–) calls this "the precession of simulacra," life in a world of copies of Plato's copies. The heightened sensitivity to semiosis — the meaning-making capacity — has occurred equally in early twentieth-century and contemporary research into metaphor, both cognitive and linguistic, and the binary semiotics of cybernetics, data encryption, logic, systems theory, chaos and complexity, DNA, and quantum physics — all of which come under the purview of semiotics.

Structuralism and Poststructuralism

Some of the aforementioned developments would not have come about in the way that they did, or as soon as they did — or perhaps even at all — if it had not been for the work of Swiss linguist Ferdinand de Saussure (1857–1913) and the collection of lecture notes his students published under the name *Cours de linguistique generale* in 1916. The founder of linguistic structuralism was the first to make a call for the development of a systematic science of signs. Saussure was building on a tradition of thought on signs, of course, that begins as far back as Hippocrates (470–410 BC), but which grew in sporadic jumps.

Saussure's conception of the sign was a strictly linguistic model, and it was intended to serve the study of linguistics. The verbal sign is thus a combination of a concept and a sound-image:

> Both terms involved in the linguistic sign are psychological and are united in the brain by an associative bond [...] the linguistic sign unites, not a thing and a name, but a concept and a sound-image. The latter is not the material sound, a purely physical thing, but the psychological imprint of the sound, the impression that it makes on our senses. The sound-image is sensory...[7]

---

7. de Saussure, in Paul Perron and Marcel Danesi, pp. 77–78.

Saussure called the concept the *signified* and the sound-image the *signifier*, and advanced the notion that the linguistic sign is arbitrary, temporally constrained, and context- and community-bound. The semiotic analysis of any text or system according to the Saussurean analysis of linguistic structures is known as *structuralist*.[8]

Reacting against this semiotic structuralism was continental philosopher Jacques Derrida (1930–2004), who wrote his doctoral dissertation on Husserl (1859–1938) and was equally influenced by the phenomenology of Husserl's student Martin Heidegger (1889–1976). Derrida is best known as a catalyst for poststructuralist approaches to theory and criticism, primarily through his development of deconstruction — a theory that is also an interpretative method.

Originally a strategy for critiquing the tradition of Western philosophy, deconstruction is about recognizing *différance* — the constant and elusive shifting of signifieds that can never be pinned down. A word never has a simple, direct, or "veridical" relationship to its meaning. Take the word "present" — did you think of this present moment, or was the present something that was given to you? Recognizing *différance* is to see the trace of prior, alternate, and additional meanings in a given sign (here, the verbal sign). "Lewis Carroll" signifies the author of *Alice in Wonderland* to you, perhaps, but to his family, it *actually* refers to Charles Dodgson. But "Lewis Carroll" may have other meanings for you too — it may connote the feelings that accompanied your reading of *Alice in Wonderland* as a child. Or, you may confuse it with "C. S. Lewis" and think that Lewis Carroll was the author of the *Narnia* series. To yet another person, "Lewis Carroll" may serve as a code that designates a certain time and meeting place, in the same way that "Star Gate" has no relationship to its literal referents whatsoever. Moreover, a sign can literally denote *two* referents, as "London" and "Paris" also refer to cities of Southwestern Ontario as well as those in Europe; and any given referent, such as the planet Venus, may have more than one *signifier* (as Saussure would say), *representamen* (in Peircean discourse), or

---

8. It is important to note the distinction often made between the history of semiotics "proper" and this comparably more recent and short-lived blip in the chronology of sign study — Saussurean semiologie, which nevertheless helped fashion the study of signs into its own discipline, primarily through the work of French cultural theorist Roland Barthes (1915–1980).

sense (as Frege referred to it): "the morning star," "the evening star," and "Αφροδίτη."

As is becoming obvious, the amount of *différance* present/absent in a single sign quickly becomes amplified with the move towards increased semiotic complexity. Thus, natural languages are full of ambiguity and constraint. The analytic philosophers tried to overcome this with symbolic logic (the previous sentence could read "$(\forall n)\ (A(n) \wedge C(n))$," where n refers to natural languages and A and C are unary predicates referring to ambiguity and constraint); whereas poststructuralists following Derrida highlighted it, celebrated it, and played with it, using-Their-(own)-"symbolic"-~~code~~. What is important is to note how both approaches have recognized the distinction between sense and meaning (in Frege's words), or form and content, or *syuzhet* and *fabula* (for the Russian Formalists). Arguably, the development of the ability to systematically analyze a sign into its component signifier(s) and signified(s) represents one of the greatest conceptual achievements of the late nineteenth and twentieth centuries.

Peircean Semeiotic

The French tradition of *semiologie* that followed from Saussure thus occupies quite an important historical and disciplinary space. But, like Newtonian physics, it does not extend into the stranger reaches of the universe. For that, we need Peirce. Often referred to as America's greatest philosopher, Charles S. Peirce (pronounced "purse") (1839–1914) wrote a history of chemistry at the age of eleven and continued to produce work of substance until the day of his death. He made great contributions to such fields as logic (where he considered himself equivalent in ability to Leibniz) and sign theory,[9] which became a fundamental part of what has been described as his "evolutionary, psycho-physically monistic metaphysical system."[10] If Saussure is considered to be the father of modern semiotics, then Peirce is considered its spirit.

Semeiotic, as Peirce called it, is the doctrine of signs, while *semiosis* refers to the sign-making, sign-interpreting process. In contrast to

9. Douglas Anderson, pp. 2–9.

10. Robert Burch, <http://plato.stanford.edu/entries/peirce/>.

semiologie and the more established field of rhetoric, and encompassing the scope of information theory, the analytic reach of Peircean semeiotic extends beyond the linguistic into the domain of the physical, biological, and non-human.

For Peirce, signs are *things*, at once immaterial and material, that stand in the place of other things. Signs signify something — *perceptible*, *imaginable*, or even *unimaginable* — for someone, and the same sign may not signify the same thing for two or more persons. Thus, the onset of an inexplicable, unexpected fever after eating some chicken may be an indication that one has contracted H5N1, or it may be a sign of God's mysterious will. Signs come to the fore in the forensic and experimental sciences, where they manifest as clues, traces, pieces of evidence *par excellence*: a diffraction pattern, a fingerprint, high levels of selenium in a dead man's liver. Rings in tree trunks and layers of rock are indexes of the earth's movement through time; a bruise is the sign of a broken blood vessel. In Peirce's semeiotic, the *world* is replete with meaning. This is what makes Peirce more relevant for a semiotic study of filters.

Unlike Saussure's, the Peircean sign is triadic and is conceptualized as follows:

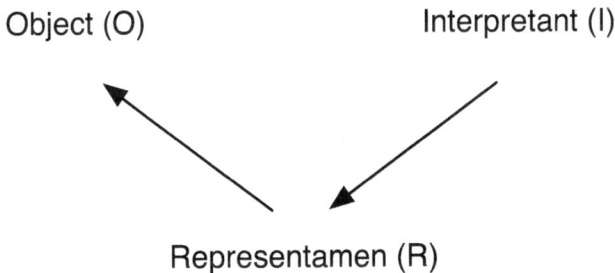

The *representamen*, similar to Saussure's signifier, is the perceptible part of the sign — for example, the written letters "b-e-l-l." The *object* is the referent of the representamen, in other words, the physical object that rings when shaken. The *interpretant* is the understanding and interpretation of this connection, similar to Saussure's signified. But the exact type, kind, and color of bell of one person's interpretant may be different from another person's interpretant. The Peircean sign does not end here, but continues *ad infinitum*. Each interpretant effectively becomes a representamen in its own right, generating a subsequent sign, which follows the same process. So we may conceptualize the process of unlimited semiosis as follows, with each interpretant also acting as the next representamen, and so on:

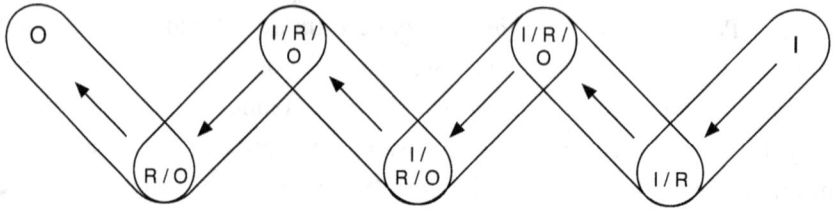

Peirce explains the sign as follows:

> A sign, or representamen, is something which stands to somebody for something in some respect or capacity. It addresses somebody, that is, creates in the mind of that person an equivalent sign, or perhaps a more developed sign. That sign which it creates I call the *interpretant* of the first sign. The sign stands for something, its *object*. It stands for that object, not in all respects, but in reference to a sort of idea, which I have sometimes called the *ground* of the representamen [...][11]

By the *ground* of the representamen (or the *precept of explanation* according to which a sign is understood as an emanation of its Object), Peirce refers to the manner in which the sign or representamen represents its Object. The representamen represents its object in one or more of three ways: *iconically*, *indexically*, and *symbolically*. Thus, an *icon* is a type of sign that represents its object by virtue of simulation of one or more qualities of the Object — it may smell the same, look the same, sound the same, *etc.* So, a child's drawing of her family is iconic insofar that the stick figures and characteristics she gave them more or less represent visually the same characteristics of people in her family. Likewise, a stand-up comic's impersonation of Michael Jackson is successful when it simulates, audibly and visibly, Jackson's audible and visible mannerisms. An *index* is a type of sign that represents its object through contiguity or

---

11. Charles S. Peirce, in David S. Clarke, Jʀ., p. 59.

causality — a cloud of slowly rising smoke in the distance is an index of the fire below it; the index finger is such because it "picks out" or refers to something by pointing to its location in time or space. A *symbol* is a type of sign that works by convention, that is, because a group of users has agreed to give it the meaning that it has. So, π ("pi") stands for a quantity that is approximately 3.14. There is no intrinsically necessary connection between the visible form "π" and the value it represents. The symbol could have been "Ξ." Likewise, the English representamen "happiness" has no inherent connection to its object. The French representamen for the same object is "bonheur."

This is a necessarily simplified and incomplete schema of Peirce's intricate and extensive typology of signs. The reader is encouraged to refer directly to Peirce's own writing or other secondary sources to glean a more detailed understanding. My point is simply to provide some foundation for understanding the systematicity of semiotics as an analytic tool. It is also important to note that, depending on the semiotician, Saussurean and Peircean terminology are often combined or used interchangeably. This is somewhat unfortunate, since they are not equivalent. Sometimes, too, Peirce's "object" is also referred to as a referent. The reader should merely note the specific definitions of terms such as "symbol," which has a much more restricted usage than it does in common discourse. Finally, it must be emphasized that any given sign often contains both iconic *and* indexical or symbolic elements. For example, the trefoil sign used for nuclear hazard warnings is both symbolic and iconic, for its usage has been implemented by convention yet the three prongs iconically represent the omnidirectional spread of radiation.

Semiotic Metaphysics

Immanuel Kant was an immense influence on the thought of Peirce, who, in college, had studied the *Critique of Pure Reason* so intensely over a period of three years that he felt he almost knew it by heart.[12] Peirce spent another two years revising Kant's list of twelve categories into three: qualities, relations, and representations. This list, which can

12. Douglas R. Anderson, p. 4.

be summarized into "firstness," "secondness," and "thirdness," Peirce considered his greatest contribution to philosophy.[13] Whereas *firstness* refers to quality, being, and existence, *secondness* refers to relations, dyads, dynamics, and brute force. *Thirdness* includes law, representations, consciousness, and all symbolic activity. Peirce observed that his triadic metaphysics makes itself manifest throughout most, if not all, systems and phenomena. "It really is so; I have tried hard and long to persuade myself that it is only fanciful, but the facts will not countenance that way of disposing of the phenomenon."[14]

Just as signs are representations and belong to the category of thirdness, so do thoughts. More precisely, Peirce maintained that *all thought occurs in terms of signs*, and thus has a partly material nature.[15] "Our mere sensations are only the material quality of our ideas considered as signs." Signs, which thus include physical biological states, are not separate from thought, which also has a material component and is subject to material constraints.[16] So, for Peirce, both signs and thoughts are partly concrete things; they are real, they have presence. For conscious agents, everything is necessarily a sign. Nothing can show itself as a phenomenon without also manifesting as a sign.

But at the same time that signs seem to be things-in-themselves, they are also filters of those things. Disagreeing with British philosopher John Locke (1632–1704), Peirce argued that our thoughts are never fully present or *immediate* to us, but always *mediated* through signs. As already discussed, each thought is merely the interpretant of the thought previous to it, and this process cannot be stopped. And as Derrida has plainly demonstrated, signs are *never* the-things-themselves. Signs always speak of *another* thing. Signs *mediate*. They condition awareness of a thing/sign, yet themselves are conditioned by other things/signs in order to be understood. This makes signs equivalent to filters.

---

13. Douglas R. Anderson, p. 12.
14. Charles S. Peirce, *Peirce on Signs.* p. 180. Since all signs are representations of some sort, all signs belong to the category of thirdness; although, complicating the matter, the manner in which each sign represents can also be divided according to the categories of firstness (icons), secondness (indices), and thirdness (symbols).
15. Charles S. Peirce, *Peirce on Signs.* p. 143.
16. Charles S. Peirce, *Peirce on Signs.* p. 54.

Is the Peircean semeiotic then merely a reformulation or extension of the Kantian transcendental aesthetic? Owing to the partly material nature of signs, might there not be some theoretical egress that could allow consciousness to escape the semiosphere? If we accept this triadic ontology, then we are faced with the task of determining how each of Peirce's categories operate in tandem to determine human experience at any level. Clearly, all categories would be present in the simplest human undertaking, suggesting that human consciousness — a deeper consciousness than the representational system involved in thirdness — may be able to move between all three levels. With an increased intensity or abandonment of intentionality, could a non-objective consciousness somehow pass beyond *thirdness* to cycle back to *firstness* at a higher level?

Semiotic Filter Analysis

Since signs form the basis of all conscious activity from sensation to complex conceptual abstractions, and since such signs are equivalent to filters, it seems wise to consider the sensory, cognitive, and psychic filters discussed by Jahn and Dunne in terms of the Peircean sign. Doing so would enable precise analysis, a calibration of disciplinary vocabularies, and, potentially, the possibility for opening the filters concept up to a greater number of individuals who may be working within yet different paradigms.

From a semiotic perspective, Jahn and Dunne make three very interesting, radical propositions, each of which opens itself to opportunities for semiotic analysis:

1. The human brain is a local unit "that serves a much more extended 'mind,' " which is the "ultimate organizing principle of the universe, creating reality through its *ongoing dialogue* with the unstructured potentiality of the Source."[17]
2. Both the sensory and the psychic channels of information have the capacity for "two-way" transmission of information. Thus, it is possible through thoughts and sensory actions to input information back

---

17. Robert G. Jahn and Brenda J. Dunne, p. 549. Emphasis mine.

into the universe. Any given sensory or psychic channel "inherently provides re-emergent information fluxes that couple the environment and the sensing complexes into bonded resonant systems."[18]

3. It is possible to alter and improve the filters through which we are connected to the subliminal seed regime.

Fortunately for this approach to the study of the "source of reality," there has already accumulated a mass of semiotic research on cultural and communication systems, owing to the influence of Saussure through such figures as Jakobson (1896–1982), Hjelmslev (1899–1965), Benveniste (1902–1976), Levi-Strauss (1908–), Barthes (1915–1980), and their students and interpreters. Insofar that we conceive ourselves to be "in dialogue" with some subliminal seed regime, or Source, with which we are co-creators of reality as we speak/read/write, then we can analyze and improve this communicative relation more systematically with some background knowledge of sign theory and analysis. If the experience of synchronicity or precognitive dreams, for example, comprises "the establishment of such resonant states between the subjective experience of a living participant and its pertinent physical and emotional environment," and "is one of the essential functions of all spiritual practices,"[19] then semiotics can aid in the study of this sort of environmental and psychic feedback, "noise reduction," and symbol interpretation.

In the process of becoming more attuned to one's dream signs and narratives, for example, one can learn to pick out the types of representamens that recur and under what *contexts* or in what *codes* they appear, in order to determine their signifieds. One may also come to specify the shift in interpretants that a given dream representamen may move through over time. Knowledge of this terminology is not necessary for dream interpretation, but it can make it more specific and help focus one's attention on the interpretative process, potentially revealing insights not otherwise available. If dream activity, as a psychic modality, is taken as a medium for the transmission as well as the reception of information, perhaps lucid dream states can act as sites of inscription upon the subliminal

---

18. Robert G. Jahn and Brenda J. Dunne, p. 553.
19. Robert G. Jahn and Brenda J. Dunne, p. 553.

seed regime. In this case, as with all other channels of communication, the semiotic choices made in self-representation can be quite important.

Jahn and Dunne raise the question of the effect caused by the sum total of all individual sensory and psychic imprints upon the subliminal seed regime. One way of approaching this question is offered by Peirce, for whom thought was made objectively real through signs and is therefore not locally confined within a subjective or physiological self.[20] Owing to the material nature of thought and signs, this seems to provide a basis for an "ethics of filter tuning." It is common knowledge that the types of thoughts we allow ourselves to think determine our interpretation of experience. Thus, it is only logical that, if consciousness is in communication with itself, the same would be true at an even deeper level. There may, therefore, be consequences attached to the dependence upon or preference for certain signs or metaphors over others, and this is something we should consider seriously and investigate further. Peirce came to a similar conclusion with respect to logic, which "is the theory of self-controlled, or deliberate, thought; and as such, must appeal to ethics for its principles."[21] An ethics of "filter tuning" seems to be required if we accept that individuals co-create reality in dialogue with a more extensive mind. Semiotic analysis can help by facilitating the focus given to sign choice, message "encoding," and interpretation.

There is another sense in which a Peircean semeiotic may help us to think about the relationship between individuals and the seed regime. It may be possible, with the help of semiotic research design, to "measure" thoughts and meanings sent and received. Just as Planck's constant measures the value of the smallest possible amount of energy x time per joule-second, it is possible to conceive of a "semiotic constant" that measures mental energy or force. Not only does thought, for Peirce, have an objective (if not physical) force on the world (including the brain), but its semiotic nature gives it a metric by which it can be "measured." Signs quantize thought by making it discrete. The semiotic materiality of thought thus allows for the possibility of considering the agency of consciousness in terms of mental force and energy. This is an admittedly

---

20. Charles S. Peirce, *Peirce on Signs*, p. 11.
21. Charles S. Peirce, in David S. Clarke, Jr., p. 62.

speculative and problematic consideration, one that veers close to computationalism, but one that nevertheless follows and finds support in the literature of pattern dynamics.[22] Moreover, the commitment to distinguish representamens from interpretants and objects could allow for the measurement of different aspects of thought, such as the distinction Baruss has made between lateral and vertical meaning,[23] or between everyday semiotic associations and their transcendental correlates.

Semiotic Interconnectedness

A semiotic approach to the filters concept fits with a more holistic paradigm founded upon the interconnectedness of all things (signs). Signs extend beyond verbal and visual language into the emotive, cognitive, and psychic registers. Most importantly, they do not lie within the exclusive domain of the human. The dances of bees, the camouflage patterns on certain fish — all living things are meaning-making creatures. It was the view of semiotician Thomas Sebeok (1920–2001), himself working in the Peircean tradition, that wherever there is life, there are signs, and *vice versa*.

In fact, semiosis is characteristic of all dynamic systems. In their study of far-from-equilibrium thermodynamics, Prigogine and Stengers often speak of the ability of a system to "sense" and "perceive" its environment. In long-range correlation, very distant particles can, as the system approaches the Edge of chaos, "communicate" with each other.[24] Likewise, radiation gathered from space is a literal, physical message from the origins of the universe. Signs themselves seem to be the stuff of the universe, insofar that the universe is held to be a conscious system.

This takes us back to the "inside/outside" problem mentioned at the beginning of this paper, and to the sort of monistic materialism characteristic of the pre-Socratics. If "all is sign," what else is there to "filter"? In other words, if there is some degree of consciousness in everything, and if consciousness is always semiotic (or in Husserlian terms, consciousness *of* an object), then can there possibly be cracks in such a semiosphere? The problem here may be that more work needs to be done

---

22. Scott Kelso, *Dynamic Patterns.* Entire work.
23. Imants Baruss, p. 22.
24. Prigogine and Stengers, p. 171.

on the nature of semiosis itself, or the status of semiosis in and for *non-objective* consciousness. Another way of thinking about this, of course, is that the semiosphere — literally, the universe as 'we' know it — is one big filter.

In any case, the usefulness of semiotic analysis for the attunement of our "information channels" to signals from the "outside" remains. In an accessible, introductory article on the semiotic method that has immediate applicability to the filters concept, Thomas Sebeok demonstrates well and clearly that any study of "filters" as such is a *de facto* semiotic one.[25] Twentieth-century semioticians have gone to great lengths to organize the "pivotal branch of the integrated science of communication."[26] To the degree that we accept that science, in spite of persistent antipathy for vitalism and teleology, is slowly evolving into a search for meaning,[27] then "the scientific study of significance" will only grow in relevance.

---

25. Thomas Sebeok, p. 448–466.
26. Thomas Sebeok, p. 451.
27. As suggested by Colin Wilson in *The Occult*.

References

Douglas R. Anderson. *Strands of System: The Philosophy of Charles Peirce.* West Lafayette, IN: Purdue University Press, 1995.

Imants Barušs. *Alterations of Consciousness: An Empirical Analysis for Social Scientists.* Washington: American Psychological Association, 2003.

Robert Burch, "Charles Sanders Peirce," The Stanford Encyclopedia of Philosophy (Fall 2005 Edition), Edward N. Zalta, ed. <http://plato.stanford.edu/entries/peirce/>.

Ernst Cassirer. *An Essay on Man.* Garden City, NY: Doubleday Anchor, 1953.

David S. Clarke, Jr. *Sources of Semiotic: Readings with Commentary from Antiquity to the Present.* Carbondale: Southern Illinois University Press, 1990.

Jacques Derrida. "Violence and metaphysics." *Writing and Difference.* Alan Bass, trans. Chicago: University of Chicago Press, 1978. pp. 79–153.

Deux ou trois choses que je sais d'elle. Jean-Luc Godard, dir. France: New Yorker Films, 1967. 90 min.

J. A. Scott Kelso. *Dynamic Patterns: The Self-Organization of Brain and Behavior.* Cambridge, MA: MIT Press, 1995.

Robert Klee. *Introduction to the Philosophy of Science.* New York: Oxford UP, 1997.

Charles S. Peirce. *The Collected Papers of Charles Saunders Peirce.* Charles Hartshorne and Paul Weiss, eds. Cambridge: Harvard University Press, 1934–36.

———. *Peirce on Signs.* James Hoopes, ed. Chapel Hill: University of North Carolina Press, 1991.

Paul Perron and Marcel Danesi, eds. *Classic Readings in Semiotics.* New York: Legas, 2003.

Ilya Prigogine and Isabelle Stengers. *Order Out of Chaos: Man's New Dialogue with Nature.* Boulder, CO: Shambhala, 1984.

Thomas A. Sebeok. "Pandora's box: How and why to communicate 10,000 years into the future." *On Signs.* Marshall Blonsky, ed. Baltimore: Johns Hopkins University Press, 1985.

Thomas A. Sebeok and Marcel Danesi. *The Forms of Meaning: Modeling Systems Theory and Semiotic Analysis.* Berlin: Mouton de Gruyter, 2000.

Colin Wilson. *The Occult.* London: Watkins Publishing, 2003.

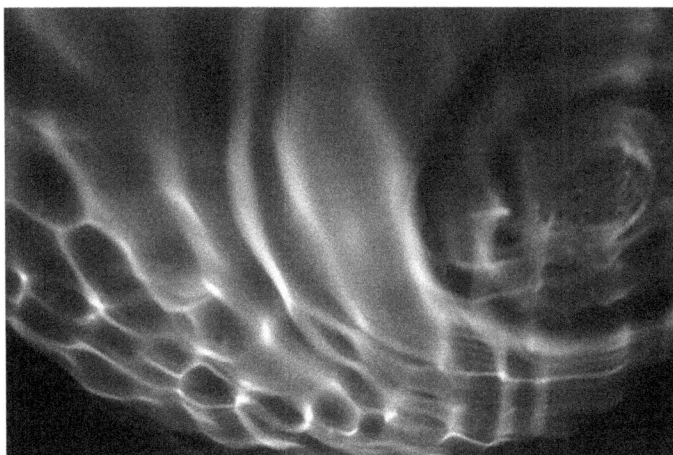

"Drops that fall into water." Image from the art-installation "Interference" by Skeel, Skriver, and Ellegaard. Esbjerg Museum of Art 2005.

Art, Mind, and Matter

CHRISTIAN SKEEL AND MORTEN SKRIVER
Artists, Copenhagen, Denmark

Prologue

"Sensors, Filters, and the Source of Reality" is the title of a theoretical paper on anomalous consciousness-related physical phenomena, but it could just as well be the title of a very interesting thesis on art. In fact, any interest in art is an interest in unusual consciousness-related physical phenomena. We don't know the nature of reality. Some celebrated quantum physicists now argue that particles might not have any mass at all: that they are in some way immaterial clicks in a counter. Our knowledge of the world has two sources: direct and indirect. Indirectly it seems that 96% of the universe is dark matter and dark energy of which we know nothing except that it has to be there for the calculations to fit. Directly we know that the world is full, that it's all there, and that we can sense it in every detail. We also know that what we see is what we are. Every human being is a reflection of the universe. How can we be different from our origins? We are all a product of the Source. We are the sensors and the filters. Between the Source and ourselves we place mirrors and paintings, text and dance, music and theories, prayers and sport, meditation and experiments, in order to be, to feel, and to learn. This is art. This is science.

Resonance

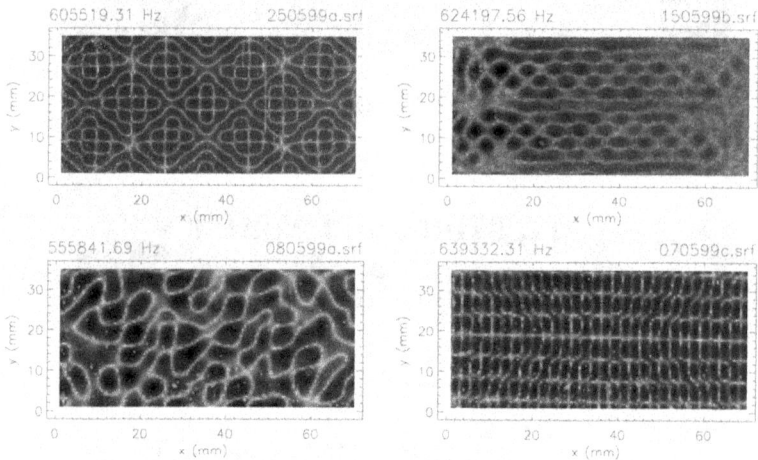

Image of acoustic waves in a quartz plate by Clive Ellegaard.

Art is basically about the interaction between consciousness and matter. In art, the artist transfers emotion and intention to the canvas. In a way that is hard to explain, the traces, emotions, and moods of our consciousness are transported *via* the nervous system through the muscles of the hand and into the shaft and hair of the brush, into the flowing paint, and out onto the absorbent canvas: a surface tension that bursts; a controlled bleeding. And there in the pigment and binder a piece of momentary, perfectly immaterial information lies, an emotional happening preserved like a print, a petrified outburst, a nervous fossil. It is neither digital nor analogue testimony, but a hidden touch, a caress in the material, waiting for the observer to unite with the essence of the painting.

To the artist and the lover of art there is little doubt that there is a mutual exchange of spirit and energy between man and his surroundings. The observer may or may not be moved by a work of art. Whether he is moved depends on whether to some extent the observer shares emotions with the creator of the work in question. We might describe the exchange of feelings between work and observer as a resonance phenomenon, just as two similarly tuned stringed instruments resonate when one of them is struck. This transfer and exchange of states of consciousness that takes place in art is hard to explain solely as a mechanical phenomenon. Not only are there too many undertones and overtones; the whole context of symbols, esthetics, and cultural contemporaneity from which art emerges acts upon anyone in its midst as a field of consciousness extending beyond the individual. Indeed, we might even describe the cultural formations, now but volatile tendencies, but which once remained stable for centuries or even millennia at a time, as a kind of self-sustaining collective arena of consciousness.

Presumably the more we open our minds and senses to these transpersonal fields of consciousness, the clearer and more frequently we will tend to sense their existence. Work on art is very much a method for opening the mind and senses to what lies beyond the scope of ordinary consciousness. In every age art has been inextricably associated with the part of the human world in which we also find dreams and visions, forebodings, prophesies, trances, and revelations. We might even say that the main trend of art since the oldest times has always been closely related to mysticism. Art has its deepest roots in shamanism: in magic signs and symbolic acts, fetish figures and sacrificial rites; the laying of blood and coloring onto stone; the magical manipulation of water, fire, oil, and ash; the invoking of spirits and conjuring of objects; amulets and things with souls. Ritual and icon were an opening into the spiritual world: an aesthetic arrangement that comprised the very centre of culture. Sound and vision, word and deed were one until the paths of art, science, and religion divided.

Today, in the modern tradition, transcendental aspects continue to be ascribed to art. The concept of transcendence in art may originate from Emanuel Kant's ideas of the sublime and of aesthetics as a special category of cognition. There is no doubt that in art, however, there is a

Interference painting. Installation image from the exhibition "Labyrinth," Charlotten-borg, Copenhagen. Skeel & Skriver 2005.

special interest in and veneration for the object that is not solely of an aesthetic nature. There is an interest in the link between object and its origin that is similar in many ways to that possessed by a Roman Catholic for a holy relic. A monochrome blue picture by French artist Yves Klein is among the most precious objects of 20th-century art. A similar paint-ing of unknown origin found in a flea market would not represent any fi-nancial value at all. But that does not mean that Yves Klein's picture does not have a special impact. On the contrary: it is generally agreed that his paintings are among the most spiritually exalting and consciousness-ex-panding works in the history of modern art. There is a special quality to Yves Klein's paintings that is hard to define and is experienced only when we actually look at them in real life. What the paintings radiate and what we see in them is the reflection of a serene, exalted state of mind closely associated with Yves Klein the man.

Like a shaman, Yves Klein might not have been particularly serene or highly developed as a person, but he was able to contact and then channel states like these to the people around him. In this way he represents a significant movement in modern art: the notion that the work can repre-sent and convey profound transpersonal spiritual states. Early pioneers of abstract art like Kandinsky and Mondrian were very much influenced by theosophical ideas of the existence of a spiritually supersensory world. The American art scene as it developed from the 1950s around Marcel Duchamp in New York is infused with Zen Buddhism and other mystical Oriental philosophy. In the 1980s the shamanist tradition seemed to culminate in the strongly Rudolph Steiner–inspired German artist Joseph Beuys, who dominated the European art scene for over a decade by his extensive artistic work, his personality, his life, and his thoughts.

The notion of art we apply today — art for art's sake — came about in the Age of Enlightenment at the same time as Romanticism. We may dub it a necessary irrational cult for the new rational science-oriented European man. Art museums that arose in the same period were sacred places. Their design and exclusive location demonstrated their exalted importance. To anyone interested in art they were places redolent with spiritual power, like temples. Anyone who entered found his senses and awareness enhanced and left a new man, his mind recharged in the same way as a believer leaves church after service. However, the way the opening of the Guggenheim Museum in Bilbao attracted millions of tourists to this provincial town in Northern Spain was not due to any special interest in or understanding of art amongst the general public: the reason was more probably a widespread, profound yearning for a collective source of spiritual nourishment to counter our material powers of production in some way. The public symbolic meaning of art consists solely in the fact that it exists; that people dedicate themselves wholeheartedly to this indefinable, open spiritual field and keep it alive.

That art is the official mystical cult of technological civilization is clear from the continuing, intense construction of art museums all over the world. A remarkably precise image of this cultural significance occurred in London just before the turn of the millennium, when the new museum flagship, Tate Modern, was opened in an abandoned power station on the Thames. The power station building itself was an impressive cathedral from the heyday of the industrial revolution. Now it was to house the production of a completely different kind of intangible energy where enormous generators had once produced raw physical power around the clock. Then the Millennium Bridge was built directly linking the temple of the modern era, Tate Modern, with the city's most important church,

St Paul's Cathedral: it has been a focal point for cultural life in London ever since.

The growing pomp and splendor surrounding art is no longer entirely countered by its inner life. From its inception at the end of the 19th century the motive force of modern art was the heroic journey of exploration. Art was an integral part of the modern upheaval in the same way as science and technology. The discovery of ever new ways of perceiving art, of new means of expression and potential styles turned art into a cultural flashpoint. It was a movement that started in principle when Cezanne began making the underlying compositional structures in his paintings just as significant as the representative layers of the motif. It only took a few decades before the Russian Malevich painted his white square on a white background. Malevich's painting was as abstract as could be, but it was also a dramatic, spiritually charged object inspired by his profound interest in the mysticism of Russian icons. At about that time Marcel Duchamp exhibited a bottle stand bought at a Parisian department store. For many years this was regarded as nothing but a provocative gesture under the anti-art label, which Duchamp himself used, but in fact it was a consistent continuation of the process that Cezanne had started. Duchamp pushed the concept of art beyond the edge of the picture, so to speak. He identified choice as the central element in art. Of all the items to be found in that department store he chose this particular bottle stand in exactly the same way as the painter chooses one color instead of another at the decisive moment. By incorporating the entire situation, process, and circumstances into the work, art was finally transformed from a craft to a particularly immediate way of being and acting in real life. At a stroke, Duchamp expanded the arena of consciousness in which art operated and transformed the concept of art in a way comparable to the influence of Albert Einstein's theories on physics.

The formal and conceptual evolution of art took place so rapidly that 50 years later, by the end of the 1930s, the possibilities for development had been discovered, but it continued with variations on existing themes until the mid-1980s. By then all styles coexisted side by side and simultaneously, and in a sense we might say that the history of art had come to a stop. Since then output has continued to rise, but artists capable of uniting and challenging the spirit of the age in the way Picasso or War-

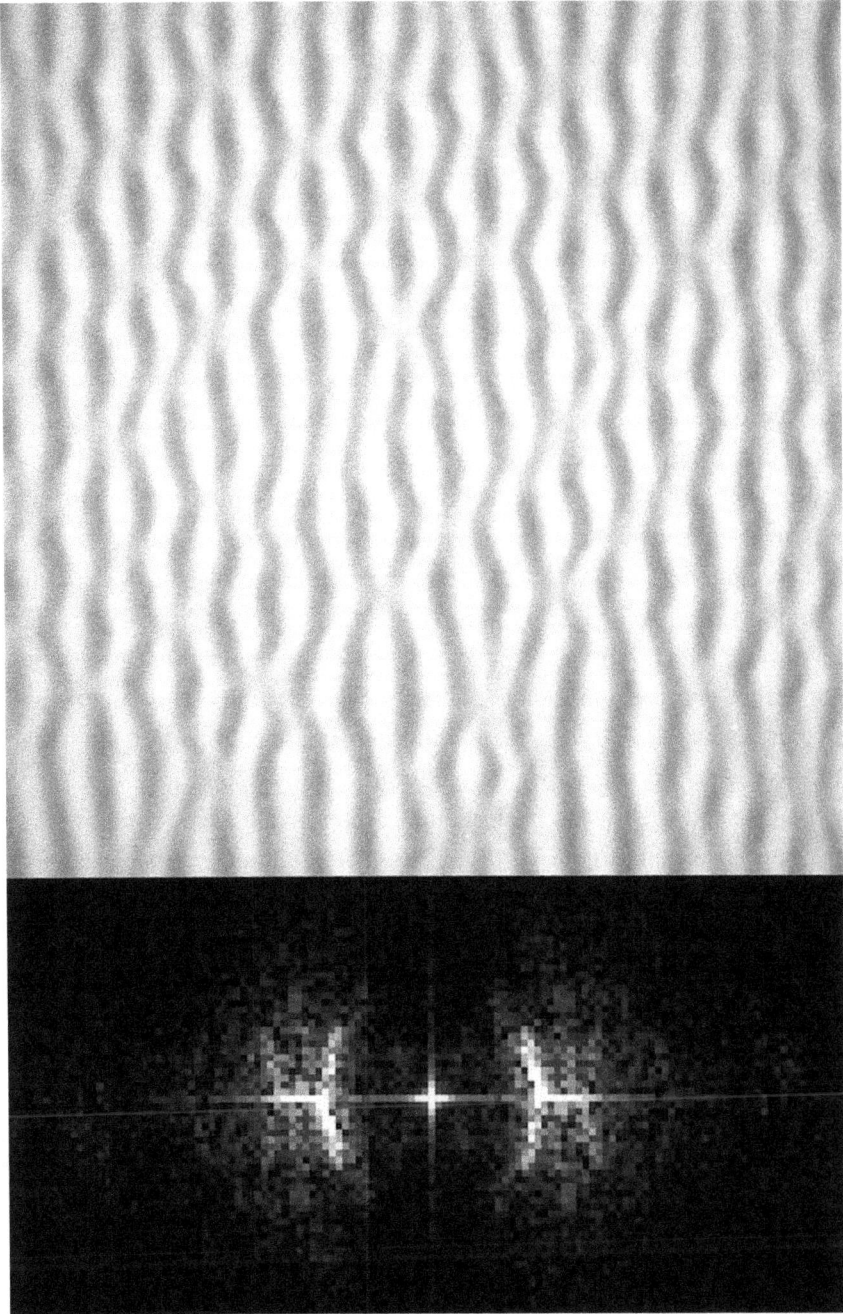

Image of a sand ripple pattern by Frederik Bundgaard.

hol did are becoming fewer and farther between. On the one hand, art is increasingly developing into purely commercial production of decorative aesthetics closely linked to fashion and advertising, and on the other, into an inaccessible, self-referring academic discipline. Indications are that art has reached the limits of its affectivity; limits already defined in the Renaissance when culture was divided into art, science, and religion as three distinct perceptive categories, each with its own language and inner logic.

Any continuation of man's cultural and civilizational evolution would seem to require the transgression of the lines dividing art, science, and religion: not in order to return to what was, but to elevate man and culture to new, higher levels of perception. Such an attempt to reunite the separate parts of our culture seems not only to be the next step in terms of logic: it also seems to be a prerequisite if we are to develop a relevant spiritual answer to the deadly nihilist materialism pervading consumer society and endangering man's very existence in countless ways. Our view of the world has been held rigid by two complementary orthodoxies for a very long time: reductionist natural science on the one hand, and the dogmatism of the great religions on the other. We need to unlock this picture and to create new ways of looking at, thinking about, and being in the world. In this regard art has a special role to play, for although it is very much closed around itself as an institution, it does provide a free zone between religion and science. If the orthodoxies of religion and science are a frozen sea, art is an opening in the ice: a free spiritual field without dogmatic ideas and rules as to how the world can or should be described.

Where Art and Science Meet

In many ways art and science are absolute opposites. They exist as separate areas because their approach to the world is fundamentally different. The ambition of science is to break nature down into its individual components with completely objective precision in order to see how they work together. The history of scientific theory is a continued series of explanations constantly spawning new questions requiring new explanations leading to new questions. Art, on the other hand, does not explain anything at all. It attempts to unify the world *via* extremely subjective, ambiguous statements. But neither art nor science can exist alone. They need each other the way the spirit needs matter in order to create a universe that can be seen, heard, and tasted. Art and science represent two complementary sides of man. So they also possess fundamental similarities. In a sense their goals are identical. They both employ intuition and intelligence to get closer to the mystery of existence. They try to create images that make sense. So the two areas must learn to talk and work together.

Of course, it is impossible to predict to what such cooperation will lead. But we might hope that art and science together could produce a continuum of understanding that simultaneously contains the abstract and the concrete, the part and the whole, subject and object, rational logic and the irrational intuition of the emotions. Perhaps this might lead to a kind of science that would not write the spirit out of nature, and a kind of art that would be a concrete instrument by which to approach the sacred. Science would, of course, continue to be good, reliable science, but its interpretations would incorporate elements from art and religion, just as art would reflect elements of science and religion through its own means of expression.

We recently worked with the physicist Clive Ellegaard and the Niels Bohr Institute in Copenhagen on a major exhibition. The exhibition explored patterns and interference in a number of different ways. The project evolved as if it had been planned by destiny. It started when a museum asked us to do an exhibition incorporating science into the field of art. Our first thought was an experiment we had chanced to see five years ago on a guided tour of the Niels Bohr Institute with Robert Jahn and Brenda Dunne from PEAR. The experiment was intended to investigate the physics of the wave patterns as for example formed by the movement of water in the sand at the edge of a beach. To us, the concatenation of technical precision equipment and the billowing sand was an amazingly poetic statement about the meeting between the analytical scientific eye and the mystery of nature. Without knowing the background of the experiment, one could clearly see that it was an attempt to chart and explain the invisible dynamic forces that shape the world at the macroscopic level: phenomena of the same kind as the Zen monks meditate upon in their sand gardens behind the Kyoto temple walls. The experimental apparatus was not conceived of as art, but for that very reason it manifested itself with clarity of expression of a kind vouchsafed only a tiny minority of works of art.

We didn't know whether the experimental apparatus still existed and we had no idea who'd set it up. But when we talked to its creator, Clive Ellegaard, we discovered that what we had seen in the experiment had also been a major motivating factor for him. As an experimental physicist, Ellegaard had been working for years on interference patterns, wave motion, and dynamic systems and he was fascinated by the aesthetic aspects of these phenomena. We really had intended only to borrow his experimental apparatus in order to use it as what Marcel Duchamp called a "ready-made," but after our very first meeting Ellegaard became an integral part of our project. Together we developed a series of apparatuses in which drops of water falling into shallow basins created different kinds of interfering patterns. *Via* a mirror at the bottom of each basin, a light projected the moving patterns onto the walls of the exhibition hall. While we were working on this installation at one of the Niels Bohr Institute labs we had moments when we felt we were approaching a point at which light waves and brain waves began to move in phase. Despite their powerful visual fascination the throbbing light patterns evinced a characteristic peace of mind. In the final installation, the apparatus and its effect were inseparable, just as the nature of the space and the consciousness of the observer played a vital part in the overall situation.

Our own interest in patterns goes back to the start of our artistic collaboration when we worked with the patterns women in parts of Southern

"Kolam" pattern made with white powder. South India 1979.

Left: Lissajous figure. Center and right: "kolam" patterns.

India draw every morning with white powdered stone outside their homes. A group of these patterns is built up of looping lines around a system of dots. By chance we discovered that in physics there is a phenomenon strikingly similar to the patterns from Southern India. This phenomenon is known as Lissajous figures. It occurs in many different contexts: for example electrical fluctuations in an oscilloscope or special kinds of pendulum movements. To us this coincidence became an image of the underlying, invisible structure of patterns within patterns to be found throughout nature and the world of man: cultural patterns and light patterns alike; throbbing, interfering patterns; patterns that determine how we act in the world and how we view it.

This perception of the concept of patterns accorded completely with Ellegaard's. He, too, was fascinated by general pattern-forming phenomena. So it was not hard for us to understand one another even though we were coming from different directions. In some sense the patterns rendered the world transparent and this transparency enabled us to see how we interfere mutually and with the environment the way different wave patterns meet and begin to affect one another. The wave movements amplify or suspend one another, thereby creating patterns and figures fundamentally different from their starting point in quality and complexity: not only the waves sound makes in the air, waves in water and light, but colliding fluctuations of all kinds possess this property, which suddenly leads from one state to another. In nature and in culture creative, shaping forces are born of the encounter and interaction between different physical and mental systems. In the same way inspiration between two or more people may suddenly lead to a new mutual understanding. Perhaps interfering oscillations between works of art and the observer are what can change our state of mind. Perhaps we might even describe love as a particularly intense form of interpersonal interference.

Our collaboration with the Niels Bohr Institute proved successful as art but what we perceived as the spiritual dimension of the project remained a metaphor in relation to science. In the context of contemporary science the spirit is an abstraction of no concrete import. The reason for this is to be found in the inner logic of science itself. It simply has no need for the notion of spirit in its definition of nature. In the natural science model the spirit of man is merely the product of chemical and electrical processes in the brain. The natural sciences explore what can be measured and weighed; the human spirit, let alone the spirit of nature, cannot be measured or weighed. It is impossible to observe because it is simultaneously that which "sees." So although the spirit is very much visible in scientific endeavor, the strange thing is that the scientific view of the world remains an oddly spiritless, mechanical affair.

Any real encounter between science and art (and religion) presupposes that the phenomenon of spirit is given a more central place in science. The spirit in the form of what we call consciousness is the only phenomenon in the universe whose real existence we can ascertain for certain. Everything else is just indirect information that reaches us through our senses. That is why for much of our history mankind has regarded the spirit as the primary dimension of nature. The great natural philosophy traditions of wisdom such as the Vedic, Taoist, Buddhist, and the Platonic schools regarded consciousness as the very foundations of the physical universe and as a phenomenon which penetrates and links everything in the universe across time and space. The innumerable accounts of unusual phenomena of consciousness (such as clairvoyant dreams) that have flourished in all cultures at all times underpin just such a perception of consciousness. Moreover, a radically extended view of the phenomenon of consciousness seems implicit in many of the ideas expressed by the founding fathers of quantum physics.

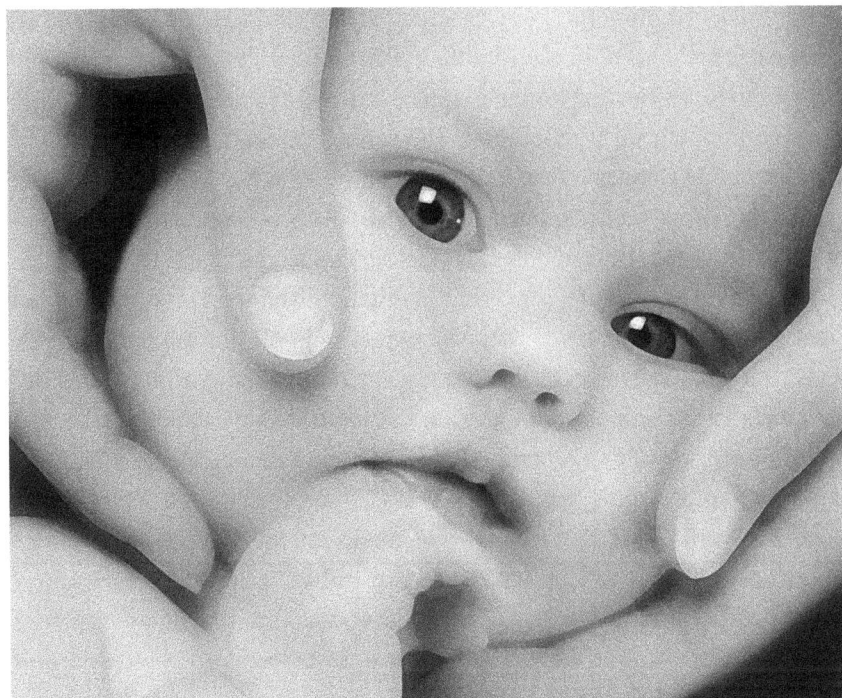

Screenshot from "The Trapholt Experiment" 2000.

The Trapholt Experiment

When we became aware of the work at PEAR in 1999, we immediately sensed that this was a fantastic invitation to a meeting among art, science, and religion. We were particularly inspired by the persistent concentrated attempts to record minimal effects of the interaction between the consciousness and various pieces of technical equipment. So we approached PEAR, suggesting that we develop an experiment of a kind that could act as science and art at the same time. Fortunately, PEAR was just as inspired by our idea as we were by their work, and a year later the experiment was complete. It was based on one of their microelectronic random event generator devices, fitted with a computer program that translated the output binary digits into evolving patterns of pixels displayed on a screen. Two display patterns that evolved randomly between a highly attractive emerging image of a baby and a random white noise background, were thus set into competition. The experiment was installed in a room of its own at the Trapholt Museum of Modern Art in Denmark.

The REG, computers, power supply, experimental log book, and so forth were located in an aluminium cupboard upon which a smaller display showed the random zeros and ones emitted from the REG. The only other component in the room was the screen displaying the dynamic of the competing images of the baby and the white noise background. Outside the room, three light displays showed the current status of the experiment: the number of trials, the cumulative result so far, and the statistical probability of this figure occurring by chance, and a sign that explained what the experiment was about. The experiment ran 'round the clock for a year. During this period, there was considerable media interest in describing the experiment and figuring out what it showed; there was also great interest from the general public in visiting the experiment and trying to influence it.

As a work of art, it was vital that the experiment appeared with absolute scientific rigor. The work was identical with the scientific apparatus, the experiment, and its design; but it was simultaneously a picture and an object of perception. The picture showed scientific endeavor and man's quest, and the forces of the universe that are concealed from our immediate senses. As an object of perception, it posed the fundamental question of what consciousness is, or perhaps more accurately, where it is in time, space, and matter. The room in which the experiment was set up was neutral, yet at the same time charged with meaning. Anyone who entered knew something special was going on that could not be seen. It was a kind of sacred place where you could contact and interact with the hidden forces of the universe. In that sense, the installation was directly linked to the oldest roots of art: to cult sites, icons, and magic signs. But at the same time, it pointed to a future possible meeting of art, science, and religion.

By definition, the results of the ongoing scientific experiment were unknown, allowing interpretations of all kinds; in this uncertainty and openness to interpretation there was room for the observer's own intuition and mental attitude. Anyone who interacted with the experiment could not fail to gain a slightly altered sense of the relationship between matter and consciousness, which led in turn to an intensification of one's perception of space and the objects that remained as one continued the tour of the museum. The Trapholt Experiment marked the extreme, paradoxical frontier post of human cognition where consciousness looks into itself and any explanation ceases to make sense. There were no longer any subject or object to be separated; no beginning or end: just timeless, directionless being.

A Kind of Conclusion

As artists, we could not form any particular views on the scientific importance of the Trapholt Experiment. We were incapable of judging its technology or the analytical methodology involved. The outcome of the experiment, however, was unimportant for the work of art. In a way, we hoped that the result would be negative because this would have confirmed that serious science was involved. But the result was somewhat ambiguous, with a statistical outcome that was marginally significant, which was even better, because it kept the picture wide open to interpretation. For art, the work at PEAR is primarily important because of the scientific endeavor behind it. PEAR's unique contribution to culture is its attempt to give consciousness a central role in the world of all science.

For 29 years PEAR has investigated various types of anomalous consciousness-related physical phenomena that are inexplicable in terms of the known models of the physical universe. Moreover, by their

"The Stockholm Experiment" 2002.

extensive experimental work, PEAR has demonstrated that under certain circumstances there is a significant probability that consciousness interacts with matter across space, and perhaps also across time. The degrees of effects measured are extremely small, however, and of a kind that makes it difficult to deduce rules for or to find patterns in the incidence of the phenomena observed. Using available experimental techniques, it has not proved possible to amplify or locate the effects observed to render them unambiguously visible as independent physical phenomena. So PEAR has been compelled to consider the psychological, subjective factors that both enter into and are part of the science the laboratory has carried out. Hence, a vitally important metascience has arisen that tries to reconceive the natural sciences themselves in its attempt to explain the apparently inexplicable.

Along with art, it is the duty of science to engender new ways of seeing the world. We will have to unify the objective and the subjective to enable harmony between our image of nature and the way it feels. As our starting point, all we know is that the universe reveals itself to man on a scale of 1 to 1. There is no reason to believe that the issue is any clearer elsewhere than here. It is here that it gathers and makes sense by way of the scent of the hawthorn blossom, Mozart's music, the swallows flitting across the sky, and a lover's caress. The deeper we look into matter and the farther we gaze into space, the more abstract and incomprehensible our observations become. We seem to be at the outer edge of the universe and at its absolute center. We cannot get farther away or closer up. Man is the best possible cosmic observatory. Nature, consciousness, and the senses form an inseparable whole. We are the universe looking at itself in the mirror of the mind.

Courting Maxwell's Demon: Filter-Shifts and Transformation in Psychotherapy

RUTH ROSENBAUM
National Psychological Association for Psychoanalysis
New York

One day my high-school chemistry teacher, Mr. Campbell, was talking about the random, yet predictable motion of gases. As he sketched little figures on the board representing molecules and atoms and electrons, he began to talk about some of the loopholes in Isaac Newton's world of perfect symmetry, of equal and opposite reactions, of causes distinctly on one team and effects on another. That was not necessarily an accurate depiction of reality, he said. It was only a matter of chance, of probability, that the molecules in the air were choreographed so that the proper life-sustaining proportion of the various gases existed in each breath. It would be possible, he said, for all the oxygen molecules to suddenly migrate to one side of the classroom, bursting blood vessels in everyone on that side, while those on the other side would be left gasping, in vain, for their lives. The class erupted into nervous giggles, melodramatic screams, and gurgling, choking sounds. At the time, I thought Mr. Campbell, who was kind of a jokester, had fabricated this vivid illustration to get the attention of a roomful of hormone-addled students. True or false, the notion captivated my imagination, not the part about dying a horrific death from a sudden shift in the patterns of molecules in the air, but the part about there being, ultimately, no fixed laws, not even for the universe. Anything was possible.

It was a valuable concept for me to keep in mind as I began working with patients over 25 years ago. I was struck by the sheer force and momentum of patterns that govern people's moods, relationships, motivation, and behavior. It seemed that for most people shifting those patterns was no less Herculean a task than grabbing the controls of a runaway locomotive traveling at 200 miles per hour and somehow getting it to change tracks without wrecking it entirely. Something beyond the expected ordering of events was needed.

Years after my high school experience, I discovered Maxwell's demon. Mr. Campbell hadn't been joking. Named after James Clerk Maxwell, a nineteenth-century physicist, this theoretical being (often depicted as an elfin/demonic figure with horns, tail, and pitchfork, sticking his hand into a container of molecules), could slip into a random, statistically predictable system, and cause it to behave in a totally unexpected, against-chance manner. It could add enough information to a system to reverse the effect of entropy, which, left to its own statistically driven devices, would bring about decay and dissipation. Eminent physicist William Thomson's description of Maxwell's demon's capability was almost identical to what I had dismissed as Mr. Campbell's fanciful embellishment:

"It is not impossible," Thomson wrote, "that one would find all the oxygen molecules in a vessel of air in the left-most fifth of [a] container" (Leff and Rex, 1990, p. 84).[1] Thomson was the first to use the name "demon" but claimed he meant it only to refer to a supernatural being and did not want to "suggest any evil intentions of the part of this being who could reverse the common tendency of nature" (p. 77).

In psychotherapy, patient and therapist engage in a process whose goal is to reverse the common tendency of human nature, that is, the tendency to repeatedly engage in life from the same set of perspectives, perspectives emerging from a maze of filters, each one of which contributes to the shaping of expectations, which, in turn, shape the kinds of experiences to which a person is open.

We accumulate filters from the time we are born; even before we are born. Our sensory systems are geared toward filtering in and filtering out, constantly shaping what we respond to. One study (DeCasper and Spence, 1986), showed that babies whose mothers read aloud a particular section of a Dr. Seuss story during the third-trimester of pregnancy responded more strongly, after birth, to hearing that particular section read, as compared to sections from other children's stories, or even different sections from the same Dr. Seuss story. So, at birth, a baby might already possess

---

1. A 2008 calculation by Brown University physicist Greg Landsberg puts the actual probability that all the molecules of air would suddenly cross to one side of a room at 10 to the minus 25 range (Collins, 2008, p. A19). (That is without a Maxwell's demon–like intervention.)

a highly nuanced filter that predisposes him to respond to *The Cat in the Hat*, for example, rather than *Horton Hears a Who!*

Each moment of our lives, each microsecond, we are accumulating filters, each one amplified or in some way colored by those that preceded it. A cruel remark in grade school can become a filter through which one experiences oneself for decades to come, and through which one experiences other experiences, even if they carry a different message. And of course, there are the dominant filters of culture, gender, religion, genetics, and family dynamics that form powerful lenses through which every other experience is shaped, in both overt and subtle, unconscious ways.

Psychoanalysis and psychotherapy concern themselves with unmasking and dismantling the filters, or selective lenses, that limit a person's realistic appraisal of self, healthy pursuit of goals, and sense of well-being and fulfillment in life. In PEAR terms, psychotherapy, by dissolving or neutralizing self-limiting filters, clears the channel through which a person can attain greater access to the "unstructured potentiality of the Source" (Jahn and Dunne, 2004, p. 549), and to an essential self in resonant communication with that Source. In psychoanalysis, filters often reveal themselves in the transference — the set of feelings, ways of relating, and assumptions that the patient carries from his past into the dynamic with the therapist.

The challenge for any patient-therapist team is similar to that of the PEAR operator-random event generator (REG) teams: to alter the predictable outcome that one might expect from the internal "programming" of a complex system of filters.[2] For example, can a woman, abused as a child and accustomed to abusive relationships as an adult, shift her intrapsychic programming enough to have a real choice in choosing relationships, rather than be governed only by the probabilities and expectations visible through the filters of her childhood?

---

2. In a typical PEAR lab experiment designed to explore the impact of human intention on the output of a random event generator's production of ones or zeros, the human subject sits in a room with a big machine and tries in some way to mesh his consciousness (or unconscious) with the workings of the machine so as to alter the expected statistical output of the machine (which according to chance would be 50% ones and 50% zeros). A meta-analysis of 832 experimental studies of the effect of human consciousness on random event generators, including some of the Princeton studies, found overall odds against chance of the impact of human intention on the machine's output of over a trillion to one (Radin, 1997, p. 140).

The sheer number and complexity of filters is mind-boggling. What makes the task of transforming this complex filter system even more difficult is that each filter can become locked into place in our physiology, imprinted in the patterns of our neural circuitry. Traumatic stress, for example, changes the levels of certain neurotransmitters, and the activation level in certain parts of the brain, which in turn serve as a filter through which a person then experiences even non-traumatic events. While medication can shift neurochemical filters and patterns of activity in the brain, thus relieving certain painful psychological states, recent studies have shown that successful psychotherapy brings about similar changes in the neural filters in certain parts of the brain without the deleterious side effects that accompany the use of many medications.

In a study at the U.C.L.A. School of Medicine, patients with obsessive compulsive disorder, which has been linked to hyperactivity of the caudate nucleus, were given either a serotonin reuptake inhibitor, such as Prozac, or cognitive behavior therapy. After ten weeks, both groups showed improvement and functioned more normally. The same changes in the brain were found in each group, mostly a decrease in the activity of the caudate nucleus, which some researchers have described as kind of "filter, sifting out extraneous thoughts and impulses" (Friedman, 2002, p. F5).

In a study comparing the efficacy of Paxil to that of interpersonal psychotherapy, depressed patients in both groups showed "nearly identical changes in their brain function, a decrease in the abnormally high activity seen in the prefrontal cortex before treatment" (Friedman, 2002, p. F5). Yet another study with depressed patients demonstrated not only that psychotherapy was as effective as medication in alleviating depression, but also that it increased activity in an area of the brain (the left side of the insula) associated with diminished feelings of depression and sadness, whereas the medication showed no effect in this area (Bower, 2001, p. 39). Clearly, the evidence for the bi-directional influence of body and mind is mounting, underscoring the ongoing interplay of the filter systems of both aspects of our beings. Because of this mutual shaping of physiological and psychological/emotional filters, I often integrate breathing techniques and biofeedback with psychodynamic therapy to help alter some of the rigid physiological filters that might be holding certain emotional patterns in place, even as shifts in emotional filters deriving from the therapeutic context help to alter physiological patterns.

The role of filters in psychotherapeutic healing is, I believe, best seen from an intersubjective point of view, with emphasis on the interaction of the filter systems of both patient and therapist, each of which is constantly evolving and affecting the other. Change and growth are most likely to occur if each member of the therapeutic dyad can expand his perspective and develop the capacity for filter-shifting, much like a well-oiled internal kaleidoscope.

To illustrate the intersubjective nature of filter-shifts in psychotherapeutic healing, I will describe three cases. The first involves Sam, a young man whose filters were so rigidly constructed that he was suffocating within them. In the second, you'll meet Seth, who challenged me to adjust my own filters in order to be able to help him. The third case demonstrates how my patient, Janet, and I consciously co-constructed a composite filter in the service of helping her.[3]

Coincidence and Filter-Shifts

When Sam first came to see me, he was seriously depressed following a significant job disappointment. He was 42, very handsome, had made a fair amount of money in his architecture business, a "golden boy" in many respects, and yet he had never maintained a relationship with a woman for more than two months. Sam's women had to be much younger, and perfect looking, and under the Sam microscope, no one came close. He had a few friends, but even they found some of his rigid views on certain issues hard to bear. Sadly for Sam, he applied the same contemptuous lens toward himself, and, at 42, his life was worth little to him because he had not fulfilled the grand vision he had for himself — not enough money, not enough status, and no perfect wife and kids.

One day, I was running a few minutes late for his session, and when he came into the office and sat down, he had a quizzical smile on his face. "I'd like to know what you think of this. I don't think this is really worth talking about, but listen to what happened. I was waiting for you and I

---

3. Patients' names and certain details have been changed in order to disguise patients' identities.

had this bag of M&Ms, and to pass the time, I tried to guess what color the next M&M would be before I took it from the bag. And, you know, I got all but one right! I mean, I don't think it's more than coincidence; I hate all that New Age-y stuff, but, it's kind of interesting."

With any other patient, I might simply have nodded and listened for what would follow. But with Sam, I recognized that this event, so outside his usual set of expectations as to how the world worked, had caught his attention. I tried not to let it wander.

"What do you find interesting about it?" I asked.

"Oh, nothing really," he backed off smugly. "I thought you might find it interesting; I think women like these kinds of things."

"Well, then, that was very nice of you to tell me about it. But, you know, if it were truly insignificant to you, if you were absolutely certain it was *mere* coincidence, I don't think you would have mentioned it," I challenged.

"I guess I was wondering if there might be something to it, I mean, do you think I might have some kind of talent?"

I knew I had to tread cautiously. To play into a belief that Sam had special powers would simply fuel the old template, and reinforce the already-existing filter — that he was worthless unless he could occupy a greater-than-mortal position.

So, I said, "I don't know about that, but I do think it means that there is something outside your usual way of seeing things that in some way intrigues you. Maybe it's liberating to think that there's something you haven't yet categorized. You know, maybe there are more things in Heaven and Earth than are dreamt of in your philosophy."

"That's from Hamlet, isn't it?" Sam asked.

I nodded.

"Well," said Sam, "I don't think that supports anything. I don't want a quote from literature. I hated all those humanities majors in college! I want a scientific explanation."

For the moment, I dropped my end of the rope in this tug of war, and Sam went on to talk about other things. But maybe Maxwell's demon was lurking. For in the next several weeks, a series of unusual coincidences, or synchronicities (depending on your filter), occurred in Sam's life. The incident with the M&Ms, which certainly could have been mere coincidence, seemed to have attuned Sam's attention to notice other odd coincidences. Sam became like an excited schoolboy bringing in material for show and tell. Clearly, something about our shared filter had changed. And then, there occurred the mother of all synchronicities.

First, some background: When Sam was depressed, he would read about the lives of famous and powerful men, hoping to find some identification with them that might kindle a spark of his own sense of worth. At one point he came across a little-known book containing George Washington's personal diary. In it were a series of prayers Washington had written for himself to provide solace and inspiration.

Sam told me about his favorite of the prayers, albeit a bit sheepishly, since, as he said, it was a little "corny" and far too religious. But if it was good enough for George Washington, it was good enough for him. He proceeded to recite the first part of Washington's "Monday Morning" prayer for me:

> O eternal and everlasting God, I presume to present myself this morning before thy Divine majesty, beseeching thee to accept of my humble and hearty thanks, that it hath pleased thy great goodness to keep and preserve me the night past from all the dangers poor mortals are subject to, and has given me sweet and pleasant sleep, whereby I find my body refreshed and comforted for performing the duties of this day, in which I beseech thee to defend me from all perils of body and soul ... (Johnson, 1919, pp. 26–27).

About the time of his discovery of the prayer, Sam, always in pursuit of hyper-macho endeavors, signed on to become a crew member of a ship on an expedition near the Arctic Circle. He was gone for over four weeks. Upon his return, he came in for his first session, smiling somewhat cryptically.

"OK, I give up," he announced. "I have to acknowledge that there are some things that can't be explained by logic or science."

I was certainly intrigued. Sam explained: Before his return to the United States, he took a side trip to Norway. On his second night in a village north of Oslo, he was having dinner at a restaurant, when a pretty young Norwegian woman drew his attention. He invited her to join him at his table. She was a college history major, and during their conversation, she happened to mention that her class was currently studying American history. One of her course requirements was that each student choose a prominent figure in American history and present a report to the class. She told Sam that she had chosen George Washington. What a coincidence, said Sam, and told her he'd recently read a book about Washington. Then, mainly to score points as a sensitive man, Sam told her of his discovery of Washington's prayers for guidance. As Sam began to recite the "Monday Morning" prayer — "O eternal and everlasting God, I presume to present myself this morning . . ." the young woman interrupted him, and took up where he'd left off. In halting English, she recited the entire first part of the prayer, the same part Sam had recited to me.

Sam looked at me. We were both speechless. Then Sam proceeded to get out pen and paper, and insisted, just to make sure we weren't getting carried away, that we try to calculate the odds against this happening by chance. And so, we went down Sam's list of questions, and tried, together, to estimate the following:

- What percentage of Americans know this "Monday Morning" prayer by George Washington?
- Of those Americans, what percentage might have travelled to a village north of Oslo recently?
- Of that small group, what percentage would have dined in the same restaurant and at the same time as the young history student who dined there that evening?

Then, we had to factor in:

- What percentage of Norwegians know of George Washington's "Monday Morning" prayer?

And of those,

- what percentage could actually recite a substantial portion of the prayer?

Needless to say, the odds we came up with were, conservatively speaking, a gazillion to one against this happening strictly by chance. And then, events of an even more improbable nature unfolded over the next several months. Without any obvious precipitating event, Sam began to question many of his fixed ideas about people and about himself. He started doing volunteer work at a hospital, and befriended an elderly man who lived near his home. He also fell in love with a woman unlike any he'd dated before, and has since married and had two children with her.

While there is no way of being certain of this, it seemed to me that our joint focus on the coincidence of his guessing the M&M colors, an anomalous experience for Sam, began a process of dismantling a very rigid set of filters that had previously locked Sam into a narrow, unsatisfying range of feelings and behavior. The filter shift began with Sam's allowing my deliberate lingering on his correct M&M guesses, and continued with his subsequent interest in other seemingly improbable coincidences. The final jolt from the Monday Morning prayer coincidence in Norway seemed to blow apart the last bit of his frozen template of filters, clearing the way for Sam's new life, supported by a new set of more flexible filters.

Carl Jung (1952/1973) tells of a case, similar in structure, where a synchronicity seemed to disrupt existing filters and open the way for transformation. Jung's patient was telling him about a dream in which she had been given a golden scarab, when they both heard a soft tapping noise at the window in Jung's office. It proved to be caused by an insect, which flew in when Jung opened the window. He caught it in his hand and found that it was a scarabaeid beetle, "the nearest analogy to a golden scarab that one finds in our latitudes," Jung wrote (p. 23). He continued:

> It was an extraordinarily difficult case to treat, and up to the time of the dream little or no progress had been made. I should explain that the main reason for this was my patient's animus, which was steeped in Cartesian philosophy and clung so rigidly to its own idea of reality that the efforts of three doctors — I was the third — had not been able to weaken it. Evidently something quite irrational was needed which was beyond my powers to produce. The dream alone was enough to disturb ever so slightly

the rationalistic attitude of my patient. But when the scarab came flying in through the window in actual fact, her natural being could burst through the armour of her animus possession and the process of transformation could at last begin to move (Jung, 1952/1973, p. 23).

The cases of Sam and of Jung's patient point to a limitation inherent in one of the prevailing filters of traditional psychodynamic theory — that a person's present dilemmas are caused by past conscious and unconscious experience, and that the key to liberating a person from his present discomfort is to follow the dots back to their origin in the past, or to discover the past in the present and release it — in other words, a linear model. While revealing unconsciously held patterns from the past is certainly crucial in most cases of psychological healing, it seems that nonlinear elements are essential as well. Whence do these nonlinear elements derive? Surely, one cannot count on the timely intervention of a golden scarab or a cooperative bag of M&Ms for a "quantum jump" in a patient's progress.

It seems as though the therapeutic relationship itself can provide an ongoing nonlinear stimulus for filter-shifts, and a scaffolding upon which words and interpretations can take hold. Just as Maxwell's demon reorganizes atoms in an otherwise predictable molecular system, and the PEAR lab operators, in subtle interaction with the REG, reorganize the pattern of expected output of the machine's ones and zeros, so does the therapeutic bond, much of it operating nonverbally, even outside conscious awareness, reorganize the intersubjective field between therapist and patient, and, in turn, expand the set of possible outcomes the patient can expect in his life.

Frame-by-frame analysis of the interaction between mothers and infants (Beebe and Lachmann, 2002) demonstrate that there are microsecond-to-microsecond shifts in both self and interactive regulation of mother and baby, with each shift serving to alter the intersubjective field, either opening up or limiting new possibilities of ways of relating. Beebe and Lachmann postulate that this mostly outside-of-awareness process is a fundamental underpinning of human communication, attachment, and psychological growth, operating simultaneously with the more conscious verbal modes of communicating. Thus, with patient and therapist there is an ongoing opportunity for reorganizing both the self-system and the self-in-relation-to-other system, and for reconfiguring the patient's (and therapist's) inner filter system, regardless of the weight of the countless linear moments leading up to that moment. This perspective is, in some ways, parallel to the Tibetan Buddhist view of the interaction of mind and reality, such that the mind is, at any point in time, capable of a nonlinear transformational interaction with, and simultaneous impact on, reality. (In this case, the dyad consists of the mind and reality, rather than of two minds.) As Ngakpa Chogyam, a Buddhist lama, has phrased it, we are always, "popping out of emptiness into the present moment" (Chogyam, 2002), so that in each new moment, anything is possible. (Emptiness, in this context, refers to the substantial, yet unformulated space that gives rise to all form.)

There is also a parallel between the intersubjective perspective of change in psychotherapy and some aspects of the PEAR random event generator studies.[4] The successful operators in the PEAR REG studies speak about entering a "third space" with the machine, in order to merge with it and gently bring about their intention of altering the machine's statistically predictable outcome. They fine-tune their own internal regulation in a way that seems to enhance the shift in the interactive field so that the REG produces its against-chance results. Similarly, each therapist-patient pair creates what Ogden (1994) terms an "analytic third" (p. 4), an essence of the relationship between each unique patient-therapist dyad that transcends a logical summation of their explicit communication. Tronick (1998) refers to the "dyadic expansion of consciousness" in psychotherapy, wherein states of consciousness emerge that encompass more than what either system (or person) alone could generate. It seems that the close relationship that develops between patient and therapist produces an "extra energy" in the system.[5] As I see it, this "extra energy", the calling card of Maxwell's demon, emerges from the attunement between patient

---

4. Relevant to this topic are the writings of psychoanalyst Elizabeth Lloyd Mayer (1996, 2007), who explored the roles of intersubjectivity and other nonlinear processes in psychoanalysis and science, as well as the implications of results emerging from some of the PEAR lab studies.

5. My use of the word "energy" and my references to Maxwell's demon are not meant to be taken in a strict physical science context, but rather are used as metaphorical illustration of the ideas presented in this chapter.

and therapist, and at the same time, effects that attunement, in a continuing spiral of filter-shifts, allowing for the alchemical transformation of insight into change. I find it interesting that many of the words used in describing the topic of intersubjective fields, such as resonance, attunement, coherence, oscillation, and perturbation of the system, are words that are also used in describing aspects of electromagnetic energy fields.

The nonlinear, nonverbal aspect of psychotherapy has increasingly been pinpointed as the focal point for change, both in evidence-based practice research and in neuroscience laboratories. Studies (Wallerstein, 1995; Klein, 2003) have concluded that a good working relationship, or what is called the therapeutic alliance, between therapist and patient, plays a larger role in psychological growth than any specific technique or theory. Following one such study by the National Institutes of Mental Health, psychologist Hans Strupp of Vanderbilt University commented that the study "indicates that the therapeutic alliance is more critical than the techniques a therapist employs or the drugs that may be prescribed. This is currently not a popular view among many researchers, and it isn't what health care insurers want to hear either" (Bower, 1997, p. 21).

Neuroscientist Allan Schore, at a conference on Neurobiology and Attachment Theory in Psychotherapy (2006), noted that recent studies of the brain (including functional MRI studies) indicate that intuitive attunement to the patient and the quality of the working alliance may be more critical in bringing about psychological change than particular techniques or interpretations. Once again, it seems as though nonverbal communication systems may be essential to the filter-shifts needed for psychological transformation.

Some of the PEAR REG studies point to a possible connection between an "extra energy" deriving from high levels of attunement between human beings, and a shift in an intersubjective field, in these instances a field consisting of two humans and a machine: It was found that two people working together with the same mental intention to impact the output of the REG produced a larger effect than a single person working alone. And couples who shared a strong bond "achieved an effect size nearly seven times larger than that produced by those same people as individual operators" (Dunne and Jahn, 2005, p. 709). One can speculate that these REG results point to an effect, though difficult to define, created by the bond between people, particularly people with an especially strong attachment or attunement, as often occurs in successful psychotherapy. I wonder if, one day, there may be measurable units of attunement that might explain both successful REG-type experiments and successful therapeutic outcome.

Physician, Open Thyself

Seth, who worked as a paralegal, came to see me in January, 2002. On September 11, 2001, he was in his office in one of the buildings near the World Trade Center when the planes hit the towers. Shell-shocked, he made his way home, one of the hundreds of ghoulish figures walking over the Brooklyn Bridge, covered in the ashen particles of buildings and bodies. For weeks following the disaster, Seth experienced what many survivors did — sleepless nights, loss of appetite, flashbacks, and difficulty concentrating. In addition, Seth cautiously told me what else he was experiencing: Every night following the disaster, he was visited by dozens of deceased souls from the Twin Towers, and they were besieging him with their anguish and confusion. Many, he said, still did not realize they were dead, and he felt it was his responsibility to help them understand this so they could move on. Others, he told me, were obsessed with unfinished business. One woman, for example, was distressed because she hadn't completed work on a big account for one of the firms, and wanted Seth to make some calls to ensure that her work would be completed. Seth had been so overwhelmed by these nightly disturbances that he went to a psychiatrist for help. The help he received was a diagnosis of "paranoid schizophrenia," a recommendation that he be hospitalized immediately for observation, and prescriptions for a total of five medications.

In his first session with me, Seth told me he had stopped taking all medication because it was "driving him crazy." Still, he wanted help. His night visitors would not leave him alone, he was not sleeping at all, and he was distracted and unfocused at his job. As I learned more about Seth, I assessed him to be a basically well-functioning individual (prior to this present crisis), with some beliefs and experiences that were beyond my habitual filter system. However, I thought, I had worked quite well with patients who were Orthodox Jews, atheists, devout Catholics, Muslims,

Evangelical Christians, even one devotee of Santería. I didn't necessarily adopt every aspect of all of their beliefs. Was Seth so different? I certainly couldn't claim to know what happens to us after we die.

As I listened to Seth, I began to see a connection between the kinds of disputes and rage Seth experienced at work and with certain friends, and the way he related to some of his deceased visitors. He would adopt a very arrogant, bossy attitude, often peppering his speech with four- and five-letter words, even as he tried to help and give useful counsel. I encouraged him to explore the dynamics from his childhood that governed his relationships with both the living and the dead. I treated the interactions he had with inhabitants of both worlds with equal concern. As time went on, Seth began to manage his anger in relationships with friends, lovers, and people at work, as well as with the Trade Center victims who crowded into his room at night.

Gradually, the nightly visitations diminished, and Seth was able, finally, to sleep. Mysteriously, a severe case of facial alopecia, which had developed after the 9/11 tragedy, totally reversed itself; Seth was delighted to have to shave once again. He also reconnected with estranged family members. This former black sheep became the family counselor, and helped several relatives to begin to deal with lingering issues of their own. Seth is now married and has attained a better position at work.

Only by expanding my filters was I able to help Seth deconstruct the filters that had been imposing real obstacles to his happiness and progress in life. This approach also allowed me to get to know a delightful human being; actually, two delightful human beings. For, as Seth tells me, his deceased grandmother, a rare mentor and beloved figure to Seth in an otherwise emotionally chaotic childhood, occasionally joins us in our sessions. Apparently, she is a fan of our work together. Who am I to argue?

A Freudian Filter — with a Twist

Though Freud (1915) said that the unconscious is timeless, I'm not sure he would have approved of my applying his statement to the following case. And yet, within the 23 volumes of work he produced over a 45-year period, Freud changed or contradicted many aspects of his theories as his thinking (and filters) evolved. Perhaps, if he were still alive, and still evolving, he might be able to accommodate this particular perspective on the timeless unconscious.

Janet, an unusually attractive, brilliant, 37-year-old corporate lawyer came to see me after the break-up of her fourth serious relationship. In all of these relationships, this super-competent, spirited woman was demeaned and devalued. In her work, though she often did the job of three people, she was routinely undercompensated and underrecognized. She suffered from many physical ailments, but would ignore her own symptoms while tending to everything and everyone else until, on several occasions, she ended up in the emergency room. Her filter regarding her own worth was so encrusted with the residue from a childhood filled with loss and traumatic events, that she truly could not see any alternative to her repetitive choices and dangerous behavior.

As intelligent as she was, and despite the considerable insight she gained in the first year of therapy, very little changed in her beliefs about herself. Often a childhood filled with trauma welds filters in place so tightly, because of the intensity of physiological responses associated with survival, that it is particularly difficult for new experiences to shift them.

At some point in the second year of our working together, Janet had a series of four dreams, each with a strikingly similar structure. An example of one of the dreams: Janet is on a battlefield. In the dream she is a male soldier. She was able to describe in detail the uniform she was wearing, the weaponry, and the surroundings. There is an artillery explosion, and she runs to aid two wounded comrades. As she does so, she looks down at her own body and discovers that her skin is black and charred, her uniform partly torn away, partly melted into her skin. She realizes that she is dead, and even so, continues to help the two dying soldiers. This theme was repeated in the four dreams in question, as it was, over and over, in her life, where she would ignore her own serious symptoms, even as she threw herself into helping others.

After describing in detail the last of the dreams in this series, Janet asked me if I believed in past lives. At the time, I was open to the idea, but hadn't arrived at a point of certainty about it. I told her that, and asked her what she thought. She was also uncertain as to her belief in reincarnation, but said that these dreams were so real-seeming, and each one so detailed as if they took place in specific eras and specific wars, that she had begun to wonder if they might actually be past life events. I, too, had been struck by the cinematic detail and vividness of these particular dreams. I suggested to Janet that we proceed as if the people in her dreams were, in fact, her previous incarnations. As I proposed this, my thought was that perhaps Janet could develop feelings for a self that was also a not-self, and that that might help her elude the deeply engrained prohibition against paying attention to, or caring for, herself.

We agreed that we would begin to include in our discourse the concept of past lives, a new filter for both of us. She even began to research some of the particulars in her dreams. For instance, one of the weapons she'd described in detail in one dream turned out to be striking in its resemblance to a Cogswell Pepper Box revolver used in the Civil War.

Though I was not at the time a card-carrying believer in past lives, I had given a lot of thought to the concept of karma. My intuitive understanding of it was that as a soul traveled through many incarnations, it accumulated patterns (perhaps in some unspecified energetic form) associated with its past experiences. When a soul incarnated into a new life, I imagined that its energy configurations would be drawn, as if magnetically, to a family or set of circumstances that resonated with, or matched in some essential way, its former experiences. So, as I envisioned it, the soul transmitted its own filters into the mind-body system at or before birth. These filters would continue to shape a person's experience in repetitive fashion, until that person could take on the challenge of becoming aware of, and changing, those patterns that were blocking the soul's full expression. Suffering in this lifetime did not mean, in my mind, that a person was being punished for past bad deeds, but rather that past experiences, past filters, as yet unidentified, could influence present inclinations, expectations, and experiences. This didn't seem so different from many aspects of psychoanalytic theory, except that the temporal-spatial frame and the sheer number of past influences reverberating in the present were greatly augmented.

Soon after Janet and I decided to apply the filter of past lives to her problems, I decided to study with a Tibetan Buddhist lama, Lama Pema Wangdak. In his class, I learned about the concept of "bag chags" (pronounced "bok chok"), which deepened my understanding of karma. "Bag chags" refers to the latent residues of habitual tendencies and inclinations, reinforced by each lifetime's experiences, which are carried forward by the soul from one lifetime to another until a person in a particular lifetime chooses to deal with those tendencies and change them, thus providing the opportunity for enlightenment and liberation of the soul from further suffering.

Janet did seem to be struggling with a karmic pattern that, as her dreams might indicate, she had been governed by many times before, even though the circumstances, location, era, and even her gender, were different than in this lifetime. (Understanding her problems through this filter did not preclude our continuing investigation of this lifetime's influences. In fact, her current lifetime's patterns simply acquired greater resonance and meaning to her, viewed from the perspective of reincarnation.)

Opening the filter of reincarnation opened Janet to new ways of experiencing herself. She was able to feel a compassion for the selves represented in her dreams that she had never before allowed herself to feel for herself in this life. She really "got" how she, in this and other lifetimes, would take her service to others, and neglect of herself, to absurd extremes. As I shared with her what I was learning in my classes with Lama Pema, she felt that if she could interrupt this karmic cycle now, she would be doing something generous, even altruistic for her future self, a self which would also be an "other," or "others," in future lifetimes. It was this subtle vision of herself as both connected to and separate from these future selves that allowed Janet to begin to extend compassion and empathy to the person she is in her current life. She felt motivated to protect herself, to speak up to people who devalued her, and to take better care of her health. Her choices in men gradually changed, and she is now engaged to be married to a man who really cares for her, rather than one who exploits her.

Unfiltered Experience

Traditional theories of psychoanalysis fostered the belief that the personality of the analyst was not a critical feature of implementing progress and change. In fact, it was the analyst's professional obligation to provide a "blank screen" onto which the patient could project his neurotic patterns. These patterns were then to be examined, and specific techniques to be applied, much as a medical doctor examines a physical body and applies a treatment. Now it is commonly agreed upon that it is inadvisable for a therapist to think of himself as a blank screen. Patients detect much about their therapists, and even a therapist who chooses to function as a blank screen is revealing a multitude of clues about his personality simply by virtue of that choice. In fact, a therapist's personal style, his way of being in relation to another, is an essential component of the intersubjective field.

As the APA Presidential Task Force on Evidence-Based Practice (2006) noted: "Because of the importance of the therapeutic alliance to outcome, an understanding of the personal attributes and interventions of the therapist that strengthen the alliance is essential for maximizing the quality of patient care" (p. 278).

I would suggest that one of the most helpful personal attributes is the therapist's ability to shift his own filters. This ability allows for enhanced attunement to the patient, and a greater ease in discovering new perspectives from which to understand the challenges facing the patient. My own training in this endeavor, with all due respect and deep gratitude to my wonderful mentors and teachers, actually began one night when I was three and half years old. I had been lying in bed for quite some time, trying to fall asleep, but feeling, as often happened, quite wide awake. This particular evening, I had already loosened the few strings that held my tenuous toddler identity together by trying to ponder the fate of my three dead siblings. After my older brother was born, my mother gave birth to three babies, each of whom died at, or shortly after, birth. All I was aware of at the time was that three children had been born, didn't survive, and then there was "me", who had survived.

Just at an age when, developmentally, I would have been learning to revel in the concept of "me", I began to question it. Who was "Ruthie"? Who was "me"? Was this "Ruthie/me" one of the other babies shifted down, a soul that had finally found a healthy body to inhabit, but had not much to do with "me" or "Ruthie" personally? (Of course, at age 3, I was not articulating my experience in this manner, but I am trying to put words to what I vividly recollect about my thoughts and experiences at the time.)

So, I continued "meditating" on this idea of "me":

"Here I am in my room," I remember thinking. "My parents are across the hallway, and my brother's in the next room. My connection to these people make me 'me'." I suppose I was locating myself in the longitude and latitude of my three-year-old reality. And then suddenly it was as if I fell beneath that grid: There was no longer a sense of "me-ness" or "they-ness." All the connections, the identifying connections — *my* family, *my* room, *my* self, that had just a moment before been so tangible — were not there at all. There was no sense of identity at all. I felt I was in a vast, unending space, except there was no "I" experiencing it. Actually, there is no way of representing this part of the experience in words; it is beyond representation, since there was no "I" to cognitively map it. Only as I came back into an awareness of "me" and began to reconnect to the things around me, only in that transition, did I sense that where I had just been, that boundless, dimensionless place, was actually more solid than the place I was coming back to. It seemed like a denser, more fundamental, and ironically, more grounding space. Rather than being frightened, I found the experience to be inexplicably exhilarating and blissful.

After that first experience, I sought, and learned, by trial and error, how to find the "secret panel" within my mind that could open onto the experience of this boundless, seamless realm. Often it would be by going back to the way it had happened originally, focusing intently on the thickness of "me", "me-ness", my parents, my house; and then, if I was lucky, the meaningfulness of all those reference points would simply fall away, and I would be in that unfiltered state, where "me" was dissolved into an ecstatic sensation of oneness.

Even though each time I returned from one of these ecstatic journeys, the fact of being "me" again precluded a totally clear representation of where I had been, I felt as though I carried something of the experience back with me, like a returning astronaut with a bit of space dust, or a chunk of an asteroid. Looking back, I am certain that there was a mutual shaping that took place between my experience of unbounded, unfiltered space and my own personal development, and that in a non-linear way, those early experiences, and many similar subsequent ones, led me to the field of psychotherapy. These mystical excursions heightened my awareness of an aspect of existence unencumbered by filters, and opened me to the filter-shifting potential of states of empathy and profound interconnectedness, whether between people, or between one's self and that which lies beyond the self.

Sometimes, as I'm sitting with a patient in my office, I experience a glimmer of that unbounded space, and of the patient and myself immersed in that space, privileged to be in each other's company at a moment in time, the limitations of our filters temporarily suspended, open to unexpected possibilities, together courting Maxwell's demon.

References

APA Presidential Task Force on Evidence-Based Practice. "Evidence-based practice in psychology." *American Psychologist, 61*, No. 4 (2006). 271–285.

Beatrice Beebe and Frank M. Lachman. *Infant Research and Adult Treatment: Co-Constructing Interactions*. New Jersey: The Analytic Press, 2002.

Bruce Bower. "Depression therapies converge in brain." *Science News, 160*, No. 3 (July 21, 2001). p. 39

Bruce Bower. "Uncovering traits of effective therapists." *Science News, 151*, No. 2 (January 11, 1997). p. 21.

Ngakpa Chögyam. "Lecture on the Nine Bardos." Bailey Farms. Millwood, N.Y. Nov. 1–3 2002.

Gail Collins. "Digging ourselves a black hole." *The New York Times*. (August 23, 2008).

Anthony J. DeCasper and Melanie J. Spence. "Prenatal maternal speech influences newborn's perception of speech sounds." *Infant Behavior and Development, 9*, No. 2 (1986). pp. 133–150.

Brenda J. Dunne and Robert G. Jahn. "Co-Operator Experiments with an REG Device." Technical Report PEAR 91005. Princeton Engineering Anomalies Research, Princeton University, Princeton, NJ, December 1991.

Sigmund Freud. *The Unconscious. Standard Edition, XIV*: 1915. p. 187.

Richard A. Friedman. "Like drugs, talk therapy can change brain chemistry." *The New York Times*. (August 27, 2002).

Robert G. Jahn and Brenda J. Dunne. "Sensors, filters and the Source of reality." *Journal of Scientific Exploration, 18*, No. 4 (2004). pp. 547–570.

William Jackson Johnson. *George Washington, the Christian*. New York: The Abingdon Press, 1919.

Carl Gustav Jung. *Synchronicity: An Acausal Connecting Principle*. Richard Francis Carrington Hull, trans. Princeton, NJ: Princeton University Press, 1973. (Original work published 1952.)

Daniel N. Klein, Joseph E. Schwartz, Neil J. Santiago, Dina Vivian, Carina Vocisano, Louis G. Castonguay, Bruce Arnow, Janice A. Blalock, Rachel Manber, John C. Markowitz, Lawrence P. Riso, Barbara Rothaum, James P. McCullough, Michael E. Thase, Frances E. Borian, Ivan W. Miller, and Martin B. Keller. "Therapeutic alliance in depression treatment: Controlling for prior change and patient characteristics." *Journal of Consulting and Clinical Psychology*, 71, No. 6 (2003). pp. 997–1006.
Harvey S. Leff and Andrew F. Rex. *Maxwell's Demon: Entropy, Information, Computing*. New Jersey: Princeton University Press, 1990.
Elizabeth Lloyd Mayer. "Changes in science and changing ideas about knowledge and authority in psychoanalysis." *Psychoanalytic Quarterly*, *LXV* (1996). pp. 158–200.
———. *Extraordinary Knowing*. New York: Bantam Books, 2007.
Thomas H. Ogden. "The analytic third: Working with intersubjective clinical facts." *International Journal of Psycho-Analysis*, 75, No. 1 (1994). pp. 3–19.
Dean Radin. *The Unconscious Universe: The Scientific Truth of Psychic Phenomena*. San Francisco: Harper Edge, 1997.
Allan N. Schore. Neurobiology and attachment theory in psychotherapy. Workshop conducted at Mount Sinai Medical Center, New York. (June 2006).
Edward Z. Tronick, Nadia Bruschweller-Stern, Alexandra M. Harrison, Karlen Lyons-Ruth, Alexander C. Morgan, Jeremy P. Nahum, Louis Sander, and Daniel N. Stern. "Dyadically expanded states of consciousness and the process of therapeutic change." *Infant Mental Health Journal*, *19*, No. 3 (1998). pp. 290–299.
Robert S. Wallerstein. "The effectiveness of psychotherapy and psychoanalysis: Conceptual issue and empirical work." In Theodore Shapiro and Robert N. Emde, eds., *Research in Psychoanalysis: Process, Development, Outcome*. Madison, CT: International Universities Press, 1995. pp. 299–312.

The Holy Undivided

JEANNINE DAVIES
Vancouver, British Columbia, Canada

Introduction

Mind is the forerunner of all things. All speech, all thought, all action.
— BUDDHA

The theme of individual existence in Buddhism is considered, at its core, inherently intersubjective. Intersubjectivity is the notion that the formation of individual identity itself is a fundamentally contextual occurrence based upon a "matrix of dependently related events," all of which function in a "state of flux" (Wallace, 2001). We may experientially realize that one's sense of self is brought into existence by the power of conceptual attribution. Such attribution happens either through the identification with the body (*e.g.*, I am thin) or through a mental process (*e.g.*, I am happy) — as well as through the confirmation of these conceptual ideations from others. This is the nature of intersubjectivity and 'dependent origination.'

Direct insight is available into the interacting constituents that form the bi-directional dynamics giving form to self and self-other. "Relational Dharma" (Davies, 2003, 2006) then, as developed by the author, is the realization of selflessness (*anatta* in Pali[1]) and change or impermanence (*anicca*), as it is experienced through the manifold of intersubjective consciousness. Through mind-to-mind contact in the *dharma*, or higher truth, and subsequent coordination upon the intersubjective terrain, a stability and momentum form. This leads to an ignition that propels experience to migrate through cumulative stages or levels as they pertain to liberation.

---

1. The perspectives in this paper are drawn primarily from the Burmese Theravada Buddhist tradition and the terminology used is that of the *Pali* language. *Pali* is the language of the Buddhist canon, known as the *Tipitika* or *Pali* Canon, and is the liturgical language of Theravada Buddhism.

Liberation in this definition refers to a progressive and increasing degree of acclimatization within freedom — the release from the gravitational pull of unconscious or conscious experience of bondage with the self-generated forces within mind that produce suffering and restriction. Concurrent with the dematerialization of conditions that form the tension of habitual psychophysical binding, mind and experience begin their ascension toward the unobstructed knowledge and recognition of itself as Source.

For Mind and Source to encounter each other is the intention of many traditions, rituals, and paths. This paper explores and models this progressive re-attunement through the illumination of specific filters and their refinement within intersubjectivity. Within the context of Relational Dharma, 'filters' refer to the gradient degrees through which Mind, while in relationship, sees its own nature. This seeing capacitates the process of purification, removing the obstacles that obscure Mind from its own innate luminosity. In the cleansing of the relational 'lenses of perception,' filters become the radiant windows into which our nature as immaculate reveals itself.

Intersubjectivity: Love's Architecture of Liberation

In the moment of love, the nature of emptiness dawns nakedly.
— URGYEN TULKU

Above all ... I was motivated ... by the most mysterious drive we ever experience — that of love. I don't think there's any influence upon my life that compares with ... love.
— BUCKMINSTER FULLER

When I met one of my Buddhist teachers for the first time, sitting in his monastery in the mystical region of Sagain Hills, an area of Northern Burma filled with nearly one thousand monasteries for Buddhist monks and nuns, preserved from the 14th century, the first words he spoke to me were in the form of a question: "What is *metta* [love]?" he asked. In that moment, and in the days that followed, the meaning of love unfolded. Through our resonance in *dharma* and instruction in the practice of *satipatthana* meditation (also called *vipassana* or insight meditation, as the practice leads to insight into the nature of selflessness and impermanence), intersubjectivity, love, and liberation were experienced as inseparable.

Wondrously, the intersubjective field between us became like a living translucent canvas upon which through our minds' interplay, self and other were imbued with color, dimension, and form. Within this heightened atmosphere of shared awareness, like a flower opening in the radiance of the sun, the conditions that give rise to self-other formation were unveiled. In our meetings each day, as our eyes would remain focused on the other's, the words that were spoken back and forth, and then relayed through a translator, ceased to be words in any way that I had known. The world upheld by concepts melted, becoming doorways leading into other dimensions. The sound of voice itself through the ear of *dharma* became like a liquid bridge that reached across the appearance of separation, eventually taking self and other, too, until all dissolved into the inter-relationship where mind, other, and love become one.

The potency of intersubjective influence within human relationship begins at life's earliest moments. Ruth Feldman's (2007) research of the parent-infant relationship shows that "synchrony," within intersubjectivity, plays an vital role in human development, directly impacting the formation and maturation of the social brain, self-regulation, and emotional resonance, symbol use, and empathy. As infant and parent commune through this closely timed mutuality of awareness, whether "concurrent, sequential, or organized," the seeds of future behavioral patterns are planted (Feldman, 2007). These discrete relational behaviors, when positively experienced and transmitted between parent-infant, and cultivated through the intersubjective immersion, set the stage for the emergent patterns that will surface within interpersonal relations later in life, dynamically impacting one's capacity for intimacy and its potential for personal transformation. As parent-infant engages in this unity of experience and coherent reflection, the baby's world is born. The self takes shape through this intersubjective resonance, through this invisible flow of love that is felt between them.

It was this power of love, that naturalist Charles Darwin also spoke of as the sinew that drove the language of life into expression. David Loye (2007) points out that in the *Descent of Man* Darwin referred to "love" ninety-five times, while "survival of the fittest" was mentioned only twice (once to apologize for ever using the term). Along with love, "moral sensitivity" was named nearly equal times, and "cooperation" (called mutual aid in his time) three times more than competition. Though prominent interpretations of evolution have conveyed otherwise, according to Loye it was love, not selfishness, that Darwin saw as the primary driver of human evolution at the level of development of the species.

Intersubjectivity is a way of naming this intimate and transpersonal terrain where mind meets mind through resonant consciousness. We may recognize this meeting as a dialogue of filters and use it consciously, as a means of tuning to wider bandwidths of experience. Within this atmosphere of shared mind can occur the release of self-identity and self-other discrimination from their familiar patterns of reference. As immersion within intersubjectivity becomes more natural, it stands as a 'residing place' for awareness to exist free of its familiar constructs. Experience, once contained by conceptual imputation and mediation through the six sense doors,[2] is released. The veils that functioned to obscure Mind's vastness lift, and experience begins its ascent toward the experiential immediacy with its own unstructured potentiality and recognition of itself as Source.

As a newborn baby feeds upon the energy of empathy within the intersubjective atmosphere between itself and its mother as a means to bond itself into a self, as the human drive to continue evolves through its reaching toward love, and as the river of liberating *dharma* opens into felt experience in relationship, this intersubjective atmosphere presents a doorway into a terrain that allows for direct contact and elaboration with our indwelling and yet-to-be-formed potentials.

Thus, intersubjectivity acting as a filter that stands between subject and object, self and other, self and Source, becomes a richly creative and pliable lens through which to see, understand, inform, and liberate our higher nature. Indeed, as we learn to swim within and grow eyes for this dynamic atmosphere, we see how causal patterns criss-cross through its terrain, informing the architectures that pattern self-other and thereby all experience. The geometry of liberation unwinds Mind from that form masking itself from its own innate luminosity.

---

2. seeing, hearing, feeling, tasting, touching, and cognition through the mind

Dharma

> *Just as the ocean has but one taste, that of salt,*
> *so too does the* dharma *have but one taste, that of freedom.*
> — BUDDHA

> *Ultimate* dharma *is that which underlies the world of concepts.*
> — VENERABLE MOGOK SAYADAW

> *Excepting immediate sensations and, more generally, the content of*
> *my consciousness, everything is a construct ... but some constructs are*
> *closer, some farther, from the direct sensations.*
> — EUGENE P. WIGNER

Dharma, an ancient Sanskrit term, has a broad and far-reaching meaning in all sects of Buddhism. In a general sense, it points to the truth of the way things are, to the specific elements of experience, and the natural laws that govern experience.

To practice *dharma* is to discern ultimate realities through direct experience. A simple example of the distinction between conventional and ultimate reality is the difference between the concept of water and the physical sensation of water. Its salient characteristics are of wetness and of a cool, warm, or hot temperature. As awareness discriminates between the concept of water and water's physical sensations, an insightful penetration into the nature of conceptual ideation occurs. Concepts are then seen as abstractions within consciousness, mental overlays born through prior conditioning.

This awareness is fostered through an intimate examination of 'name' and 'form.'[3] Name (*nama*) refers to mental phenomena and to the mental components of feeling, perception, mental formations, and consciousness. Form (or *rupa*) refers to the body, physical phenomena, and sensations; and becomes attributed through the "six sense doors." In this way, one may come to unveil the world that exists beneath concepts. 'Name' and 'form' may be seen respectively as objective and subjective measures. *Nama*, being abstraction and projection, lies at the heart of objective measure. *Rupa*, being the embodied and immersed sensation, lies at the heart of subjective measure.

---

3. "Name and form" (*nama-rupa*) is the 4th link in dependent origination (*paticca samuppada*) and is conditioned by consciousness, and forms the condition of the six sense-base.

Parallel to the progression of insight[4] into these two realities, transpersonal and transconceptual awareness is cultivated. As this awareness becomes progressively embodied, it leads to a lessoning of fixation in perceiving or interpreting self-identity and reality as experienced through the six sense doors. Through cultivation of this method of introspective observation, mind becomes pliable, transparent, and open. This, in turn, leads to factors of awakening whose symmetry serve to nurture an advancement toward freedom — the relaxation and eventual extinction of the mental impurities (*e.g.*, greed, aversion, and delusion) that function to restrict and cloud the mind from its deeper nature.

Embedded within the conceptual architectures that incline the mind toward entry into the *dharma* is the immediacy of their results. Within the experience of their geometry and structures, path and goal are recognized as one. In this way, *dharma* is not bound by linear time. Yet, paradoxically, its visibility emerges through time. This emergence is made possible by the alignment of attention and observation within the direct experience of discernible qualities of 'name' and 'form.'

Through the continuity of attention on mind-body processes, a new intelligence is born. This intelligence illuminates the simultaneity of mutual dimensions holistically co-emerging through all appearances. Like looking into a stream that has sediment clouding the surface, at first all one sees is sediment. And then, as the sediment clears, that which is in the stream, and the stream itself, become visible. This can be likened to how *dharma*, and what is seen and known through *dharma*, ascends into awareness. The awareness within the intersubjective fills the mind-to-mind gap, promoting a kind of elasticity as the proximity between self and other merges into Relational Dharma.

---

4. Insight (*nana*) refers to "knowledge," comprehension, and intelligence, and is a synonym for wisdom (*panna*).

Relational Dharma

> *Don't you sense me, ready to break into being at your touch?*
> — RAINER MARIE RILKE

> *If you look at anything carefully, deeply, enough, you discover the*
> *mystery of interbeing, and once you have seen it*
> *you will no longer be subject to fear —*
> *fear of birth, or fear of death. Birth and death are only*
> *ideas we have in the mind,*
> *and these ideas cannot be applied to reality.*
> — Thích Nhất Hạnh

In contrast to attuning to the *dharma* through purely introspective ob-servation, Relational Dharma focuses on heightening and refinement of awareness *via* the interactive interplay of experience in human relation-ship. The intersubjective field that connects minds illuminates a matrix of filters, and becomes the means to inspire spiritual momentum. Through the progression of insight, these filters lead to a further revealing of Mind's deeper substratum and organizing mechanics.

The realizations that emerge through Relational Dharma are in ac-cord with the *satipatthanasutta* (*vipassana*, or insight meditation), the most revered of all discourses in the Theravada Buddhist tradition. The insights that unfold through understanding its spectrum are considered fundamental to what Wallace (2001) refers to as "the cultivation of a multi-perspectival view of oneself, others, and the intersubjective rela-tions between oneself and all other sentient beings." The fundamental shifts in perspective that arise eradicate the notion of a separate self that resides along a fixed sense of continuity. Although masked by the ap-pearance of continuity, impermanence, as unveiled through the filters of awareness and insight into relationship, is seen as real and ubiquitous. Reality itself is recognized through continuous movement or change, with no ultimate core, or centrality. Through the practice of *satipatthana* within shared awareness in relationship, an anchoring upon the actual ex-perience of self in relation with other is adhered to and sustained. The continuity of this anchoring emerges as a transparency that brings direct clarity to experience by seeing into the actual nature of other.

The liberating insights into the nature of mind and reality that gradually unveil emptiness or no-self *(anatta)* and impermanence *(anicca)*, and the nature of how suffering *(dukkha)* arises in relation to the fixed belief in a self that is permanent or unchanging (also referred to as the three characteristics of existence), emerge through the intersubjective view, enabling a transpersonal exploration of the mutuality and development of spiritual insight as "inextricably tied to relational movement" (Jordon, 1997). Liberation is achieved at the confluences of our most intimate and precious folds of interdependence — the endlessly wondrous, human relationship itself.

We need the vision of interbeing, we belong to each other; we cannot cut reality into pieces. The well being of 'this' is the well being of 'that,' so we have to do things together. Every side is 'our side;' there is no evil side.
— Thích Nhất Hạnh

In traditional *satipatthana* practice, one uses the physical sensation of the breath or the abdomen as "object of meditation," or attention. In contrast, the practice of Relational Dharma utilizes the full breadth of experience, as it arises in connection with another. In this way, the alignment within the "four foundations of mindfulness" (which include contemplation of the body, feelings, states of mind, and mind objects) as experienced intersubjectively, becomes the ongoing "object of meditation." Not conditional on the body being in any defined posture or locality, the whole of the practice relates with the attunement to one's experience of mental and physical occurrences as they intersect in relationship. As such, it is an attitudinal posture, not confined or contingent upon any form other than the employment of awareness on relations. As the Burmese mediation master Sayadaw U Pandita was fond of expressing in regard to opening the mind to liberation, "Although the form is helpful, it is awareness that liberates."

As continuity in this intersubjective atmosphere gains further momentum, awareness begins to coordinate with the immediacy of what is occurring as present experience. As deeper transconceptual natures of self and self-in-relation-with-other are progressively un-layered through Relational Dharma, the mind and heart soften and open. This malleability gives way to a further synchronization, and the experience of self and other as either objective or subjective, or separate and outside of oneself, transforms. Through shared *dharma* resonance, an increasing sense of spaciousness and simultaneous connectedness occurs. The resonance permeates and occupies the intersubjective mind-to-mind atmosphere, and this permeation causes the nature of 'other,' as existing outside of oneself, to progressively dissolve. By knowing this permeation, we may see the arbitrary and illusory nature of the parameters that form divisions in the mind and that function to restrict and/or divide Mind's capacity to encounter an unobstructed flow of experience.

Whether through individual, couple, or group practice, as awareness coordinates directly with the nature and experience of other, perception of other moves through progressive filters. These filters reveal gradients through which mind, sustaining mindful awareness in relationship, sees its own nature while involved in the process of purification from that which obscures it from its own innate luminosity. In the cleansing of the relational 'lenses of perception,' filters become radiant windows through which our immaculate nature reveals itself. When awareness moves into accord with the nature of how other is directly experienced, we have allowed ourselves to *be touched*.

Phottabba speaks to the essence of being touched. To touch, or experience phottabba, is to know through direct non-conceptual experience, the primary elements: earth, fire, air, and water. When coordinated with experience, these elements are perceived by the body as solidity and hardness, heat and maturing, distension and motion. The water element, which is cognized by the mind, brings a feeling of cohesion and liquidity to these bodily sensed features.

In this relaxation of solidity, or opaqueness, the transition of experience from gross to subtle filtering begins. Mind becomes able to lean into or against the mind of another, feeling the vibrational texture that forms the contour of the perceived ending of self and beginning of other. In addition, as experience moves from gross to subtle filters, the capacity to tolerate increasing degrees of uncertainty is gained, which helps nurture a shift from habituated associations that rely upon identification with self, to immersion in a transconceptual intersubjective atmosphere. Through this sensed vibrational touching, mind-to-mind contact deepens and the progression of relationship in *dharma* continues through gross, subtle, and refined levels. At the refined level, mind interpenetrates mind and "mingles into oneness" (Kunsang and Schmidt, 2005).

Gross, Subtle, and Refined filters represent three discernible structures of experiential transition through purification within Relational Dharma and the terrain of intersubjectivity. Though experiential, they can be conceptualized as follows:

Gross Filter

At the initial gross level of intersubjective filtering, the primary feature is a structure of self defined by separateness and autonomy. The matrix of self is referenced as local, contained, and relatively constant, while other is experienced as outside and separate from this containment. As bare attention (a mental posture of non-activity that is characterized by receptivity, focus, and wakefulness) is brought toward, and progressively aligned with mental and physical processes experienced in relation with other, a discerning clarity and familiarity arises. The distinctions between one's feelings and thoughts (mental) and sensations of the body (physical), as they intersect with mental projections of the other, become intuitively more punctuated and discrete. As this intimacy within the awareness of relationship continues, "momentary concentration" is achieved, further supporting a partial absorption in the objects of attention, and awareness is able to "close in upon and fix on whatever object is being noticed and the act of noticing will proceed without break" (Mahasi). This partially interpenetrating and forward-leading attitudinal posture flexes the experiential envelope past the parameters that previously had limited its extension. Like having one foot move into a door while the other foot extends out the door, the subjective and intersubjective dimensions are now encompassed in parallel. While self is still experienced as predominately separate from other, a co-joining dimension of awareness arises where self-other form is less fixed and more mutual.

Subtle Filter

At the subtle level of filtering, the quality of bare attention that rests on mental and physical processes becomes significantly more acute and strong as they intersect with other. This agility facilitates a close proximity and timing in the meeting of mind-body experience as it arises in tandem with the objects in awareness that formulate the composite of other. Within this immediate lucidity and strength of awareness, experience adheres with and anchors upon the features of other, causing an illumination of the interactive dynamics to pervade holistically across mind in an effortless way. This ease leads to tranquility, as awareness, so filtered, is able to attend to and directly align with any of the arising objects for any desired length of time. Within this lucid proficiency, insight is able to penetrate the objects and experience illuminates the arising and dissolving formations of mind-body cognition.

Awareness of how the pairing of a material process (seen as object) and a mental process (the action of knowing it) co-occurs illuminates how self and other are fabricated through this activity. There is a realization that when visual consciousness arises, both the sense door of the eye and the visual object of the other are co-present. This is true of each of the six sense doors. In noticing or reflecting upon an object that is a formation of the composite of other, consciousness becomes engaged in noticing, thinking, reasoning, or understanding.

Mahasi notes that "Consciousness arises in accordance with each object that becomes evident. If there is an object, there arises consciousness; if there is no object, no consciousness arises," leading to "knowledge by comprehension through direct experience" that objects noticed are impermanent and impersonal (Mahasi). As the dynamics of impermanency are directly experienced, a co-arising association within intersubjectivity is enhanced.

From the vantage point of the intersubjective, the surfaces of self and other are penetrated, and form is seen as impermanent and without an inherent or solid existence. The undivided field of Relational Dharma is experienced and inhabited as these moving patterns of change and impermanence are realized. Self-other form appears as translucent emanation co-occupying the unbound nature of intersubjective awareness: that which remains in and through the arising and passing of all formation.

Refined Filter

At the level of refined filtering, observance on mind-body processes remains continuous, along with equanimity within the arising and passing of formations. This experience reveals a deeper transparency — objects disappear or extinguish immediately at their moment of initial emergence. Here, the awareness of change, or the arising of mind-body processes, is no longer visible and the appearance of form emerges as one that is already vanishing or disappearing. Perceiving the dissolution of appearances gives way to a pleasure and freedom that reinforces the continuity of observance.

In the awareness of the action of perceiving, two factors are always present: an objective factor and a subjective one, *i.e.* the object noticed, and the mental state of knowing it. According to Mahasi, these vanish or dissolve by pairs, one pair after the other. Within any given moment of the arising there is a multiplicity of numerous processes. In this detailed observance, it can be seen that within the very arising of form its dissolving is already occurring. The dissolving is part of the motion of arising: in the moment-by-moment appearance of the other; in the movement of its body and form; in its sound as it meets the ear; and in the direct experience entwining within the relational motion of formation. Like a semi-translucent mirage being pervaded by the sun's light, its opacity giving way to a fading transparency, emptiness and form are seen as one.

Concurrent with the filters refinement and the release from the circuitry that propels self and separation, spiritual ignition (*samvega*) grows. The momentum supports the progression through each level of filter upon a terrain of gradual departure from the binding with self-correlates.[5] This terrain is felt to occur in five interwoven stages, and traveling between them is seen as a release that happens in parallel to the progression of the filters. The stages unfold naturally and occur in proportion to the progress of insight achieved through the refinement of the filters.

The stages are represented as follows:

1. Part-time liberation.
2. Liberation by distancing the impurities.

---

5. the karma of past conditions and the aggregates

3. Total eradication of the impurities (path consciousness).
4. Quieting down the impurities.
5. Total liberation.

Although the last of the five stages represents knowledge leading to complete release from the psychophysical bonds of constriction, neither it nor the preceding four stages should be regarded as hierarchical, linear, or mutually exclusive.

With the release of psychophysical constrictions, insight into their conditioned nature becomes recognized — the emerging view of dependent origination. The flowering of the mind through the gross, subtle, and refined filters and parallel 'stages of liberation,' reveals a deeper topography of filters. These link and inform the pattern of Mind itself, and its causal motion in the architecture of self and other.

Paticca Samuppada: **The 12 Links of Dependent Origination**

All sects of Buddhism subscribe to the notion that there is a fundamental unity to life. This unity, or *dharma*, expresses itself through cause and effect relationship described by the doctrine of *paticca samuppada*[6] (which translates as dependent co-arising, or dependent origination) and was realized by the Buddha on the eve of his enlightenment. The understanding of a bi-directional causality between observer and Source is an elementary reflection of this doctrine.

Paticca samuppada is considered as both an abstract statement of a universal law and as a means to resolve suffering through its direct experiential application. As a universal law, it can be seen as a meta-matrix of relationships created by the interpenetrating dynamics of mutually woven

---

6. The meaning of *paticca samuppada* has several translations, including dependent co-arising, conditioned co-production, causal conditioning, causal genesis, and conditioned genesis (Macy, 1991, p. 34). The breakdown of the meaning of *paticca samuppada* is as follows:

Uppada is the substantitive form of the verb *uppajjati*, which means "arising." *Sam-uppada* means "arising together." *Paticca*, as the gerund of *pacceti* (pati + i) means to "come back to" or "fall back on," and is used to denote "grounded on" or "on account of" (p. 34). Therefore, the compound means "on account of arising together" or "the being on account of arising together" (Macy, 1991, p. 34).

causes. In the abstract description, dependent co-arising is "equivalent to the law of the conditioned genesis of phenomena ... it expresses the invariable concomitance between the arising and ceasing of any given phenomenon and the functional efficacy of its originative conditions" (Bodhi, 1980). It is said that the Buddha defined *paticca samuppada* as "that according to which co-ordinate phenomena are produced together" (Macy, 1991a).

As a means of resolving the problem of suffering and transcending conventional existence, a formula of 12 links can be identified that serve as a vehicle to encounter its dynamics through direct experience. These 12 links, each like a filter, interact to form the constituents that give rise to the character of human experience. As the formula becomes intuitively realized, mind disentangles from conditioned experience and comes face-to-face with the freedom inherent in its own direct nature.

In a sense, the links form an intersubjective map for seeing the way mental components[7] and sense media[8] interact in relationship with 'other' in co-generating interdependent projections. The formula seeks to illuminate the "causal nexus responsible for the origination of suffering" (Bodhi, 1980) by invoking a scale and composition where one may recognize, and eventually penetrate, the nature of interdependent causal movement.

Although the links are arranged as 12 specific factors, insight into the formula's meaning is not conditional on a specific arrangement. In the most common version, the map starts with ignorance; another starts with the interrelation between name (*nama*) and form (*rupa*); and yet another with consciousness (*vinnana*). The 12 links comprise the "factors of existence" and are therefore considered to give rise to the "wheel of existence" or the "round of becoming" (Macy, 1991a). Each of the psychophysical factors of existence provides the conditions for the subsequent 12 factors — thus indicating the wheel, or cyclical nature, of life as it arises within interdependent conditions. When certain conditions are present, they give rise to subsequent conditions, which in turn give rise to other conditions, and the cyclical nature of life in *samsara,* or *the round of rebirth,* can be seen as a transition of states between filters.

---

7. or aggregates — which include feeling, perception, volitional formations, consciousness, and sense media.
8. including the inner sense organs: eyes, ears, nose, tongue, body, and mind, and the outer sense media and their respective objects.

The classical ordering of the 12 links, as stated in the Pali texts (*Samyutta Nikaya*, SN 12.2), and their account of the arising of the wheel of existence and life are as follows:

- From ignorance (*avijja*) as a requisite condition come fabrications (*sankhara*).
- From fabrications (*sankhara*) as a requisite condition comes consciousness (*vinnana*).
- From consciousness (*vinnana*) as a requisite condition comes name-form (*nama-rupa*).
- From name-form (*nama-rupa*) as a requisite condition come the six sense media (*salayatana*).
- From the six sense media (*salayatana*) as a requisite condition comes contact (*phassa*).
- From contact (*phassa*) as a requisite condition comes feeling (*vedana*).
- From feeling (*vedana*) as a requisite condition comes craving (*tanha*).
- From craving (*tanha*) as a requisite condition comes clinging/sustenance (*upadana*).
- From clinging/sustenance (*upadana*) as a requisite condition comes becoming (*bhava*).
- From becoming (*bhava*) as a requisite condition comes birth (*jati*).
- From birth (*jati*) as a requisite condition, then aging and death (*jara-marana*), sorrow, lamentation, pain, distress, and despair come into play.

Such is the origination of this entire mass of stress and suffering. (Access to Insight, 2006)

As these factors occur in an arising cycle, so too do they occur in a cycle of fading and cessation:

- From the cessation of fabrications comes the cessation of consciousness.
- From the cessation of consciousness comes the cessation of name-form.

- From the cessation of name-form comes the cessation of the six sense media.
- From the cessation of the six sense media comes the cessation of contact.
- From the cessation of contact comes the cessation of feeling.
- From the cessation of feeling comes the cessation of craving.
- From the cessation of craving comes the cessation of clinging/ sustenance.
- From the cessation of clinging/sustenance comes the cessation of becoming.
- From the cessation of becoming comes the cessation of birth.
- From the cessation of birth, then aging and death, sorrow, lamentation, pain, distress, and despair all cease.

Such is the cessation of this entire mass of stress and suffering (Access to Insight, 2006).

This dynamic pattern of dependent co-arising can be seen reflected through all conditioned phenomena. The causal motion across formation provides the architecture through which the patterns of genesis organize and manifest into form. Within Relational Dharma this interlinked, bi-causal motion is illuminated through the experiential, intuitive, and perceptual interface between self and other. In this meeting, the mechanics that form the 'genetics' of intersubjectivity are brought into astounding illumination.

In the pursuit of deliverance, there exists an intuitively conjoined motion of release. This conjunction is similar to the interdependent patterns of conditioned genesis, from which arise a bi-directional function. The bi-directionality encountered is itself a transcendental staircase, leading both 'into' and 'out of' conditioned existence. Nurturing experiential understanding of this bi-directionality generates the capacity to inform and create new patterns of evolution within genesis.

Perceiving Inter-Relationships

Filters can be seen to inform the interactions that pattern dependent origination. They illuminate how phenomena materialize and dematerialize
through a relationally mutual reciprocity. In this way, events do not occur
through a linear causality; "rather they help each other happen by providing an occasion, locus, or context" (Macy, 1991b). As events are enabled
within a given context, an entwining motion occurs, which in turn influences the events. This relational, wave-like reciprocity can be seen to permeate all phenomena, informing and forming their arising and passing.
The motion of formation does not originate in any specific event, but in
the relationship between events.

The bi-directional motion of dependent origination informs the ongoing linkages between that which produces *nama-rupa* (name and form,
mind and matter, mentality-physicality, subjective and objective). From
this union of mental (*nama*) and physical phenomena (*rupa*), emerges the
materialization of the five aggregates (feeling, perception, volitional formations, consciousness, and sense media), highlighting the crucial link in
the causal chain of dependent origination. In the direct experiential investigation of what comes into being through the interplay of mind and matter within consciousness, the physics of intersubjectivity can be perceived.
Through this direct realization, one can recognize the existence of a 'circuitry' that conditions the 'template' of interrelated causes and establishes
the conditions of the physical and psychological 'genetics' of formation.

Insight into these mechanics enacts a kind of formula for undoing
of the causal linkages within consciousness that lead to habitual 'self-
generation.' Stepping into this nonlinear momentum makes it possible to
recognize and see through the organizing patterns that give rise to the
experience of self. Perception of this dynamical pattern, or architecture,
reveals a dependently co-arising experience of the relaxation of previously unnoticed mental rigidity, and provides a subsequent release from
habitual circuitry. In this way, by entering this 'calculus' of filters' motion, habitual associations can be recognized and released.

The matrix of dependent co-arising can be described as a holistically inclusive system of accordance, with the operation of the matrix
likened to psychic 'software.' The filter functionality of this software illuminates the perceptual mechanics that typically obscures Mind from

its relationship with Source and brings Mind into direct touch with what lies beyond. Not recognizable through linear thinking, this perspective of mind is bi-directional, holding its tension between a backward and forward entwinement. A unity, or continuum, is thus perceived in the process of change.

The broadened scope, breadth, and depth that this kind of seeing produces enables the human mind to encounter new manifolds of awareness — affordances provided by the matrix of filters. As one's reference to these stabilizes, it becomes progressively easier to climb out of the circuitry of conditioned and habitual responses and one awakens into another sphere of identification that immediately and directly influences one's own freedom.

To Perceive Wholeness

This view of *paticca samuppada,* and the Relational Dharma by which we may encounter it, involves an overarching awareness that stretches to encompass a meta-symmetry of filters that manifest through deep, multilayered causality. To touch and be touched by its architecture is to step away from linear reasoning, intellectual judgment, conventional modes of thought, and our usual ways of deciphering information. As Macy (1991a) stated, "It is not a dissecting or categorizing exercise of the intellect." Buddhist scholar Herbert Guenther (1989) described this as a movement away from a "mechanistic linguistics," and a requisite for encountering the immediacy involved in this kind of experiential knowing. He described it as a "shift in attention and interest away from the surface of sensuous and mental objects and toward the dynamic background and source of all that is."

Beneath the colorful rendering of deities in classical Tibetan Buddhist art, there lies a specific geometrical grid, or *tigse,* that is associated with each deity. The grid is topological, providing the structure for the image and establishing the guidelines for what it represents. This sacred structure underscores all Buddhist forms. Though conventionally invisible in the final visual creation, it can be recognized once the eye is attuned to this sacred geometry.

In a similar way, as filters of awareness become attuned, the geometry of dependent co-arising emerges. When we see into reality with the recognition of its layers and dimensions of filters, existence itself becomes like an array of multi-tiered lattices, transparently interrelating tapestries of dimensionally and vibrantly creative movement. We are released from the confines of superficial perception.

> *Profound and tranquil, free from complexity,*
> *Uncompounded luminous clarity,*
> *beyond the mind of conceptual ideas.*
>
> *In this there is not a thing to be removed,*
> *nor anything that needs to be added.*
> *It is merely the immaculate looking naturally at itself.*
> — NYOSHUL KHEN RINPOCHE

In contrast to the notion of a fixed truth, Relational Dharma can be viewed as an *accordance structure* for deliverance. Its conceptual framing seeks to support a *liberating linguistics* through which direct experience encounters its release. Within the Relational Dharma model, specific processes (*i.e.* filters) are illuminated as a means to parameterize and illustrate a phenomenology for degrees of insight — liberating Mind from the forces of ignorance and self-generated suffering. As Mind moves into greater proximity with liberation, a deeper substratum of causality becomes visible. These relationships can be seen to link and inform the patterns that give rise to the nature and formation of Mind itself, and its causal motion in the architecting of self and other.

Through this recognition, experience releases from the gravitational pull of conditioning and becomes propelled toward the potentiality of full liberation. As liberation is touched, filters cease to obscure experience from an intimate and direct relationship with itself as Source. In the relational accordance with Source, filters become translucent and pliable canvases upon which emerge the colors of luminosity, compassion, and wisdom — in an ongoing alchemy toward the nature and expression of higher human freedom.

References

Access to Insight. Paticca samuppada vibhanga Sutta: *Analysis of dependent co-arising* (SN 12.2) T. Bhikkhu, trans. 2006. Retrieved July 14, 2006, from http://www.accesstoinsight.org/tipitaka/sn/sn12/sn12.002.than.html.

Anita Barrows and Joanna Macy, trans. *Rilke's Book of Hours: Love Poems to God.* New York: Riverhead Books, 1996.

Bhikkhu Bodhi. *Transcendental Dependent Arising: A Translation and Exposition of the* Upanisa Sutta. Kandy, Sri Lanka: Buddhist Publication Society, 1980.

Jeannine A. Davies. Experiential Physics: Explorations in Modern Physics, Consciousness and the Meditative Mind. Thesis, Bachelor of Arts. Montpelier, VT: Vermont College, 2003.

———. *Re-Visioning the Ancient Buddhist Doctrine of Causality into a Modern Matrix of Transformational Interrelatedness.* San Francisco, CA: unpublished manuscript, Saybrook Graduate School & Research Center, 2006.

Ruth Feldman. "Parent-infant synchrony and the construction of shared timing; physiological precursors, developmental outcomes, and risk conditions." *Journal of Child Psychology and Psychiatry, 38,* Nos. 3 and 4 (2007). pp. 329–354. Retrieved November 20, 2007 from PsychINFO.

Herbert V. Guenther. *From Reductionism to Creativity: rDzogs-chen and the New Sciences of Mind.* Boston: Shambhala, 1989.

Erik Pema Kunsang and Marcia Binder Schmidt. *Blazing Splendor: The Memoirs of Tulku Urgyen Rinpoche.* Hong Kong: Rangjung Yeshe Publications, 2005.

David Loye. *Darwin on Love.* Carmel, CA: Benjamin Franklin Press, 2007.

Joanna Macy. *Mutual Causality in Buddhism and General Systems Theory: The Dharma of Natural Systems.* Albany, NY: State University of New York Press, 1991a.

———. *World As Lover, World As Self.* Berkeley, CA: Parallax Press, 1991b.

S. Mahasi. *Discourse on* Paticcasamuppada. n.d. Retrieved September, 28, 2005, from http://web.ukonline.co.uk/buddhism/mahasip1.htm#1.

———. *The Progress of Insight.* n.d. Retrieved August 5, 2008, from http://www.accesstoinsight.org/lib/authors/mahasi/progress.html.

Jean Baker Miller. *Toward a New Psychology of Women.* Boston: Beacon Press, 1987.

Thích Nhất Hạnh. "Interbeing." *Resurgence Magazine Online.* 2006. Retrieved March 1, 2006, from http://www.resurgence.org/resurgence/articles/interbeing.html.

———. *The Heart of Understanding: Commentaries on the* Prajnaparamita *Heart Sutra.* Berkeley, CA: Parallax, 1988.

U Pandita, S. *On the Path to Freedom: A Mind of Wise Discernment and Openness.* Malaysia: Buddhist Wisdom Center, 1995.

B. Alan Wallace. "Intersubjectivity in Indo-Tibetan Buddhism." *Journal of Consciousness Studies, 8,* No. 5–7 (2001). pp. 209–30.

Emotional Armoring as a Filter of Consciousness

RICHARD BLASBAND, M.D.
Center for Functional Research
Sausalito, California

Introduction

In their article, "Sensors, Filters, and the Source of Reality," Robert Jahn and Brenda Dunne postulate that there are ". . . resonant channels of communication between the mind and its source environment," the source being the well known aspects of the external world that excite our five senses, plus various more subtle sources of information such as intuition, inspiration, and instinct, as well as other domains of intangible physical reality wherein function forces and entities variously labeled "Qi," "prana," "orgone energy," "implicate order," and "zero-point vacuum," among others. The authors further postulate that full and direct experience of these realms is constrained by a variety of "filters," among them "muscular armoring".[1] Here we will attempt to elucidate the nature of armoring.

Emotional armoring, as discovered and defined by Wilhelm Reich, M.D., has two variations that operate in synchrony with each other: character armoring and muscular armoring. Character armoring manifests as habitual ways of walking, talking, and behaving, and originates out of the attempt to solve conflicts between one's instinctual urges and the constraints of society. It serves to absorb anxiety and act as an interface with the external world. Muscular armoring is the functional counterpart of character armoring, manifesting as patterns of chronic muscular tension.

Since the armoring serves to dull sensation wherever it is present, it will attenuate and may even totally block incoming information from one's perceptual apparatus. If the brain itself is armored, which is not

1. Robert G. Jahn and Brenda J. Dunne. "Sensors, filters, and the Source of reality." *Journal of Scientific Exploration, 18*, No. 4 (2004). pp. 547–71.

unusual in armored people, perception itself may be blocked, resulting in a filtering of excitations, whether of internal or external origin. In mild cases, sensation and perception of the excitation intensity is diminished; in severe cases, as in catatonia, there may be massive blocking of sensation and perception. The result, in either case, is reduced contact both with oneself and with the outside world. Since 95% of adults in the Western World are estimated to be armored, this compounds to a serious filter of our appreciation of reality.

The Origin of Armoring

Emotional armoring begins in childhood. Clinical evidence from patients in therapy indicates that we are born with basic tendencies that can serve as potential defensive patterns. When the outside world blocks our natural impulses and we are faced with intolerable anger or anxiety, we call upon these tendencies to help us protect ourselves. Over time, the reinforced tendencies compound into rigidities that become our defensive psychological "character structure," and its complementary somatic counterpart — chronic muscular tensions.[2]

To understand how armoring serves as a filter, we must examine its different components in some detail. Both character armoring and muscular armoring arise out of conflicts between one's instinctual impulses and the outside world. At an early age, impulses such as sexual love and natural aggression pressing for expression are met by "verbotens" (*forbidding*) from parents and social institutions: schools, church, *etc.* The child naturally experiences this as frustrating, and reacts with anger. The anger, however, is also forbidden, as the parent or agents of society threaten retaliation or abandonment. The vulnerable child cannot afford either, and so becomes conflicted about whether or not to continue to express his/her anger. Ultimately, the conflict is internalized as the attitude of "If you can't fight them, join them," and the external conflict is replaced by a partially resolved internal conflict. In the process of this internalization, the child changes something within himself, and the anger and associated threat are suppressed and cease to be a conscious problem.

---

2.   Wilhelm Reich. *Character Analysis.* NY: Orgone Institute Press, 1949. p. 145.

On a psychological level the internalized prohibition is used to block the original impulse. This is, however, only a partial solution to the conflict: an aspect of the original impulse still presses for expression, albeit in a muted, distorted form.

In a similar process, the natural rage at being frustrated in the urge to move out into the world and secure for oneself the right of self-determination, is smothered and is frequently replaced by chronic complaining and/or meanness. Since these behaviors are also not ordinarily permitted, the child, once again threatened by abandonment or retaliation, represses the complaining and/or meanness by further internalizing the prohibiting "No." The complaining/meanness diminishes, leaking out only now and then as "secondary impulses," or they may stop completely. This process may continue through several iterations, depending upon what the family/institutions can tolerate. Most often, however, the child ends up as someone who has lost his capacity for full emotional expression, as well as contact with both his "core" and the outside world. He loses his capacity for self-determination and the ability to go after what he rationally needs to establish personal independence.

Here we must differentiate the behavior and attitudes of the armored individual from one who has been permitted to express his natural aggressive and sexual needs in a rational and responsible way. In the latter, there are no compensatory attitudes, no cover-up of natural aggression with passivity, reactive neurotic aggression, pornography, *etc.* The child retains self-determination, which allows the internal freedom to express needs, depending upon the strength of inner impulses and a sense of the capacity of the external world to satisfy them.

Contactlessness

At each point where a prohibition blocks an impulse, the individual cuts himself off from his deeper self. He loses contact with himself and replaces his natural contact and sense of self-assuredness with a substitute contact, which still permits some relationship to the outside world — albeit a relationship lacking the full depth of expression of whom he truly, deeply is.

By adulthood we have then created the average armored individuals of our society. Through sequence after sequence of inhibiting natural and secondary impulses, and developing increasing layers of contactlessness, they have developed a "façade" that cuts them off from their core and their natural inner impulses, and have lost the capacity to establish full contact with the outside world. Depending upon the exigencies of their lives, the character armoring will consist of either a simple or complex network of sequences. Whereas unarmored individuals experience life as exciting and themselves as lively, armored individuals experience life as dull and mechanical and they themselves as having an inner void behind their façade.

The treatment of character armoring requires analysis of the patient's character structure. Rather than focusing on the *content* of the patient's verbal productions as is usually done in psychoanalytic therapy, the character analyst focuses on the *way* those patients express themselves. Consistent and repeated observation and analysis of the way the patients talk, walk, hold themselves, their facial expressions, *etc.*, yield more direct penetration to their psychic depths, the spontaneous release of blocked impulses, and eventually, the reestablishment of full psychic contact.

Anchored Armoring

Character Analytic Treatment underwent a significant transformation when Reich found that in patients who had strong stubborn defense, the character armor could be "anchored" in patterns of chronic muscular contraction. By constantly calling these patients' attention to their "stiff-necked stubbornness," for example, he could get them to drop their defenses and let their necks relax, which produced a sensation of being flooded with alternating sympathetic and parasympathetic excitations and feelings. Reich thus learned that in addition to the patients' ideation, behavior, and postural attitudes, their stiff-necked stubbornness was simultaneously and literally manifested in a rigidity of the muscles of their necks, and that the muscular armoring was laid down in definite patterns that corresponded to emotionally expressive segments of the body. The segments include the ocular, oral, cervical or throat, chest (including the back and arms), diaphragm, abdomen, and pelvis (including the legs). Since the muscular armor is a functionally identical, complementary facet of the character armoring, it serves the same purposes as the latter, as a means of sustaining contact with the outer world as well as providing a defense against inner impulses.

Segments tend to be armored transverse to the long axis of the body. They form a ring of chronic muscular contraction that, depending upon the individual, can penetrate to the depth of the organism, including all glands, mucous membranes, organs, and nerves within that segment. The contraction is sustained by chronic hypersympathetic tone[3] and serves to absorb the anxiety that the person would experience if the armor were not present. In therapy, one works on the muscular armoring as a complementary approach to character analysis. This is done by consistent and methodical pressure on the armored muscles, combined with the restoration of natural respiration, until the organism releases its bound emotions. By working systematically from the head toward the pelvis, armoring is released, more rapidly bringing patients into contact with their core functioning and their genital excitations.[4]

By now the reader should have at least a glimpse of how armoring can serve as a filter between the individual and his perception of his deeper self and of the outside world. To understand fully the depth and extent of the filtering process, however, we must describe Reich's discovery of spontaneous plasmatic pulsation as a fundamental life process.

Plasmatic Pulsation

Reich's detailed investigation of the sexual life of his patients in psychoanalysis, and of non-patients who he thought were emotionally healthy, led him to conclude that the orgasmic experience is characterized by four fundamental "beats." The first is an initial building of mechanical tension as organs fill with fluids and become tumescent. It is followed spontaneously by "bioelectric charging" at the erogenous zones. At the climax of the orgasm, with the onset of involuntary muscular tremors and clonisms, bioelectrical discharge takes place. This is followed by mechanical relaxation as fluids redistribute themselves back into the larger corpus of the body, away from the erogenous zones. This sequence — tension, charge,

---

3. There are some illnesses, such as asthma, however, where chronic parasympathetic tone dominates. This is most often a defense against anxiety, a sympathetic function. Some gastrointestinal disorders also appear to have this kind of dynamic. Elsworth Baker. *Man in the Trap*. N.Y.: Farrar, Straus, & Giroux, 1967. p. 202.
4. Baker. *Man in the Trap*.

discharge, relaxation — also appears in all pulsatory organs, the heart, bladder, bowel, *etc.*, as well as on an individual cellular level, as microscopic investigation reveals.[5]

Reich's bioelectrical studies on humans expressing a variety of emotions supported the importance of spontaneous pulsation in that context. A direct current milli-voltmeter was used to measure changes in DC potentials on the skin surface while subjects felt and expressed various emotions. These measurements revealed that during so-called "expansive" states of anger and sexuality there was in increase in bioelectrical potential at the skin surface, while the opposite was true during "contractive" states such as anxiety or sadness.[6]

Further experiments along this line indicated that the reaction of an organism to a stimulus is not so much a function of the intensity of the stimulus, but, above all, of the readiness of the organism to respond. These reactions are similar to those found when stimulating microbiological organisms. If you prick an ameba with a needle it contracts its pseudopodia, forming a small, tight, ball. After a short period, the organism will venture out again, extending pseudopodia. But if you prick it again, it will withdraw for a longer period before opening up. Repeated insults, consequently, will result in increasingly prolonged withdrawal. Spontaneous pulsation, the *sine qua non* of life, is diminished. Such reactions occur in multi-cellular organisms, including humans, on cellular, individual organ, and total organismic levels. Armoring against emotions may be superficial, affecting principally the striated musculature, or it can involve a dampening of organismic responsivity and excitability all the way down to the cellular level of internal organs. When the dampening penetrates to the cellular nuclear level, degenerative illnesses, including cancer, often follow.[7]

---

5. Wilhelm Reich. *The Function of the Orgasm*. NY: Orgone Institute Press, 1942. p. 79.

6. Reich. *The Function of the Orgasm*. p. 326. It is interesting that directional changes in REG output while patients in therapy were expressing emotions showed a direct correlation with the quality of the emotion expressed: increased output during the expression of anger, an expansive emotion; decreased output with the expression of sadness or anxiety, contracted states. Richard A. Blasband. "The ordering of random event generators by emotional expression." *Journal of Scientific Exploration*, *14*, No. 2 (2000), Summer. pp. 195–216.

7. Wilhelm Reich. *The Cancer Biopathy*. NY: Orgone Institute Press, 1948. p. 182

Armoring of Consciousness

Disappointment reactions, anchored in characterological and muscular armoring, frequently involve sluggish or non-existent responses to external stimuli. This is the biophysical basis of the dulling of excitation that we find in armored people. Correspondingly, it is also the biophysical basis for a filtering of consciousness. Unarmored organisms respond to external stimuli, no matter what their nature, with appropriate sensory response and excitation. They perceive what is out there with internal excitations that are accurately perceived by the brain and the organism as a whole.

Armored organisms, on the other hand, do not respond in this kind of open and straightforward way. If heavily armored, they register little or no reaction, as in the extreme case of catatonic freezing. If the individual is moderately armored, as most Western humans are, they will experience distorted perceptions of inner excitation and/or external stimuli. These distortions generally take two forms. Heavily or moderately armored individuals will project their own inner perception of "deadness" and their lack of spontaneous liveliness onto the outside world, creating a mechanistic worldview where all things, living or non-living, are understood as being a simple or complex concatenation of dead parts. Indeed, because of the ubiquitousness of such armoring, the reductionistic mechanical worldview among Western scientists is simply accepted as being "correct thinking," despite its having led mankind into an extremely precarious situation with respect to our survival in the eco-world. We think in a particulate, binary, either/or way, with a physics that is isotropically invariant, and a cosmos that is static and empty. Nature, however, tends to express itself most often in spontaneously excitable, pulsating waves that change gradually and anisotropically, and are responsive to external influences, including thought.[8,9]

For the sake of clarity, I have presented the armoring process and its effects as somewhat monolithic. In reality, the degree of armoring in any individual is a function of their being in a relatively bioenergetically

---

8. Wilhelm Reich. *Ether, God, and Devil.* Orgonon, Rangeley, ME: Orgone Institute Press, 1949. p. 118.
9. Nicolai Levashov. *The Final Appeal to Mankind.* Privately published, 1997. Vol. 2. (Also at www.Levashov.info.)

"expanded" or "contracted" state at any given moment, and of the pre-vailing exigencies of the outside world. As Reich maintained, there are "holes" in the armor, which permit sensations to be reasonably accurate-ly perceived. Depending upon one's character structure and the degree of inhibiting pressures from the outside world, one may be capable of relatively immediate and direct perception of certain things, while other things, especially those that are emotionally threatening, are usually dis-torted. One may be able to thrill to the sounds of a Beethoven symphony while retaining an irrational antisexual bias with respect to adolescent love. Or one may be quite rational with respect to the latter, but rather ir-rational with respect to political opinions.

As indicated above, the filtering process due to armoring can produce a dampening of sensory excitation that can sometimes penetrate all the way down to the cellular level. This means that organs circumscribed by an armored segment *literally* will be compromised in their functioning. If the organ is the eye, an extension of the brain, which may also be ar-mored, it could mean a loss of visual acuity, an inability to see accurately what is literally in front of one's eyes, especially if the object to be viewed has emotional significance.

Biophysical and clinical examples involving the loss of three-dimen-sional vision can shed light on the relationship between cognitive processes and filters. Clinical experience has demonstrated that most neurotics have lost three-dimensional perception: they think they see three-dimensionally because of past experience with perceptual visual clues, but they really do not. In therapy, with the dissolution of armoring in the ocular segment, the eye (and brain) can recover the capacity for spontaneous plasmatic pulsa-tion. The eyes brighten, and visual acuity and three-dimensional vision re-turns. When this happens, the patient may exclaim about how differently they now see, how everything now has dimension, whereas before this, they now realize, "... things looked flat." Because vision and the brain are so co-functional, a loss of the visual function can extend to the domain of thought. Observations and conclusions that are readily evident to one per-son may be extremely difficult for the ocularly armored individual. They literally cannot *see* your point. Obviously, this process can extend to the inability to entertain radically new points of view and the implication of

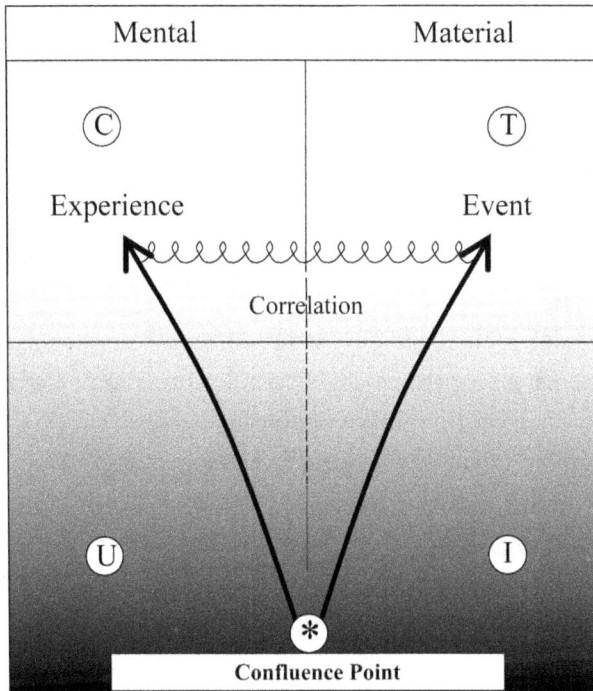

Figure 1. The M⁵ Model after Jahn & Dunne.

anomalies in nature. This is the biophysical basis for so-called "cognitive dissonance."

With therapy, and the dissolution of the ocular and brain armoring, the patient becomes capable of entertaining ideas that may have seemed totally impossible prior to therapy. A concomitant manifestation of the softening of armoring in the ocular segment is the perception of a restoration of spontaneous pulsation in the neurons of the brain. Patients report that they feel their brain "moving," something that they may initially experience as frightening. They begin to think more functionally, less mechanistically. Also, with therapy, political views can move from the extremes to the center. Those who were socialistic in choice become less strident in their views and can even entertain some conservative views. The opposite holds for those who tended toward arch-conservatism prior to therapy. Advocates of both sides of the political spectrum lose their knee-jerk reflexive attitudes and truly begin to make choices out of a rational consideration of the issues at hand and the needs of their community.[10] As therapy progresses, the individual moves more deeply into restoring contact with his true self; increasing contact with oneself and the outside world is tantamount to changing one's filters.

To understand the relationship between the changes that take place on a biophysical level and complementary changes on the mental level it is useful to invoke the M^5 model of consciousness described by Jahn & Dunne (Fig. 1).[11]

In this model, mental and physical events are described as two parallel, complementary processes with a shared source. In one of these, conscious mental activity (C) has an unconscious substrate (U), and in the other the tangible physical domain (T) has an intangible physical substrate (I). Since the model applies to armoring as a filter, muscular armoring on the tangible physical level is a complement of character armoring, as described above. (I) comprises those "forces" and "energies" that sustain muscular armoring on (T). Complementary processes in (U) are manifested in dreams and unconscious psychic processes that sustain the character armoring. Both parallel processes arise from a "source," an "ultimate autonomous reality". At the interface of (U) and (I) there are places of confluence, of merging, where all distinction between the two domains disappears.

It is precisely at these points that armoring, and the filtering of consciousness due to armoring, is created — and with therapy, dissolves.

Conclusion

This paper has described the development of a filtering process in consciousness that takes place in growth and development, whereby the average person in Western society becomes insensitive to the world around him and to his inner excitations. Wilhelm Reich described this process as a form of armoring, and detailed how it happens and how it can be dissolved through the analysis of one's character and the softening of corresponding muscular contractions. Both character and muscu-

---

10. Baker. *Man in the Trap.* p. 153.
11. Robert G. Jahn and Brenda J. Dunne. "A modular model of mind/matter manifestations (M^5)." *Journal of Scientific Exploration, 15*, No. 3 (2001). pp. 299–331.

lar armoring have been shown to influence, and frequently distort, the perception of and response to the impulses arising within the individual and from the external world. As such, they may be regarded as fundamental filters of reality.

References

Elsworth Baker. *Man in the Trap*. N.Y.: Farrar, Straus, & Giroux, 1967.

Richard A. Blasband. "The ordering of random event generators by emotional expression." *Journal of Scientific Exploration, 14*, No. 2 (2000), Summer. pp. 195–216.

Robert G. Jahn and Brenda J. Dunne. "A modular model of mind/matter manifestations (M^5)." *Journal of Scientific Exploration, 15*, No. 3 (2001). pp. 299–331.

————. "Sensors, filters, and the Source of reality." *Journal of Scientific Exploration, 18*, No. 4 (2004). pp. 547–71.

Nicolai Viktorovich Levashov. *The Final Appeal to Mankind*. Privately published, 1997. Vol. 2. (Also at www.Levashov.info.)

Wilhelm Reich. *The Function of the Orgasm*. NY: Orgone Institute Press, 1942.

————. *The Cancer Biopathy*. NY: Orgone Institute Press, 1948.

————. *Character Analysis*. NY: Orgone Institute Press, 1949.

————. *Ether, God, and Devil*. Orgonon, Rangeley, ME: Orgone Institute Press, 1949.

Sensors, Filters, and the Objects of Perception: A Direct Realist, Multidimensional State Space Model

IGOR DOLGOV
New Mexico State University
Las Cruces, New Mexico

Introduction

The question of whether perception is direct or indirect has remained a topic of debate since the early days of western philosophy. It is currently being readdressed by modern psychology in the context of a debate between the constructivists who take a representationalist view of perception (Fodor and Pylyshyn, 1981) and ecological psychologists (Turvey *et al.*, 1981) who consider perception to be direct. Representationalism, also called *indirect* realism, states that in perception one is aware only of indirect objects, specifically sense-data (or qualia) that correlate with the external objects existing in the physical world. While this worldview has been the *sine qua non* of western philosophy and is the dominant paradigm utilized by most scientists today, this perspective is not shared by everyone.

The Scottish Enlightenment philosopher Thomas Reid believed the representationalist viewpoint to be guilty of a genetic fallacy[1] in describing the process of perception, and consequently proposed a *direct* realist perceptual model. His account treats perception as immediate and direct, with the objects of perception being the actual external objects, qualities, and events that populate the world. Reid argued that the alternatives to direct realism, grounded either in phenomenalism or skepticism, were both absurd in their denial of the grounded nature of perception and,

---

1. A genetic fallacy is a logical fallacy that consists in evaluating a thing or process in terms of its earlier context, disregarding development and dynamics, and then carrying over that evaluation to the thing in the present.

by *reductio ad absurdum*, must be rejected.[2] The opposition to indirect realism was further bolstered by pragmatist thinkers like John Dewey and William James, and was recently rejuvenated eloquently by Mark Johnston (2004) in *The Obscure Object of Hallucination*. Johnston's analysis begins with a situation in which a seemingly hallucinatory object is superimposed over a real one and matches its appearance, making them perceptually indistinguishable. He undertakes both conjunctive and disjunctive accounts of this predicament and ultimately concludes that "the objects present in veridical sensing are not exhausted by those that could be given to a mere hallucinator" (p. 114).

While mainstream psychology continues to operate on a constructivist model of perception rooted in indirect realism, several other notable psychologists have rejected this worldview. John Dewey (1896), the eighth president of the American Psychological Association, first pointed out the false assumptions of the indirect realism–based reflex arc concept in psychology that still serves as the basis for the overwhelming majority of research done today. J. J. Gibson (1966, 1979) challenged the indirect realist model by proposing an ecologically motivated theory of perception. The central notion of Gibson's theory is that perception of the world is rich, immediate, and most importantly, direct. While he was predominantly a theoretician, empirical findings, such as the ubiquitous use of τ (retinal expansion parameter) by humans and animals, have confirmed the ecological model's basic assumptions. Definitive empirical support for the direct realist account of perception comes from the field of kinesiology, specifically *via* the rediscovery[3] of the research of Russian movement physiologist Nicholai Bernstein on the development of motor coordination and expertise (Bernstein, 1967; *cf.* Thelen, 1995).

Although the direct realist worldview remains unaccepted by mainstream western psychology, many principles of Gibson's theory have existed as tenets in a variety of eastern and animist traditions for several

---

2. This objection is not seen as valid by phenomenalists like George Berkeley, Frank Jackson, and David Chalmers. Furthermore, the skepticist viewpoint also has some appeal, as evidenced in *The Matrix as Metaphysics*, where Chalmers (2003) outlines and defends the credibility of just this sort of viewpoint.
3. Nikolai Bernshtein and Ivan Pavlov were both Russian neurophysiologists in the early part of the 20th century. Due to the popularity of Pavlov's classical conditioning work, much of Bernstein's work was suppressed and not translated into English until 1967.

millennia. The established beliefs and practices of these cultures embody a collection of valuable insights for any theory of perception, and can directly inform the ecological model. One ubiquitous characteristic of these pagan and animist cultural practices is a long history of appeal to altered states of consciousness (ASCs) for guidance and assistance in various aspects of everyday life. The types of intentionally initiated ASCs that are utilized by such cultures are generally not pathological, but rather benign and purposeful. The remainder of this chapter will refer to the subgroup of ASCs characterized above as functional altered states of consciousness (fASCs).

Although Gibson's theory of perception is well developed, it does not dutifully entertain perception as it occurs in a functional altered state of consciousness. Gibson views the unadulterated perceptual state as privileged, with any shifts in perception due to imagination, illusion, hallucination, or any alteration in the mundane state of consciousness as being maladaptive. He dismisses any utility of such perceptual phenomena with the comment, "I remain dubious" (1966, p. 261). Similarly, traditional western approaches consider fASCs to be maladaptive hallucinatory phenomena, again failing to recognize the value of the information that is perceived in the context of a ceremonial fASC. Alternatively, by adopting an open-minded empirical strategy and examining the information available in fASCs, perceptual and cognitive theorists could gain a broader understanding of the spectrum of the information that can be perceived and obtain some insight into underlying psychological mechanisms.

The remainder of this work begins by summarizing the core principles of Gibson's ecological theory and observing that many of these same principles are accepted tenets in indigenous cultures around the world. The production, characteristics, and functions of fASCs will then be reviewed, with a focus on perceptual shifts and the veridicality of the perceived information. Lastly, this chapter will posit a simple extension of the ecologically motivated paradigm that treats perception as a dynamic process existing in a state space where certain channels of information transfer are weighted to emphasize salient information patterns. Such a formulation of perception naturally extends to defining perceptual and cognitive filters as weighting mechanisms that emphasize certain aspects of the ambient energy array present in the physical environment, while retaining the ability to access other features of the information array by rearranging the subjective weighting scheme employed by an observer.

Basic Principles of Gibson's Ecological Paradigm

Gibson (1966, 1979) begins his theory of perception by defining the subjects and objects of perception as simply those organisms capable of perception, namely animals endowed with sensory, neural, and generally motor mechanisms. The objects of perception are those that are contained within the ecological niche of the observer. Gibson (1979) is careful to point out that the animal and the environment are interdependent, stating that "... the words *animal* and *environment* make an inseparable pair. Each term implies the other" (p. 8). This relationship entails that ecological properties are relational in nature, a fact that has several implications, most important of which is an inherently subjective conceptualization of reality. He goes on to state that perception is immediate and direct, and that what is perceived is relational, meaningful information about the observer's environment.

It is important to be aware of the distinction ecological theory makes between two common meanings of the verb "to sense": (1) to detect something; (2) to have a sensation. In the ecological case, the first meaning is reserved for perception, whereas the second meaning literally means the response of the sensory organs. Perception, rather than sensation, is considered to be primary in the perceptual chain of events, with the rationale that perception can often be sensationless, as in his example of "[a] blind man [who perceives] the wall in front of him, without realizing what sense has been stimulated" (Gibson, 1966, p. 2).

The above distinction of two meanings of sense highlights an important difference between the constructivist and ecological paradigms in their accounts of the chain of events that underlie the perceptual process itself. The mainstream view is based on the classic reflex arc paradigm that defines sensation, perception, and cognition as parts of a serial process that is initiated by a passive sensory response to a physical stimulus and proceeds by constructing conscious experience from inherently impoverished sensory data. Meaning is then assigned to this information through a variety of higher cognitive mechanisms. On the other hand, the ecological approach asserts that the functional role of the perceptual mechanism is not to detect and decode neural activity patterns (neural correlated of consciousness), but rather to perceive the *meaning* encoded in the structure of the available and pertinent information contained in the environment (Gibson, 1966, 1979). Perceived information is practical, tangible, and affords the organism an opportunity to act to satisfy its needs.

Furthermore, mainstream psychology assumes sensation, perception, and cognition to be distinct individual processes that interact to produce behavior. Ecological theory regards this approach as misguided because it fails to account for the highly interdependent nature of perception and action. Gibson observes that perceptual systems are constantly active and that the process of perception requires perpetual action. For Gibson, perception and action are really two aspects of a single dynamic perception-action mechanism that comprises a gamut of active perceptual systems that resonate[4] with information patterns in the environment. To determine the nature of information that is directly perceived, he again addresses the question in ecological terms. Thus, the information that is perceived by an animal depends on its biology and psychology, and is that which is required for survival in its niche.

In the visual case, the animal perceives the structured layout of the surfaces in the environment, which in turn *affords* the animal various possible actions. Gibson states:

> The activity of an observer that is afforded depends on the layout, that is, on the solid geometry of the arrangement. The same layout will have different affordances for different animals, of course, insofar as each animal has a different repertory of acts. Different animals will perceive different sets of affordances. Therefore, the perception is of practical layout, not theoretical layout, but it is nonetheless geometrical for all that (Gibson, 1972, p. 37).

For non-visual perceptual mechanisms, the rules of solid geometry no longer apply, and one needs to rely on the pertinent structural paradigm.

---

4. For a full discussion of perceptual/sensory systems and the resonance mechanism, see Gibson 1966, 1979.

Ecological theory defines the units of perception to be quantifiable, relational in nature, and on the scale of the perceiver. An essential point of the theory is that the units of the environment are not independent, but rather exist in a nested structure so that smaller units are embedded in the larger. Gibson states, "There are no atomic units of the world considered as the environment. Instead, there are subordinate and superordinate units. The unit you choose for describing the environment depends on the level of the environment you choose to describe" (1979, p. 9). Standardized, abstract, and non-relational units of measurement which are based on conceptual and computational convenience are not considered relevant to explaining a general ecological theory of perception. Moreover, events and animals in the environment obey certain natural and ecological laws rather than many of the abstract laws espoused by physics and mathematics.

Similar to learning strategies currently being employed in backpropagation artificial neural network models, the ecological paradigm characterizes learning as a series of incremental adjustments of the aggregate perception-action mechanism. Persistence and change embody events, which are the basic units of the temporal flow of perception. According to Gibson, "The flow of abstract time, however useful this concept may be to the physicist, has no reality for a [non-human] animal. We perceive not time but [nested] processes, changes, [and] sequences ..." (1979, p. 12).

The perception of the environment has a certain quality of stability even though it is constantly changing: "The permanency underlies the change ... some properties are conserved and others are not ... for invariant and variant, each term of the pair is reciprocal to the other" (1979, p. 13). By perceiving both the changing and locally permanent properties of the environment, an animal's perception-action system enables it to act effectively by detecting those regularities in the ambient stimulus flux that encompass the environment's affordances and impending dangers.

Ecological Psychology and Indigenous Cultural Practices

When Gibson proposed his ecological approach to perception in 1966 (and more forcefully in 1979) it was a radical theory that contradicted many aspects of the established behaviorist and emerging cognitive schools of psychology. Yet, core Gibsonian principles resonate well with timeworn eastern traditions like Buddhism and Hinduism, as well as the beliefs and practices of a number of animist tribal cultures. The five principles listed below are shared by ecological psychology and the world-views of the aforementioned cultures, as evidenced by their mythology, rituals, and mundane practices:

- The environment is governed by natural laws.
- Nothing is permanent. The environment world both remains constant and changes.
- The animal and its environment are interdependent and complementary.
- Sentient organisms (directly) perceive meaningful information about the real objects in a structured environment (not sense data).
- Perceived information is pragmatic and practical rather than theoretical.

One highly relevant shared aspect of cultures that adhere to the above beliefs is their common appeal to functional Altered States of Consciousness (fASCs) as a valuable source of information that is unavailable in mundane conscious states.

Functional Altered States of Consciousness

Many pagan and animist cultures employ functional rituals in which practitioners enter a mystical trance by consuming some form of hallucinogenic preparation or participating in some physically demanding rite, thereby achieving an altered state of consciousness. On the other hand, most Eastern traditions employ various mental control techniques, such as meditation, for similar purposes. While the characteristics and production of fASCs do vary among cultures, there is a highly salient common factor that is evident in their purpose: in fASCs, practitioners are said to be able to perceive information that is otherwise typically inaccessible.

Ludwig (1960) suggests that an ASC can be defined as: "[A]ny mental state(s) induced by various physiological, psychological, or pharmacological maneuvers or agents, which can be recognized subjectively by the individual himself (or by an observer of the individual) as representing a sufficient deviation in subjective experience or psychological functioning from certain general norms for that individual during alert, waking consciousness" (p. 9). Functional ASCs represent a subset that includes only those states that satisfy the above definition, while also being intentional, purposeful, and generally benign. The following is an abridged and modified description of the production, characteristics, and functions of fASCs based on the scheme laid out by Ludwig (1966) in Charles Tart's classic volume, *Altered States of Consciousness.*

Production of fASCs

Altered States of Consciousness may be produced "in any setting by a wide variety of agents or maneuvers which interfere with the normal inflow of [exteroceptive] or proprioceptive [information], or the normal outflow of motor [processes], the normal "emotional tone," or the normal flow and organization of [perceptual and] cognitive processes" (Ludwig, p. 10). Specifically, fASCs can be produced *via*:

a. *Significant increase/reduction of exteroceptive and proprioceptive information and/or motor activity.* This category includes mental states resulting primarily from a significant increase or reduction of available stimulation and activity. In some cultures, fASCs are achieved *via* dance rituals that increase levels of stimulation and activity to produce a trance, whereas other cultures appeal to monitored infliction of superficial pain. On the other hand, Buddhist monks achieve fASCs through passive meditation, a process that reduces both stimulation and activity.

b. *Significant increase/decrease in alertness or mental involvement.* This approach includes mental states that result from focused or selective hyper-alertness, such as the states of intense concentration utilized in Zen Buddhist meditation (Badiner, 2002) and the Hindu practice of Samadhi. On the other hand, some animist cultures achieve states of hyper-alertness through long periods of sensory deprivation.

c. *Presence of somato-psychological factors.* This approach includes those mental states that are a result of alterations in body chemistry or neurophysiology. In many indigenous cultures fASCs are frequently observed in the practice of purposeful administration of various psychoactive preparations (Badiner, 2002; Devereux, 1997). There are also examples of such fASCs in kundalini-awakening states, which are achieved only by long-time practitioners of mind and body control.

General Characteristics of fASCs

An interesting observation about fASCs is that while they tend to produce many similar physiological effects they remain profoundly variable experientially. Some of the more common shifts in mentation observed in fASCs are:

a. *Alterations in perception.* The most evident subjective changes are in the perception of the external environment, which is an aspect of fASCs that is extremely relevant to our discussion. Mainstream psychology treats these perceptual phenomena as instances of delusory, non-veridical perception. In contrast, eastern and animist cultures that adhere to fASC practices treat the information that is perceived in such states as veridical and generally place great value on information obtained in this way. Perception of the flow of time is also often altered in a profound way, while the notion of abstract time often becomes meaningless.

b. *Alterations in cognition.* This category encompasses a variety of subjective changes in concentration, attention, memory, and judgment. The rules of rational logic may be loosened or abandoned, making certain abstract cognitive tasks very difficult. One of the most common and interesting aspects of a fASC is a sense of increased meaning and significance attributed to events and insights.

c. *Alterations in emotional state.* Emotional experiences are often amplified, with emotions being more primordial and intense than in an unaltered state.

d. *Sense of the ineffable.* The qualitative experience of a fASC seems to be profoundly different from the reality experienced in an ordinary state of consciousness, and is generally uniquely meaningful, thereby making it very difficult to describe to those who have not had similar experiences.

Purposes and Functions of fASCs in Eastern and Animist Cultures

Functional ASCs are utilized in a number of ways in traditional eastern and animist societies:

a. *Enhanced understanding.* Arguably, the most valuable contribution of fASCs is their ability to expand one's consciousness and achieve states within which one can gain new knowledge and understanding of oneself and the nature of the world, along with other illuminating insights (*e.g.*, Huxley, 1954; Strassman, 2001). Moreover, there is ample evidence that fASCs served as catalysts in the foundation of many prevalent religious and spiritual movements (Badiner, 2002; Devereux, 1997; Merkur, 2001).

b. *Enhanced perception and survival.* As well as gaining greater self-understanding, fASCs have been employed for perceiving pragmatic information, such as ascertaining the medicinal properties of certain plants or the location of game or nearby sources of water. Indigenous agricultural practices are also often based on information obtained while in fASCs. In fact, the net yield of indigenous South American gardens planted based on information acquired in fASCs frequently have been shown to produce greater yields than are achieved by modern agricultural techniques. Furthermore, Hindu yogis and Tibetan Buddhist monks are reported to be able to control various body processes, such as heart rate, metabolism, respiration, and body temperature. These mind-over-matter techniques allow them to survive for extended periods in extreme conditions that would kill other people (Schmicker, 2001).

c. *Healing.* Throughout human history, fASCs have also played an important medicinal role, as evidenced by their use for purposes of spiritual and physical healing by a variety of religious and spiritual figures, as well as some modern-day psychotherapists. Shamans are known to enter fASCs in order to diagnose the cause of an ailment and to determine remedies and healing rituals. Additionally, abundant anecdotal evidence exists of puzzling recoveries of ill individuals who were healed by medicine-men or in modern labs by researchers administering traditional hallucinogenic compounds (for a comprehensive review, see Winkelman and Roberts, 2007).

d. *Social bonding.* Certain fASCs seem to facilitate the process of community building and are used during rites of passage in many cultures.

e. *Reconnecting with the environment.* As Gibson points out, most people who live in the civilized world have little connection with the natural environment. An experience of a fASC often endows the practitioner with a sense of communing with nature. This often results in an increased appreciation for other people, animals, and the surrounding environment, and frequently a more sustainable attitude toward life.

The above characterization of functional altered states provides a general idea of the various roles they serve in indigenous communities where practitioners undertake these states in the context of ceremony, not as recreation. There is no doubt that perception in certain maladaptive ASCs is indeed non-veridical; however, the appeal to functional ASCs for guidance has a long historical precedent and is almost universal among ancient cultures. Therefore, we must consider the possibility that some instances of perception in fASCs are indeed veridical in nature. The founder of the American psychological and psychical research movements, William James, firmly believed in the validity and profound value of altered states of consciousness. In his *Varieties of Religious Experience* (1929, pp. 357–358), he states:

Our normal waking consciousness ... is but one special type of consciousness, whilst all about it, parted from it by the filmiest of screens, there lie potential forms of consciousness entirely different. We may go through life without suspecting their existence; but apply the requisite stimulus, and at a touch they are all there in their completeness, definite types of mentality which probably somewhere have their field of application and adaptation. No account of the universe in its totality can be final which leaves these other forms of consciousness quite disregarded. How to regard them is the question — for they are so discontiguous with ordinary consciousness. Yet they may determine attitudes though they cannot furnish formulas, and open a region though they fail to give a map. At any rate, they forbid a premature closing of our accounts of reality.

The above reflects the opinions of a number of the modern era's most influential scientists, philosophers, writers, artists, and religious leaders, such as Gustav Fechner (1879), Fredric Jameson (1990), Aldous Huxley (1954), Salvador Dali (Moorhouse, 1990), and the Dalai Lama (Gyatzo, 1994). Furthermore, effects similar to the kinds of anomalous perception phenomena observed in fASCs have also been widely reported in Psi research (Bardens, 1987; Cardeña, Lynn, and Krippner, 2000; Jahn and Dunne, 1987, 2001, 2005; Radin, 1997; Schmicker, 2001; Tart, 1977; White, 1976).

A Multidimensional State Space Model of Perception

To explain the existence of the types of anomalous perceptual phenomena that occur in fASCs, ecological theory can adopt the position that perceptual set/aptitude is dynamic, and that the perception-action system shifts its various resources according to the demands of the task at hand. Gibson (1979) believes that perceptual ability is enhanced through learning, an adaptive iterative process that occurs as a result of the perceptual systems gradually achieving better resonance with the most pertinent information in its environment. While he does not specify exactly how this process occurs, he proposes that the perceptual tuning process undergoes a series of incremental steps that further the scope and acuity of the perception. Gibsonian theory correctly specifies that in terms of their physical response to stimuli, the sensory organs remain mostly unchanged throughout the lifespan of an organism, and that therefore "no new sensations can be learned. The information that is picked up, on the other hand, becomes more and more subtle, elaborate, and precise with practice. One can keep learning as long as life goes on" (Gibson, 1979, p. 245).

Ecological psychology emphasizes the fact that the available ambient information is structured. Therefore, a perceptual system with improved pattern detection ability would perceive (i) more information about familiar units of the environment (improved acuity), and/or (ii) totally novel information sources that were unavailable in mundane states (larger scope). An interesting phenomenon that occurs in fASCs is an experienced enhancement in perceptual ability, often partially realized as an improved ability to perceive structure in the ambient stimulus array (for an example see Aldous Huxley's account of his first experience with peyote, *The Doors of Perception*).

Aside from the already cited sources, there are numerous anecdotal reports of psychedelic experiences resulting from the consumption of entheogenic substances that enhance familiar patterns and reveal novel ones in the surrounding world. The mechanism for this sudden perceptual shift can be modeled as an extension of Gibson's account of enhancing perception through learning, with the main differences being the duration and permanence of this enhanced perception. In his adaptive learning model, the process is dynamic and the perceptual system improves steadily with exposure to novel environments and can decline only through injury or age. However, in fASCs the perceptual system is suddenly and significantly shifted; the duration and intensity of this shift are determined by the particulars of a given experience.

A *state space* model of perceptual attunement provides some clarification and a possible mechanism for a perceptual system's capacity for both gradual and sudden shifts. A state space is an n-dimensional hypercube of discrete states which can formally be defined as the n-tuple [N, A, S, G] where N is the actual set of states, A is a set of arcs connecting the states, S is a nonempty subset of N that contains start states, and G is a nonempty subset of N that contains the goal states. We propose that the perception-action system can be modeled to exist in a state-space that defines the observer's mental set and perceptual ability. The fundamental assumption of such a system is that perceptual aptitude can be decomposed along a series of vectors that correspond to the various energy patterns (and likely pattern types) perceivable by organisms. This array of vectors can be thought of as a battery of sensors, or perhaps more properly, perception-action units. Certain patterns of the ambient energy array are positively weighted to bring relevant aspects of physical reality into an observer's conscious awareness. Given limited psychological resources, aspects of the array that are not essential to an observer's performance in the environment are weighted negatively and do not arise into consciousness. The positive and negative weighting of ambient information provides the necessary filtering of the environment that allows organisms to act successfully to achieve their goals.

Perception begins with a robust ambient energy array which is filtered at several stages in the process. Although first-order qualities are perceived directly, initial filtering of the energy array is realized by the physiology of the perceiver. Second-order qualities are perceived indirectly through a filtering process which attempts to integrate immediately perceived information with existing mental models. The inflow of information is then segmented into elements which are used in future mentation or discarded. Embodied cognition theory illuminates the determinants of the latter stages of process. For example, the perception of other people's actions (movements and intentions) is accomplished through the neural activation of the observers' premotor and motor cortexes. The active neurons include mirror neurons, which also show activity when the observers perform the action themselves (Barsalou, 2008). Glenberg (1997) and colleagues have also shown that this kind of complementary modal reactivation occurs not only in action perception, but also in the perception of emotion and in language comprehension, and is the overarching principle governing memory. When we perceive the actions of others, our neural activity approximates a pattern which is typically present during our own actions. In effect, our filters consist of our physiological apparatus, our ecological adaptations, and relevant personal experience.

The nominal conscious state in which organisms perform daily activities likely represents a global optimum of a given cost function within the perception-action state space. However, as is the case with complex state spaces, there typically are many local optima. These minima and maxima in the state space represent different information weighting configurations that can be useful for tasks characterized by specialized demands on the perception-action system. Access to these local maxima may not always be available and may require a perturbation in the system, such as entry into an altered state of consciousness. In the current model, fASC states make available a new subset of arcs (A_l) that enable specific adaptive shifts in the perceptual state space. Such shifts would consequently allow for the perception of information in fASCs that is not available in mundane states of consciousness.

Conclusion

Researchers of functional altered states of consciousness and related phenomena like Psi have long encountered opposition from the mainstream scientific community (Jahn and Dunne, 2005, 2008). The true value of a direct realist and multidimensional state space model of perception is that these phenomena can be couched within a scientific model that does not rationalize away their existence as products of delusion or imagination. Within an ecological framework, the operational assumption is that the environment is richer than what our specialized perspective typically reflects. Many different organisms have evolved to function within our ecological niche, and although the range of evolved perception-action systems is highly heterogeneous; each equally valid perceived reality reflects eons of evolutionary pressures on an organism's genetics, as well as the environment that shaped its development.

While certainly less succinct than the reductionist model of a single veridical reality, a holistic direct realist approach may be more fruitful. In modern psychology, the failure of the reductionist model is emphasized by the lack of a comprehensive account of conscious experience by neurocognitive researchers in spite of an abundance of replicable laboratory-acquired data (Glenberg, 1997). Alternatively, the ecological and embodied paradigms argue for a recentering of psychological theory on grounded, modal experience as a platform for modeling mental processes.

Mark Johnston's (2004) philosophical argument for the primacy and immediacy of the perception of first-order qualities emphasizes the difference between the hallucinatory (nonveridical) and mundane (veridical) objects of perception. Similarly, the fields of mainstream medicine and psychology have adopted a pathological evaluation of altered states of consciousness with minor exceptions. On the other hand, modern anthropological, ethnobotanical, and nontraditional medicinal disciplines record a number of functional, adaptive indigenous, and modern practices that successfully utilize altered states (for a comprehensive review see Winkelman and Roberts, 2007). The question must then be asked: What are the objects of perception in fASCs, and do they more resemble Johnston's objects of hallucination or the objects of mundane perception? Many researchers would likely reject the idea of veridical perception in fASCs, and it has thus far been the standard to take the weak position that the objects of perception in such states lay on a continuum somewhere between hallucinatory and veridical perception. However, ecological theory has the potential to argue for a stronger position, one which asserts that objects of fASC perception are like mundane ones, in that they exist in the environment.

Departing from Gibson's views, but remaining in line with basic ecological theory, we argue that if perceived information is relational in nature, each individual's reality is unique, which implies the nonexistence of a single veridical reality. Thus, the shifting of perceptual filters as weighting schemes in altered states does not invalidate the reality of perception in such states. Just as for mundane perception, the objects of perception in fASC exist in the ambient energy array. Information perceived in such altered states is not delusory in nature, but rather perceived through perceptual shifts that take place as a result of adaptive filtering of the ambient energy array. The reported richness of the phenomenology of fASCs is likely due in part to a shift of the experiencers' reality criterion, a signal detection theory–based threshold for perception of an object in the environment (Dolgov and McBeath, 2005).

References

Allan Hunt Badiner. *Zig Zag Zen: Buddhism and Psychedelics.* San Francisco: Chronicle Books, 2002.

Dennis Bardens. *Psychic Animals: An Investigation of Their Secret Powers.* London: Robert Hale, 1987.

Lawrence W. Barsalou. "Grounded cognition." *Annual Review of Psychology, 59,* No. 1 (2008). pp. 617–645.

Nikolai Aleksandrovich Bernshtein. *The Co-Ordination and Regulation of Movements.* London: Pergamon, 1967.

Etzel Cardeña, Steven Jay Lynn, and Stanley Krippner. *Varieties of Anomalous Experience: Examining the Scientific Evidence.* Washington, DC: American Psychological Association, 2000.

David John Chalmers. "The matrix as metaphysics." Philosophy Section of www.thematrix.com, 2003. Reprinted in Christopher Grau, ed. *Philosophers Explore the Matrix.* New York: Oxford University Press, 2005.

Paul Devereux. *The Long Trip: A Prehistory of Psychedelia.* New York: Penguin Putnam, 1997.

John Dewey. "The reflex arc concept in psychology." *The Psychological Review, 3* (1896). pp. 357–370.

Igor Dolgov and Michael K. McBeath. "A signal-detection-theory model of normal and hallucinatory perception (in reply to Collerton *et al.*)." *Journal of Behavioral & Brain Sciences, 28,* No. 6 (2005). pp. 761–762.

Gustav Theodor Fechner. *Die Tagesansicht gegenüber der Nachtansicht* [*The day view compared to the night view*]. Leipzig: Breitfopf & Hartel, 1879.

Jerry A. Fodor and Zenon W. Pylyshyn. "How direct is visual perception? Some reflections on Gibson's 'Ecological Approach'." *Cognition, 9,* No. 2 (1981). pp. 139–196.

James Jerome Gibson. *The Senses Considered as Perceptual Systems.* Boston: Houghton Mifflin, 1966.

———. "The affordances of the environment." 1972. In Edward S. Reed and Rebecca Jones, eds., *Reasons for Realism: Selected Essays of James J. Gibson.* Hillsdale, NJ: Lawrence Erlbaum Associates, 1982. pp. 408–410.

———. *The Ecological Approach to Visual Perception.* Boston: Houghton Mifflin, 1979.

Arthur M. Glenberg. "What memory is for." *Journal of Behavioral and Brain Sciences, 20,* No. 1 (1997). pp. 1–55.

Tenzin Gyatzo. *The World of Tibetan Buddhism: An Overview of Its Philosophy and Practice.* Boston: Wisdom Publications, 1994.

Aldous Huxley. *Doors of Perception.* London: Chatto & Windus, 1954.

Robert G. Jahn and Brenda J. Dunne. *Margins of Reality: The Role of Consciousness in the Physical World.* San Diego: Harcourt Brace Jovanovich, 1987.

———. "A modular model of mind/matter manifestations (M^5)." *Journal of Scientific Exploration, 15,* No. 3 (2001). pp. 299–329.

———. "The PEAR proposition." *Journal of Scientific Exploration, 19,* No. 2 (2005). pp. 195–246.

———. "Change the rules!" *Journal of Scientific Exploration, 22,* No. 2 (2008). pp. 193–213.

William James. *The Varieties of Religious Experience: A Study in Human Nature: Being the Gifford Lectures on Natural Religion Delivered at Edinburgh in 1901–1902.* New York: Modern Library Press, 1929.

Fredric Jameson. *Signatures of the Visible.* New York: Routledge, 1990.

Mark Johnston. "The obscure object of hallucination." *Philosophical Studies, 120*, Nos. 1–3 (2004). pp. 113–183.

Arnold M. Ludwig. "Altered states of consciousness." 1966. In Charles T. Tart, ed., *Altered States of Consciousness: A Book of Readings.* New York: John Wiley & Sons, 1969. pp. 9–22.

Daniel Merkur. *The Psychedelic Sacrament: Manna, Meditation, and Mystical Experience.* Rochester, VT: Park Street Press, 2001.

Paul Moorhouse. *Dali.* London: PRC Publishing, 1990.

Jeremy Narby. *The Cosmic Serpent: DNA and the Origins of Knowledge.* New York: Penguin Putnam, 1998.

Dean I. Radin. *The Conscious Universe: The Scientific Truth of Psychic Phenomena.* New York: Harper Collins Publishers, 1997.

Michael L. Schmicker. *Best Evidence: An Investigative Reporter's Three-Year Quest to Uncover the Best Scientific Evidence for ESP, Psychokinesis, Mental Healing, Ghosts and Poltergeists, Dowsing, Mediums, Near Death Experiences, Reincarnation and Other Impossible Phenomena That Refuse to Disappear* (2nd ed.). Lincoln, NE: Writers Club Press, 2002.

Alexander Shulgin and Ann Shulgin. *Phenethylamines I Have Known and Loved (PiHKAL): A Chemical Love Story.* Berkeley, CA: Transform Press, 1991.

Rick J. Strassman. *DMT: The Spirit Molecule: A Doctor's Revolutionary Research into the Biology of Near-Death and Mystical Experiences.* Rochester, VT: Park Street Press, 2001.

Charles T. Tart. *Altered States of Consciousness: A Book of Readings.* New York: John Wiley & Sons, 1969.

———. *Psi: Scientific Studies of the Psychic Realm.* Syracuse, NY: E.P. Dutton, 1977.

Esther Thelen. "Motor development: A new synthesis." *American Psychologist, 50*, No. 2 (1995). pp. 79–95.

Michael T. Turvey, Robert E. Shaw, Edward S. Reed, and William M. Mace. "Ecological laws of perceiving and acting: In reply to Fodor and Pylyshyn." *Cognition, 9*, No. 3 (1981). pp. 237–304.

Rhea A. White. *Surveys in Parapsychology.* Metuchen, NJ: The Scarecrow Press, 1976.

Michael Winkelman and Thomas Roberts, eds. *Psychedelic Medicine: New Evidence for Hallucinogenic Substances as Treatments.* Portsmouth, NH: Greenwood/Praeger, 2007.

Out-of-Body Experiences:
An Exploration of Non-Local Filters

NELSON ABREU
International Academy of Consciousness
South Miami, Florida

Introduction

The ability of consciousness to acquire information and experience about places and events beyond the usual physical senses has been reported since the beginning of recorded history and described in many cultural traditions. In recent times, these phenomena are referred to as "Out-of-Body Experiences" (OBEs), and are closely related to those described as "Near Death Experiences" or "Remote Perception," among other labels. While still regarded with skepticism by mainstream science, a substantial number of scholarly studies and subjective reports have attested to their reality and raise important questions about the nature of consciousness and its interactions with the physical universe. This evidence suggests that consciousness can not only transcend the physical body, but also reduce or modify the effects of the physiological, cultural, and psychological filters that limit and color this mind-Source communication. The out-of-body experience and allied phenomena also suggest the existence of subtle "bodies" and dimensions that need to be explored and integrated into our current models of consciousness.

Out-of-Body Experiences

After a stressful day, John lies exhausted in bed. He falls asleep almost immediately, but regains some awareness when he hears a dog barking. He realizes he is feeling some unusual sensations — his body is very numb and light and he discovers he is unable to move. Just before panic sets in, exotic tingling and electricity-like vibrations spring up throughout his body. Wonder partially overcomes fear, and soon he feels like his body is floating upwards. The vibrations get increasingly intense until a pressure at the back of the head propels him out of the bed accompanied by a strong sinking sensation. The vibration ceases and he can see his physical body resting in bed. John feels wonderful with the liberation from matter and breathing.

He becomes aware of a very pleasant and kind presence and gets a strong wish to see his mother at the hospital. He flies out through the wall and finds himself immediately at his mother's bedside. The presence, or guide, instructs him to send healing vital energies to his mother. He perceives that her non-physical body is floating a few inches above her physical body and he helps her to awaken in the astral dimension. Soon afterwards, his deceased grandfather comes to greet them. With a single embrace, John and his grandfather exchange so many thoughts. John is so overcome with emotion that he feels immediately drawn back into his body. The next day, his mother tells him of a "dream" where she relates some similar details of the previous night.

A typical OBE could progress something like this account. Also known as astral projection, or projection of the consciousness, this widespread phenomenon has been reported throughout history. It is the intentional or spontaneous separation of the consciousness from the physical body. In recent decades, the OBE has entered the domain of scientific exploration beyond the confines of religion and mysticism. It is now more common for the everyday individual and the scientist alike to have OBEs and other related experiences in order to arrive at a more logical understanding of the aspects of life that transcend the physical senses and rules.

According to "lucid projectors," those who have frequent OBEs with some degree of awareness and control, it is possible to have joint projections with others who are able to corroborate the recollections of their shared extraphysical events. As in PEAR's remote perception research, in these cases one can frequently make accurate, visual observations of physical reality while consciously but invisibly present at a scene in the astral or extraphysical dimension. Some lucid projectors can use this as a way to access more subtle realities and even to obtain a glimpse of life before birth or after physical death (the *final* projection). They are reported to observe others preparing for their next physical existence or undergoing the deactivation of their physical bodies.

More extensive study of OBE phenomena could allow us to explore psychical processes from a multidimensional perspective that might reveal processes hidden from our usual awareness and reveal characteristics of the subtle filters that can be tuned or unblocked to develop our non-physical perceptions. One of the major difficulties in studying such processes is that the scientist cannot simply be an observer. Just as one cannot really understand human/machine random event generator (REG) interactions without first-hand experience, investigators need to serve as their own subjects and undertake many OBE expeditions to confirm the reality of the phenomenon. Only then can they begin to understand the nature of the experiences and what they can reveal about the nature of consciousness, including so-called anomalies and other subtle processes that affect our daily lives. Not every OBE attempt is successful, any more than every REG interaction will produce an extra-chance result. Serious evidence can be accumulated only from a collection of many repeated attempts.

Most consciousness researchers today wonder "how consciousness can arise from biology," but the evidence from consciousness-related anomalies research suggests that this needs to be rephrased as "how does consciousness communicate with biology?" "Sensors, Filters, and the Source of Reality" models the information exchange between consciousness (in the sense of mind or awareness) and its Source. The study of out-of-body experiences can augment this model by the imposition of intermediary subtle "bodies" and realities; *i.e.* different levels of filtering between awareness and the Source. For example, during an out-of-body experience, one feels like one is utilizing the *psychosoma*, a subtle body related to emotions, commonly referred to as the "astral body". If emotions originated in the body, then the consciousness would be free of emotionality during such experiences, and after physical death. However, the opposite seems to occur: in OBEs and near death experiences emotions, previously attenuated by the dense mortal vehicle, or soma, are now reported as being felt more intensely. Many times projectors feel they are drawn back to the soma, or even lose consciousness, when they become overly emotional, which can cause a severe reduction in the experience of lucidity and, in some cases, physical effects on the associated soma.

One of the most intriguing experiences is the so-called partial projection, where a part of the psychosoma — such as the astral head or an astral hand — disconnects from the physical body. In such a situation, it is possible to perceive simultaneously both the physical and non-physical body. The psychosoma is described as being connected to the body through a subtle energy system, frequently called the etheric body or *energosoma*. This "bioenergy" could be related to the teleological connection postulated in "Sensors, Filters, and the Source of Reality." This seems to be the case with all psychical phenomena, according to the model termed "projectiology," proposed in the 1980s by Brazilian researcher Waldo Vieira, MD, and described in his tome *Projections of the Consciousness*, and later in *Projectiology*. In my own experience, I have found that I was able to achieve greater success in my OBE attempts once I was able to gain better control of the subtle energy that serves as the information channel between the body and the psychosoma, but can also

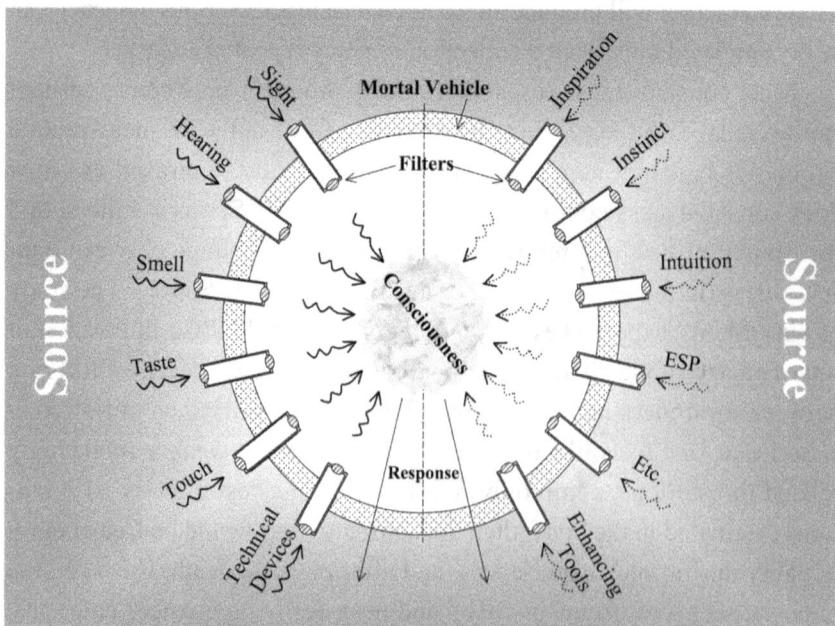

Figure 1a: Depiction of information exchange between awareness and its normal and subliminal source ("Sensors, Filters, and the Source of Reality," Jahn and Dunne 2004)

act as a sort of "glue" or inhibitor when it is stagnant or blocked. More controlled flows of bioenergy have also increased the occurrence of other psychical perceptions.

The existence of this energosoma is most apparent during an out-of-body experience, when the energy channel appears to consolidate into what is popularly called the "silver cord" that is presumed to link the physical and nonphysical heads. This connection that vitalizes the body until death can sometimes be visualized through clairvoyance in the waking state, but it is much more easily and naturally perceived when out-of-body. One of the my earliest experiences was that of a partial projection in 1999, when I sat up in bed in my energy body, reached back with my right astral-arm, and felt the silver cord with my astral-hand. It

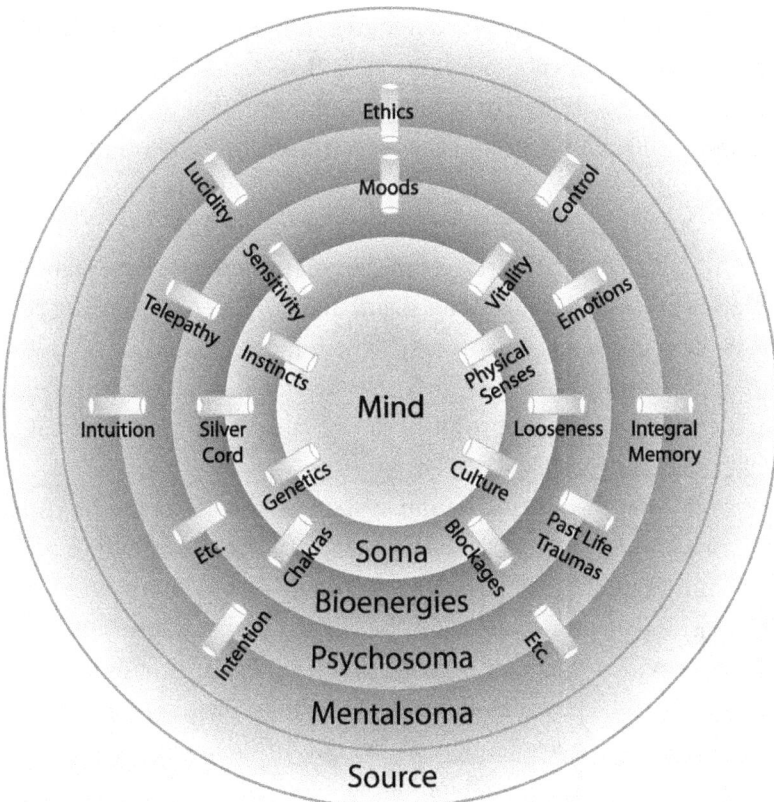

Figure 1b: Augmented model of levels of information exchange with additional vehicles and some of their sensors and filters (illustration by Manori Sumanasinghe).

felt very real, and I felt it form and propel my astral, or para-head out of my physical head.

Another way the energosoma is apparent in OBEs comes in the energetic pre-projective sensations, which can include the experience of vibration: a sense of resonance state between the energosoma, including the aura, and its sense organs (*chakras* or meridians) and pathways (*nadis*). Respected lucid projectors Robert Monroe and Waldo Vieira both indicated that this vibrational state could be induced intentionally. Vieira describes how the partial disconnection between the body and the psychosoma produced by the vibrational state facilitates non-sensory perceptions and the OBE, as if tuning and opening up the appropriate channels. Out-of-body telepathy can also be understood as the exchange of information *via* bioenergy encoded in thoughts, ideas, intentions, memories, sentiments, and emotions (or *thosenes* — theoretical units of manifestation of *th*ought-*sen*timent-*energy*). Sometimes this energy can be exchanged out-of-body for therapeutic purposes as well.

A more subtle "body" or vehicle of manifestation of the consciousness has also been proposed — the *mentalsoma*, or body of discernment — that becomes apparent in some rare out-of-body experiences through the consciousness, rather than through the more common physical sensations. This advanced OBE projects the consciousness into a world beyond space and time as we understand them, and is related to experiences of *samadhi* or "cosmic consciousness," where the mind and its Source are in direct communication. Such experiences have been hypothesized as being the locus of our integral memory of successive past physical and non-physical existences.

We can refer to this compound system of somas, as the *holosoma*. If the consciousness has more than one type of vehicle of manifestation, then the mind-body problem may be revised as the *consciousness-holosoma* (Sassoli de Bianchi 2005). In this view, the many forms and levels of energy provide a range of sensory channels that are conditioned by a variety of filters — physical and non-physical — that allow for communication between our cosmic Source and our different modes of manifestation and awareness. Understanding and controlling the holosoma can help us achieve greater communication with Source, both in and out of the body.

Projective Perceptual Filters

Even though we cannot prove that we dream, we do not have difficulty persuading others that we do. On the other hand, the out-of-body experience is much more difficult to talk about to parents, educators, health professionals, and friends. Surveys throughout the world indicate that less than 1% of humanity has experienced repeated lucid projections, while as many as 10% can recall at least one OBE in their lifetime. Unfortunately, the pressures of society, dissemination of misinformation, and the lack of a scientific explanation of such phenomena, encourage most people to avoid the subject and its potentially important implications by dismissing such experiences as simply very vivid dreams, or by filing it away in the unconscious realm of one's mind where it ceases to disrupt prevailing beliefs.

Many more people, however, relate sensations and perceptions associated with the out-of-body experience, usually without recognizing it as such, *e.g.* the sensation of flying, seeing one's "dead body on the bed" or shared "dreams" (Trivellato 2002). Experienced projectors claim that all of us float slightly above the physical body in our astral body as part of natural sleep. In other words, it would seem that 100% of humanity has out-of-body experiences without being aware of them.

Why, then, does the consciousness usually black out when the body goes to sleep, if it does not have to? From the time we are children, we are conditioned to have our minds go to sleep along with our body ("sweet dreams!"). "Time to put your body to sleep! Remember, today we are visiting granny. See you on the other side, kiddo!" How often do parents say something of this sort? It is also possible that we black out as a reflexive reaction to the fear, anxiety, and trauma of death, where the OBE would not conclude with a return to the physical body. Interestingly, most people who have near-death and out-of-body experiences report that they have lost their fear of death as a result.

While people can find more time for leisure activities, education, and self-study in today's modern world, several psychosocial factors can interfere with the experience of lucid OBEs. Many are not ready to consider the possibility that our consciousness can function beyond the physical body during and after biological life. Others have a set of priorities or beliefs that make them uncomfortable with concepts of multidimensionality, or with a world encompassing a continuum of increasingly subtle dimensions of reality that are more and more remote from space-time conventions. These cultural and psychological filters not only create a resistance to accepting the reality of OBEs and other anomalies, such as those studied at PEAR, but they can actually inhibit their manifestation.

On the other hand, most people could start having OBEs within just a few weeks with consistent and intelligent practice. There are many anecdotal accounts from people who have their first experience the night or morning after attending a lecture, reading a book, or having a long conversation about the OBE. Many times, simply becoming aware of the very notion of projectability can counteract the "consensus trance" (Tart 2001) that maintains us in a "paracomatose" state. Sleep represents almost one-third of our life span that many regard as serving no real purpose beyond physical rest. But what if we could eventually achieve the ability to maintain a condition of continuous consciousness: continually aware, alternating between in- and out-of-the-body life?

The objective at hand, however, is to learn how it is possible to unblock and properly tune the multidimensional sensors of our holosoma to have OBEs with better awareness, control, frequency, and recall. Ideally, one would be able simply to lie down, relax, and shift into an OBE without breaks in awareness, have sufficient energetic control to deal with a variety of extraphysical situations, go to a desired location and acquire a sufficiently clear perception of it, and then have enough recall to transfer the information to the brain upon returning, to create a physical record before the fragile recollections deteriorate. Our subtle channels would then be sufficiently unfiltered or unblocked that we could simultaneously perceive the physical, energetic, and extraphysical realities and how we interact with them. Unfortunately, this level of OBE is usually achievable only through long-term self-training.

There are many cases where a group of projectors have reported the ability to convene in a collective OBE with lucidity, only to recall the experience with different levels of success. Some will remember only fragments, or will pay more attention to certain aspects of the events, probably due to their personal filters. Others will remember the experience *en bloc*, while still others will have absolutely no recall. Imagine going to work and not remembering having been at the staff meeting the day before! Interestingly enough, it seems possible to recall a previous projection on a subsequent OBE. This is just one of several indications that we seem to have memory outside the brain, an integral memory that stores all our experience: physical, projected, and extraphysical (before and after biological death).

It is worth pointing out that in OBEs our focus of attention and level of lucidity can fluctuate much more and more quickly than while in the physical body. In the waking state the perceptual sensors and their filters seem more rigid and difficult to control. Hence, the projection of the consciousness inevitably trains us to harmonize our cognitive and emotional reactions. In contrast, in the out-of-body state we notice that thought involves immediate action, communication, and rapport. We also learn to be aware of the kind of *thosenes* that we produce, or the morphic field we create (as proposed by Rupert Sheldrake). With more open channels to telepathy, there is less possibility for unnoticed fake smiles and silent judgments in OBEs. Of course, if our attention is constantly shifting, or our mind is constantly wandering, we could find ourselves teleporting from place to place in the middle of interactions and getting sidetracked from the objectives of our extraphysical agenda.

With time and experience, the developing projector realizes that many OBEs are only partially conscious. Such diminished lucidity can interfere with realization that one is projecting, such as in the so-called lucid dream, which tends to be a semi-conscious OBE, characterized by a mixture of evanescent thought-forms, oneiric dream imagery from the brain, and real extraphysical sensations and perceptions. Lucidity seems to be channeled through a sensor originating beyond the physical environment, one closer to the Source. The consciousness, during a typical lucid dream, enjoys high enough awareness to enable the dreamer to realize that he or she is dreaming, but not enough to perceive reality as clearly as during a waking state. Once the person is able to increase his or her lucidity, it is not uncommon for the dream imagery to dissipate and reveal the actual situation, with the psychosoma already partially projected in the physical base, usually the bedroom. This is not so rare an occurrence; in various surveys some 20% of people have reported lucid dreams.

If physical perceptual sensors and filters are intricate and highly individual, imagine how complex extraphysical filters can get! By comparison, physical senses seem like gross attempts to replicate "paraperception," but the visual flavor of such non-physical perceptions can allow us to "see" in 360 degrees simultaneously; to observe the door of the closet on the 3rd floor of the building next door, the molecules of the wood, the color of the clothes inside the closet, the room behind that closet, the outline of an important document folded in the pocket of one of the shirts, and to view the owner's current whereabouts and then transport our awareness to that location.

Some factors that may contribute to poor recall of OBEs are weak lucidity, exceptionally long duration, disorienting abrupt return to the physical body, or extreme remoteness from familiar surroundings. We also may encounter "colors," "sounds," and many other sensations that simply do not map to the physical senses. It is an interesting feature of anomalous perception and communication that the information (ideas, intentions, emotions, memories, propensities, *etc.*) acquired in such experiences can sometimes be interpreted *via* a variety of senses, even simultaneously in a sort of non-pathological "parasynesthesia." For instance, I could arrange to meet someone at a public event for an extraphysical community of environmentalists. The "speaker" at this event could telepathically transmit an emotion that I perceive sympathetically but interpret visually, while the other participant might interpret the same stimulus in terms of colors, sounds, or body sensations.

PEAR's research, and that of others, has identified subjective correlates as being more significant than physical variables, such as distance and time. The latter do not seem to affect the tangible results, but qualities like intention, emotional resonance, or personal meaning have been shown to be important factors in achieving positive results. Similarly, lucid projectors, OBE practitioners, and other psychically sensitive people, have observed through direct experience that what we term bioenergy plays a central role in almost all psi phenomena, and that its reach is quite insensitive to spatial and temporal distance. Significant differences are seen, however, with rapport among the participants: a clearly subjective and intersubjective variable. It appears that the stronger the affinity between two consciousnesses, the easier it is for them to establish a transcendent bond that consequently enhances telepathy, synergy, and joint projections.

Even for persons of sophisticated perceptive capability, however, there can arise clouded or distorted imagery, due, for instance, to an excessive load of physical features or aroused emotions. These distortions of anomalous acuity have been found in remote perception research at both PEAR and at the International Academy of Consciousness (IAC). PEAR engaged pairs of participants, an "agent" at target location and a "percipient" applying what could be termed traveling clairvoyance. IAC employed either traveling clairvoyance or OBEs to target a computer image in a known location: an adjacent room for its Projective Field experiment (Alegretti 2002) or an office in Miami for its Image Target Project (Medeiros 2002). Results in both cases varied from photographic precision, to partial correspondence of environment and/or its components, to complete inaccuracy. Major geometrical distortions, deformations of the ambience, differences in emphasis of parts of the scene, and descriptions of targets from future trials were occasionally reported. For example, in one instance several percipients described the image of a thermometer as if it was turned upside down, as a "tall narrow jar."

Projective Filter Tuning

Projective filters are easily detected but poorly understood in virtually all forms of anomalous perception. In IAC classes students often perform exercises where they have the opportunity to practice a common clairvoyance modality. First, the students relax their physical bodies as best they can, by relaxing muscular and psychological/cerebral tension and are encouraged to remain immobile. Next, they are guided through a series of basic exercises to unblock, balance, and loosen the *energosoma*. The psychophysiological relaxation, physical immobility, and enhanced pliability of the energetic field naturally promote a partial disconnection between the soma and psychosoma to facilitate the OBE, which in turn enhances the influx of extraphysical energy and information — in this case of extraphysical "visual" information: seeing either the energetic dimension (observing different layers, the fluctuations, shapes, colors of the "aura," bioenergetic emissions, chakra activity), or the extraphysical dimension ("seeing" extraphysical presences, or observing technological devices, for example). It is interesting that a group utilizing clairvoyance to observe the same target person may tune into slightly different "channels" and layers of the multidimensional event and describe different aspects of the target individual. It is also common for people to interpret the same energy aura in terms of different colors. Other things that frequently have been noted in large group experiments include perceptions of apparent breaks in the auras, which could signify energetic couplings between the physical person and an extraphysical one, or impressions of the characteristics of extraphysical faces.

In the tuning of perceptual filters the theme of resonance comes up repeatedly. Though it is a common spontaneous pre-projective sensation and state, the initial vibrational state can be induced at will, producing a resonance within the entire energosoma that can be felt quite intensely and can facilitate anomalous perceptions or the flow of information between the extraphysical dimension and the physical brain. This vibrational state typically induces the aforementioned partial projection condition and serves as a projective technique as well. In this case, the resonance involved is among the different levels of components of a single individual's being, rather than between different individuals or between an individual and his or her physical environment.

As people fall asleep and start to project naturally, albeit only slightly, they can often begin to hear extraphysical conversations in the vicinity. Startled, they may awaken (reconnect) and the voices disappear. When they fall back asleep, however, the clairaudience resumes. This kind of partial disconnection marks the beginning stages of an OBE, which can also be described as a reduction of the physical body's restriction of the consciousness. Have you ever felt like you were falling while sleeping, and awakened with a jerk-awake sensation? This is another example of what might be described as an interrupted OBE, or a physical repercussion of the rapid reconnection of the consciousness and the astral body that had been floating a few inches above the physical body. The physical sensation of falling is transmitted through the energetic connection between the soma and psychosoma and the brain interprets the signal by creating a short dream of you falling down a cliff. As you regain consciousness, you wake up with a start from the falling sensation and jerking of the body caused by the abrupt reconnection. In view of such relatively common experiences, it is quite possible that the psychosoma may project whenever we are unconscious in order for our energy bodies to recycle their life-sustaining processes.

A related example of the multiple body (*holosoma*) model can be seen in the striking reduction of success during telepathy or remote viewing when the participant's mind is too active and is trying too hard to read the target. Such cognitive activities are thought to impede the flow of unconscious information, imagery, or intuition. Excessive activity of the biological brain appears to inhibit the opening of the paraperceptual channels, perhaps by maintaining the inflexibility of the ordinary consciousness filters. Often an individual can achieve deep physical relaxation, but remains too mentally active, perhaps due to anxiety, excitement, or other mental or emotional factors.

Finally, we observe that through the increased ability to direct one's bioenergy, and thus one's capacity for controlled projection, a natural increase in psychical sensitivity occurs. Some random event generator (REG) users have reported that they became more aware of their energy fields as a result of their interactions with the device. The multidimensional, multi-body model offers a holistic and elegant framework that can lead to more detailed self-understanding through direct experience. In limiting the scope of anomalies research to the traditional parapsychological categories of extrasensory perception or psychokinesis, many other phenomena are overlooked, along with the more ambiguous experiences where the distinctions between those conceptual categories become blurred. More importantly, such rigid categorization precludes exploration of the many overlaps and commonalities that relate many anomalous experiences. For example, as we noted at the beginning of this paper, the numerous similarities among such phenomena as OBE, lucid dreaming, near-death experiences, and remote perception, among others, suggest that these distinctions are themselves filters that emphasize the differences among these experiences at the cost of recognizing their common origins, and thus limit the possibilities for their better understanding.

By better understanding of the processes and mechanisms surrounding these transcendental non-local phenomena, we may be able to eliminate the fear, misinformation, romanticism, and mysticism that attend any events that are imbued with uncertainty. Such insights would have far-reaching implications for the study of consciousness well beyond the facilitation of OBEs. For example, might the acquisition of willful control of bioenergy, which seems to facilitate projections, enhance consciousness-machine interactions? Moving further afield, the out-of-body experience could illuminate the role that bioenergy plays in physical health and healing, in our interactions with other people and with the environment, in our level of self-awareness and self-defense, and in our overall capacities for communication, awareness, and perception. It could provide us with the realization that different levels of experience involve different kinds of filters, which in turn could clarify the role that filters play in our constructions of reality. If we could, with experience, learn to develop a multidimensional awareness, to become simultaneously aware of what is occurring on the physical and non-physical planes of experience, we could come to see space and time themselves as filters of consciousness. We could then be able to detach ourselves more easily from the filtered experiences of space-time and move closer to cosmic unity in what Jahn and Dunne describe as "unmediated dialogue with the Source."

References

Wagner Alegretti and Nanci Trivellato. "Quantitative and qualitative analysis of experimental research project into out-of-body experience." *Journal of Conscientiology*, 4, No. 15S (2002). pp. 153–188.

Robert G. Jahn and Brenda J. Dunne. "Sensors, filters, and the Source of reality." *Journal of Scientific Exploration*, 18, No. 4 (2004). pp. 547–570.

Rodrigo Medeiros and Patricia Sousa. "Image target research project: A methodology to support research on remote perception phenomena." Proceedings of the 3rd International Congress of Projectiology & Conscientiology; *Journal of Conscientiology*, 4, No. 15S (2002). pp. 111–130.

Massimiliano Sassoli de Bianchi. "Letter to the editor." *Journal of Conscientiology*, 8, No. 29 (2005). p. 53.

Charles Tart. "Waking up: Overcoming the obstacles to human development — Selections from the book." 1991. URL: http://www.paradigm-sys.com/ctt_articles2.cfm?id=18. Accessed September 1, 2009. p. 2.

Nanci Trivellato. "Benefits of conscious projection." Online article; International Academy of Consciousness. 2002. URL: http://www.iacworld.org/English/Resources/Articles/BenefitsOfTheConsciousProjection.aspx. Accessed September 1, 2008.

Waldo Vieira. *Projectiology: A Panorama of Experiences outside the Human Body*. International Academy of Consciousness, Miami, May 2002.

———. *Projections of the Consciousness*. Rio de Janeiro: International Institute of Projectiology and Conscientiology, May 1981 (Port.), 1997 (Engl.).

Mind and Biological Evolution

Antonio Giuditta
Department of Biological Sciences,
University of Naples Federico II, Italy

Preface

Some 25 years ago, long before I became aware of the existence of the PEAR group and of their pioneering data on the influence of human mind on the random output of different types of machines (Dunne and Jahn, 2005), I proposed an alternative to the neo-Darwinian view of biological evolution (Giuditta, 1982). According to this neo-Lamarckian model, philogenetic evolution implied the existence of a spiral flow of information between the environment, the phenome, and the genome of evolving organisms, rather than the hypothetical mechanism based on random genomic mutations and natural selection.

The postulated involvement of subconscious mental events in PEAR's anomalous effects reinforced my opinion that the impressive repertoire of biological diversities hardly could be attributed to random events, but might be due rather to the capacity of biological systems to filter and elaborate information derived from the environment. Indeed, the global nature of most philogenetic variations suggested that they could not be reduced to independent changes of single organismic features, but might be the result of overall computing operations such as those supporting mental activities and integrated functions and behaviors, notably those modulating ontogenetic development.

It is worth noting that even human creative capacities may be attributed to brain algorithms when viewed from the outside, although they definitely belong to the category of subjective events when experienced from the inside. In any case, as human mental capacities must be included in the category of biological features, their origin should be traced back along the uneven path of biological evolution. Hence, computing capacities of non-human organisms, irrespective of their degree of complexity, may be regarded as due to brain algorithms, but also as mental events, presumably subconscious.

Introduction

According to the prevailing neo-Darwinian hypothesis, the outstanding diversity of living and extinct organisms is due to the effects of random genomic mutations, eventually expressed in somatic traits and physiological and behavioral patterns. Due to their random nature, only a fraction of genomic mutations is capable of eliciting changes inducing a better fit of the organism to the environment, hence longer survivals and higher reproductive rates. Most mutations are indeed irrelevant or deleterious. In addition, evolutionary relevant effects are assumed to be caused only by mutations affecting germ cells (gametes), as they are responsible for the inheritance of individual traits. Conversely, random mutations concerning somatic cells cannot influence germ cells, as prescribed by the cellular dogma that genomic information is transferred from germ cells to somatic cells, but not the other way around. Such a hindrance is compounded by the central dogma of molecular biology (the molecular dogma) that states information may only flow from DNA, *via* RNA, to proteins (that is, from genome to phenome), but not *vice versa*.

In sharp disagreement with neo-Darwinism, the neo-Lamarkian hypothesis maintains that evolutionary changes first occur in the organism's phenome (that is, in the integrated complex of structures, functions, and behaviors), which is directly modified by environmental changes. Somatic variations are assumed to be eventually transferred to germ cells, presumably following their encoding in DNA base sequences (Giuditta, 1982). The latter process is fully denied by neo-Darwinism in view of the persistent belief in cellular and molecular dogmas. It should be recalled, however, that the inheritance of acquired organismic changes has been demonstrated in several experiments (Landman, 1991; Jirtle and Skinner, 2007; Tsankova *et al.*, 2007). These effects do not appear to be mediated by variations in DNA sequences, but by selective changes in the operations performed by the epigenetic system, the complex set of proteins and RNAs that modulates the expression of DNA segments in each cell (Wolffe and Matzke, 1999). These demonstrations weaken the conceptual basis of neo-Darwinism as they challenge the validity of cellular and molecular dogmas.

Irrespective of their substantial differences, both neo-Lamarckian and neo-Darwinian hypotheses attribute a key role to environmental conditions which are assumed to shape evolutionary changes, albeit

with substantially different mechanisms. According to the neo-Darwinian view, phenomic variations elicited by random genomic mutations are
bound to follow diverging evolutionary paths depending on their degree
of fitness to the environment: organisms with a lower degree of fitness
being differentially eliminated by natural selection, while those with better fitness are warranted a higher probability of survival and reproductive
capacity. A radically different opinion is held by the neo-Lamarckian hypothesis, which maintains that environmental changes directly generate
adaptive somatic variations. In so doing, they behave as multidimensional
templates of organismic changes.

It should be added that the emphasis on the influence of environmental changes stressed by either hypothesis runs the risk of overshadowing
the evolutionary role of additional factors, notably those which are intrinsic to the organism itself. Indeed, if it is true that the dynamic interplay
among different organismic components lets them generally oscillate
around a permissible balance, it is equally true that stronger oscillations
might possibly attain threshold values leading to a novel equilibrium.

Natural Computing and Biological Diversity

We have not yet mentioned a third view that explains the outstanding diversity of living forms by attributing it to the creative capacity of an omnipotent being. We refer to creationism and its disguised version of "intelligent design," which cannot be considered scientific hypotheses since
they both resort to a transcendent being. In addition, in view of their failure to adequately support the existence of biological evolution, creationism and intelligent design have been rejected strongly by the scientific
community, which criticizes their lack of a sound rational basis.

It appears nonetheless indubitable that structural features, functional
systems, and behavioral patterns of living beings (from prokaryotes to humans), exhibit an extraordinary degree of sophisticated intelligence and
beauty that cannot be marginalized. Even a superficial knowledge of biology is sufficient to support this statement. As even closely related species differ from each other by complex sets of differences, these qualities might have conditioned the belief in a transcendent entity imposing a
novel unitary coordination on several individual variations. The need for

such coordination cannot be marginalized even within the context of evolutionary perspectives. Differences among species are not limited to single traits, but they appear rather as integrated changes of structures, functions, and behaviors requiring the complex reprocessing of data pertaining to ontogenetic interactions (Giuditta, 2008). To envisage the existence of this class of natural events foreshadows a demanding research task, which is necessary, however, to attain a credible evolutionary theory.

The output of such complex set of processing operations hardly may be attributed to random genomic mutations followed by natural selection, notwithstanding the putative accumulation of beneficial mutations. Indeed, even the simultaneous occurrence of a few mutations is considered an unlikely event. A more encouraging perspective is offered by the neo-Lamarckian belief that environmental changes induce variations on the organism's structures, functions, and behaviors in direct fashion. As these integrated features are already in a dynamic equilibrium with the environment, they appear well suited to adapt just as comprehensively to impinging environmental changes, provided they remain below given thresholds of intensity and rate of manifestation. In such a view, the organism is assumed to use the environment (and its modifications) as a source of precious information contributing to its adaptive response, as a kind of multidimensional mold instructing the organism's attempts to adapt (Giuditta, 2008)

It is worth noting, however briefly, that a modified organism will interact with its environment in a different way, thereby inducing environmental changes that, in turn, will eventually modify the interaction of the environment with other species of that ecological niche, including those that were modified initially. From a wider perspective, environmental changes may be considered to modify to a different degree all organisms of an ecological community, leading to overall modifications in that community. In brief, interactions between organisms and environment, and among organisms, will promote the evolution of ecological communities by positive and negative feedbacks. As these processes are time-dependent, they may be described as spiralling flows of information leading up or down according to the overall increase or decrease of information content (Giuditta, 1982). It follows that limiting attention to the evolution of a single species is a gross oversimplification: what is evolving is the entire biocenosis.

Natural Computing in Learning and Memory

What proposals might be advanced with regard to the processing operations playing a role in biological evolution? As a mere beginning, one might consider the comparable operations that take place during the life cycle of an organism and are responsible for experimentally verifiable effects, such as those induced by learning. This process is widely present in mammals and man, but also in primitive organisms such as bacteria (Tagkopoulos *et al.*, 2008). Learning implies acquisition of new information from the environment which eventually leads to the solution of a problem. In the present context, the concept of problem is extended to include all challenges posed by sets of items implying the existence of a meaning that may be identified if fragments are placed into a coherent whole.

If we examine the intellectual capacities of humans, notably those underscored by the conscious mind, it readily will be admitted that operations of acquisition, processing, and generation of new data are continuously underway, either during the flow of familiar thoughts and behaviors or their novel genesis. Comparable operations are at work to support the strikingly wide and diversified range of subconscious activities. The latter operations are involved in the integration and coordinated output of vegetative functions and instinctive behaviors, but they also closely underpin conscious events. Control and modulation exerted by nervous and hormonal systems reach down to cellular and molecular levels. In brief, they include vital domains which are much more widely extended and essential (or comparably essential) than those of our conscious experience.

An eloquent demonstration of the efficiency of our subconscious mind in generating adaptive solutions is provided by a study in which waking and sleeping subjects were compared with respect to their capacity to identify an implicit rule leading to a faster solution of a mathematical task (Wagner *et al.*, 2004). In this experiment, a simple repetitive exercise was presented to two groups of subjects who were requested to perform a more extensive version of the same task after comparable periods of sleep or waking. When intergroup performances were compared, the number of subjects who identified the implicit rule turned out to be three times larger among those who were allowed to sleep than among those who were kept awake. This is consistent with the common experience that daytime worries are more likely to find solutions after a good night of sleep. In addition, it bears striking similarities to functional elements of unconscious filters addressed in this volume. In evolving organisms, environmental changes are likely to generate an incongruous match between impinging stimuli and response capacities of the organism. The problem might be solved by (unconscious) adaptive modifications of organismic responses leading to a novel balance.

Of special relevance for the evolutionary process is the suggestion that subconscious mental activities also are present in animal species less complex than man. When one of the most elementary features of mind, that of perceiving stimuli, is used as an index of the presence of mental activities throughout philogenetic evolution, no threshold of biological complexity is identified below which mental events may be excluded. Hence, subconscious mental processes have been considered widely distributed in the biological world (Giuditta, 2004). This conclusion is supported by the consideration that subconscious mental events, notably those related to problem solving, may be attributed to complex processing operations controlled by algorithms, that is on what is now referred to as natural computing. These operations are extensively distributed in the biological world, as recently detailed in a unicellular ciliate (Ehrenfeucht *et al.*, 2007).

In this respect, it may be of interest to recall the experience reported by the Nobel laureate George Wald (Wald, 1987) when he happened to watch a movie on the feeding behavior of ciliate protozoa, single-celled animals that go about, digest, reproduce, and do everything a multi-cellular animal does. "I remember particularly a protozoan going at a microscopic piece of meat. It fastened onto one of the muscle fibers and then backed up to pull it away, and it would not come. So it went in again, and backed up at another angle, and went in again and backed up at another angle, worrying off this fiber. And I was thinking, that is exactly what a dog would do, trying to deal with a chunk of meat. Was this single-cell aware of its activity and the purpose of that activity? For that matter, is a dog aware? Again, no scientific confirmation or disconfirmation of the question is possible."

In brief, irrespective of the objective or subjective criterion adopted, natural computing (or mental processing) appears widely distributed among biological entities in which integrated functions and behaviors play a key role. Since the activation of algorithms is modulated by environmental conditions (to mention a relatively simple example, consider the switching of functions and behaviors associated with circadian oscillations), it seems reasonable to expect that when they exceed familiar boundaries, organismic responses will be modified depending on the range of available resources and physical constraints. Under these conditions, the organism is confronted by a problem which is not formally different from those encountered and adequately solved in its previous evolutionary history. The organism's capacity to process data may thus be assumed to be instrumental in allowing it to attain a novel solution capable to reset its unbalanced interaction with the environment.

Natural Computing and Biological Variations

It should be noted that any novel balance attained by solving an evolutionary problem rests on a different way of modulating and integrating cellular and molecular components of the organism, notably those of the epigenetic system. It follows that, granting that computing operations enacted by the organism deal with signals and retrosignals, their ultimate effects are not likely to be limited to information transactions and meanings. Indeed, signals and retrosignals require physical supports in both natural and artificial computing, but in natural computing the diversity of systems and subsystems composing or surrounding the organism (from elementary particles to ecosystems) makes the identification of physical supports of natural computing rather uncertain. Even if consideration is limited to the molecular level, the great diversity of individual components crowding this domain makes their identification as physical supports of computing operations very unlikely in view of their great heterogeneity. Comparable difficulties are raised when natural computing is considered to be involved in levels of organization below and above the molecular level.

These thoughts may relate to not only the putative involvement of natural computing in the generation of evolutionary novelties. They also concern the acquisition of novel biological features by an organism, as it takes place during learning, exposure to a sensorially enriched or impoverished environment, and chronic changes in habits. Under these conditions, the physical effects of natural computing have been objectively verified, as animals undergo changes in brain synapses and neuronal circuits (Bruel-Jungerman *et al.*, 2007; Kim and Linden, 2007; Neves *et al.*, 2008). A wealth of observations certifies that acquisition of novel data does not merely concern the abstract realm of information transactions, but likewise affects the bodily structure of an organism. Hence, the proposal that natural computing may lead to structural modifications during philogenetic evolution is not lacking experimental support, since it relies on a wealth of data concerning comparable organismic processes.

Natural and Artificial Computing

These considerations call attention to what appears to be a substantial difference between natural and artificial computing. While the physical structure of man-made computers (hardware) is not substantially modified by computing operations generated by programs (software), computing operations taking place in biological systems do modify their physical support, as hardware and software coincide. Experience leaves a trace in biological systems: brain synapses may be potentiated, depressed, or eliminated, and neural circuits may be modified in shape and size as a result of experience. In addition, as computing operations may be expected to occur at each level of biological organization, biological systems also appear to differ from man-made computers in so far as their computing capacities extend across several organizational levels, while man-made computers rely on only a single level of physical support.

While it is not easy to assemble evidence of the role of natural computing in evolutionary events, its putative participation is in agreement with two well-accepted features of philogenesis: the general presence of intraspecific variants (strains or races), and the similarity of traits of closely related species. The relatively limited degree of these differences indicates that the original organismic asset has been modified only partially, as expected from integrated changes due to computing operations concerning the adult stage. Conversely, when evolutionary changes interfere with the basic plan of an organism, natural computing is likely to have operated at earlier stages of ontogenetic development.

The generally held belief that environmental changes lead to less substantial variations of the adult organism calls attention to a seldom-presented problem: do somatic variations occurring in an adult organism result only from the adaptive response of somatic cells, or do they derive from appropriate changes in their related stem cells. Even assuming that the former alternative is more likely, it cannot be forgotten that modifications of the adult organism have been inherited by the progeny (Landman, 1991; Jirtle and Skinner, 2007; Tsankova *et al.*, 2007). Hence, they have been able to influence previous developmental stages. In addition, the adult organism can hardly be considered an evolutionarily useless entity. It follows that adult experiences are likely to modify ontogenetic pathways leading to terminal differentiation. If this is the case, what mechanism may allow signals stemming from a "later" developmental stage to be back-shifted to a "previous" stage (that is, from differentiated cells to stem or germ cells)? Reliable observations of this putative backward transfer do not seem to be available.

Conclusion

The postulated participation of computing capacities in the process of biological evolution should not be considered as attributing these features to the will of an omnipotent god. Indeed, any such intervention is unlikely to have led to the relatively limited diversities between closely related species. The involvement of unlimited powers should have solved, once and for all, all problems plaguing organisms. To the contrary, philogenetic evolution demonstrates that butterfly species derive from butterfly species, and that present-day horses originate from horse progenitor species. In other words, biological evolution has progressed by small steps yielding living forms similar to the initial evolving species, as expected from its limited computing capacities.

If the astounding repertoire of nature's creative acts cannot be attributed either to supernatural interventions or to random genomic mutations, the remarkable computing capacities of organism's integrative functions become a plausible explanatory option. These capacities, notably those coordinating organismic responses to the environment, utilize complex algorithms that modulate biological performances at all levels of organization. The same algorithms (and their related mental events) reasonably may be assumed to be capable of identifying emerging incongruities between environmental stimuli and organismic responses, and of suitably modifying potential resources to match environmental modifications.

References

Elodie Bruel-Jungerman, Sabrina Davis, and Serge Laroche. "Brain plasticity mechanisms and memory: A party of four." *Neuroscientist, 13,* No. 5 (2007). pp. 492–505.

Brenda J. Dunne and Robert G. Jahn. "Consciousness, information, and living systems." *Cellular and Molecular Biology, 51,* No. 7 (2005). pp. 703–714.

Andrzej Ehrenfeucht, David M. Prescott, and Grzegorz Rozenberg. "A model for the origin of internal eliminated segments (IESs) and gene rearrangement in stichotrichous ciliates." *Journal of Theoretical Biology, 244,* No. 1 (2007). pp. 108–114.

Antonio Giuditta. "Proposal of a 'spiral' mechanism of evolution." *Rivista di Biologia, 75,* No. 1 (1982). pp. 13–31.

———. "Essay on the nature of mind." *Rivista di Biologia, 97,* No. 2 (2004). pp. 187–196.

———. "Natural computing and biological evolution: A new paradigm." *Rivista di Biologia, 101,* No. 1 (2008). pp. 119–128.

Robert G. Jahn and Brenda J. Dunne. "Sensors, filters, and the Source of reality." *Journal of Scientific Exploration, 18,* No. 4 (2004). pp. 547–570.

Sang Jeong Kim and David J. Linden. "Ubiquitous plasticity and memory storage." *Neuron, 56,* No. 4 (2007). pp. 582–92.

Randy L. Jirtle and Michael K. Skinner. "Environmental epigenomics and disease susceptibility." *Nature Reviews. Genetics, 8,* No. 4 (2007). pp. 253–262.

Otto E. Landman. "The inheritance of acquired characteristics." *Annual Review of Genetics, 25* (1991). pp. 1–20.

Guilherme Neves, Sam F. Cooke, and Tim V. P. Bliss. "Synaptic plasticity, memory and the hippocampus: A neural network approach to causality." *Nature Reviews. Neuroscience, 9,* No. 1 (2008). pp. 65–75.

Ilias Tagkopoulos, Yir-Chung Liu, and Saeed Tavazoie. "Predictive behavior within microbial genetic networks." *Science, 320,* No. 5881 (2008). pp. 1313–1317.

Nadia M. Tsankova, William Renthal, Arvind Kumar, and Eric J. Nestler. "Epigenetic regulation in psychiatric disorders." *Nature Reviews. Neuroscience, 8,* No. 5 (2007). pp. 355–367.

Ullrich Wagner, Steggen Gais, Hilde Haider, Rolf Verleger, and Jan Born. "Sleep inspires insight." *Nature, 427,* No. 6972 (2004). pp. 352–355.

George Wald. "Consciousness and cosmology: Their interrelations." *Bergson and Modern Thought: Towards a Unified Science.* Andrew C. Papanicolaou and Pete Addison Y. Gunter, eds. Chur: Harwood Academic Publishers, 1987. p. 349.

Alan P. Wolffe and Marjori A. Matzke. "Epigenetics: Regulation through repression." *Science, 286,* No. 5439 (1999). pp. 481–486.

Complexity, Interdependence, and Objectification

VASILEIOS BASIOS
University of Brussels
Brussels, Belgium

There are powers and thoughts within us, that we know not till they rise
Through the stream of conscious action from where the self in secret lies.
But where will and sense are silent, by the thoughts that come and go,
We may trace the rocks and eddies in the hidden depths below.
— JAMES CLERK MAXWELL[10]

1 Introduction

During the last twenty years or so, the investigation of fundamental aspects of complex systems in connection with the observer's participatory role in determining their understanding has brought forth a novel perspective in science. The characteristic quality of complex systems to unfold their dynamics in a wide range of space and time scales and thus admit various different, irreducible but compatible, levels of description prompts us to search for the appropriate level of description in which unification and universality can be expected. It becomes more and more evident that the different levels of description possible for a complex whole point to a common origin on a deeper level. As a matter of fact, one might argue that certain filters — conceptual, epistemological, or methodological — are inevitable if one engages in the description and/or explanation of complex entities which are given as a certain whole. The mere choice of the particular mode or framework of examination is what will permit the unfolding of any anticipated explanation or description for complex phenomena. The Protean nature of complexity though, forces us to let something escape. We are coming of age in acknowledging, more often implicitly than explicitly, this fact.

The main thesis of this presentation is that Complex Systems lend themselves to many distinct levels of description. Some are dynamical, structural, geometrical or topological, metric or probabilistic. Others represent a hybridization of the above. Moreover, especially for living complex systems, any observation necessarily will be partial and always dependent on the observer's choices, due to incompressible initial conditions and/or approximate parameter estimations. It becomes evident that no single set of known mathematical or other formalisms can yield a description of a complex whole that is both complete and consistent.

It means that a new double-edged approach is needed. On the one hand, we need a concerted approach which will synthesize and unify all relevant elements at different levels, by using different tools and descriptions. On the other hand, we need to discriminate between two things. The first is the several given aspects of the facts under scrutiny. The second is how these facts were acquired based on the specifics of sets of objects and relations which led to their conceptualization in the first place.

We are fast approaching the point where we need to concern ourselves not only with the study of nature, but with the nature of that study.

Being aware of the limitations of our descriptions we can describe the limitations of our awareness. That, as a consequence, will outline the search for a Science towards the limits, as William James called it. It will consist of a scientific endeavor capable of reflecting not only on its own abstractions (a discourse that *epistemology* already provides), but on its fundamental objectifications (a discourse that goes one step deeper into what can be described only as a 'pre-epistemology').

Let us take a rude example to fix the main idea: Imagine the bees. Each one of them is an individual with certain functions, genetic information, brains, and other organs, among which some facilitate their intercommunication. A colony of bees, though, is more than a bunch of them together. Each bee lives its own life but also lives the life of the colony. The emergent dynamics of the hive is totally compatible but never entirely reducible to the dynamics of each individual and *vice versa*. The story that the social-behavioral biologist narrates is based on facts filtered out of the total given facts for bees and hives to match his level of description. The geneticist will focus on how genetic material and gene expression is affecting the hive. A physicist will try to model the collective behavior based on the communication signals they exchange and how these trigger collective behavior. The ecologist will seek out environmental factors responsible for the well-being of bees and hive. The list of experts that could engage in the studies of bees would be endless. What we have come to realize recently, due to the leading complex systems approach, is that all these levels of description are interconnected, interdependent, and sometimes what one emphasizes the other ignores. Some other times when one becomes aware of this 'filtering of facts' at work, novel realizations emerge, new paths and bridges are forged, and a fresh common ground is discovered to lay beneath our previous conceptual foundations. That is another 'bonus' of complexity studies: the highlighting of the importance of being interdisciplinary.

2 What Is Complexity That We Should Be Mindful of It?

> *Mais quand une règle est fort composée,*
> *ce qui luy est conforme, passe pour irrégulier.*
> *(But when a rule is extremely complex,*
> *that which conforms to it passes for random.)*
> — LEIBNIZ, DISCOURS DE MÉTAPHYSIQUE, VI, 1686

Looking into Webster's dictionary the word 'complexity' is defined as 'the quality or state of being complex.' Furthermore under 'complex' we read:

Main Entry: (1) **complex**, Function: noun, Etymology: Late Latin complexus totality, from Latin, embrace, from complecti, Date: 1643, (1): a *whole* made up of complicated or interrelated parts.

Self-referential as this definition may seem, it places the emphasis on 'whole' and 'interrelated parts.' We have come to realize that something complicated is not necessarily complex, although a complex system can be complicated. The terms 'whole' and 'interrelated parts' emerge as fundamental notions on which the *nonlinear* relations among constituent parts rely and are identified. This has been the case mainly in the physical sciences. But it is not necessarily restricted to these alone. Indeed, the connection between complexity studies and nonlinear science allows us to bridge the divide between subjective and objective narration in fields as diverse as physics, chemistry, biology, cognitive and consciousness studies — not to neglect sociology and economics.

In complex system studies one is confronted with nonlinear relations which usually give rise to a great number of states. In most cases this signifies many levels of ongoing processes of a different temporal and spatial scale. Complexity manifests through the presence of multi-stationarity and/or chaotic regimes of motion with emerging dynamics in a wide spectrum of characteristic times and lengths.

All these states unavoidably lead to the breaking of symmetries both in the spatial (pattern formation) and the temporal (irreversibility: what does it mean?) domains. It is now well understood that the above emergent patterns and rhythms are due to 'nonlocal' effects in a dual sense. The first is that the correlation lengths of the emerging patterns and rhythms are many orders of magnitude larger than the correlation lengths of their constituent parts. The second sense expresses itself through the concomitant limited horizon of predictability arising from *sensitive dependence on initial conditions and parameters* — which is the indispensable defining aspect of chaotic motion.

Of course, complexity of form and structure is not a new or strange concept in the field of scientific investigations. Intricate patterns and forms — structures with great beauty and delicate design — have captured the attention and admiration of scientific thinkers since the dawn of time. A classic reference remains D'Arcy's *On Growth and Form*.[1] Recently, studies of structural complexity in relation to information processes, from physico-chemical and biological systems to man-made networks such as electricity's power-grid, the World Wide Web and the internet, various social groups, *etc.*, have made an impact on the scientific literature and created lively discussions (see, for example, [2, 3] for an introduction; specialized references can also be found therein).

Nevertheless, in addition to the structural aspects of complexity, its dynamical aspect has been the object of path-breaking research since the sixties. Owing to the early, seminal, contributions of Hermann Haken, Ilya Prigogine, Brian Goodwin, their co-workers, and many others, the role of nonlinear relations and fluctuations in self-organization, synergetics, pattern formation, irreversibility and, in general, to what now tends to be called 'emergence' has been amply elucidated. For an overview of their work, one might consult [4, 5, 6].

These pioneering contributions go well beyond qualitative descriptions, analogies, and metaphors. They address fundamental issues such as the interplay of structure, function, and fluctuations; they invoke a nonclassical — sometimes circular — causality (since the parts collectively determine the macroscopic order parameters and the macroscopic order parameters determine the behavior of the parts' collectivity) and they offer a new apprehension of the fact that determinism does not necessarily imply predictability (a corollary due to sensitive dependence on initial conditions *and* parameters).

Through the analytical tools of theoretical physics and mathematics, unexpected relations between topological and geometrical aspects (*structure*), dynamical laws (*functions*), and stochastic processes (*fluctuations*) were discovered in the heart of complex systems.

3 Fallen Doctrine of Classical Determinism: (Classical) Objects Misbehaving

A curious thing about Complexity — often hailed as 'the third revolution of physics' — is that it did not occur as a paradigm shift over unaccommodated data and unexplained facts. Definitely it is not the brainchild of a single investigator, like Relativity, and has not been followed by explosions threatening mankind, like Quantum Mechanics. Although its technological and conceptual advances are being harvested by the widest known array of disciplines in science, it constitutes a community of ideas and workers with a quite well-defined area of studies and a fertile laboratory of new concepts. Both of these are characterized by an explicit interdisciplinarity and an intrinsic multitude of approaches.

Probably it was the spectacular and rapid advance of Quantum Mechanics and Relativity that attracted attention away from the developments of nonlinear science in the turn of the previous century. Indeed, it is commonly believed that classical determinism had to be revised after the advent of the uncertainty principle[1] and the ever-present, fundamental-in-nature, 'quantum leaps.' But this statement, although commonly accepted, tells only the story from the viewpoint of Quantum Mechanics. As John C. Sommerer, one of the very early workers in chaos theory, put it:

> To cast the situation as a mystery, classical determinism was widely believed to have been murdered (maybe even tortured to death) by quantum mechanics. However, determinism was actually dead already, having been diagnosed with a terminal disease 10 years earlier by Poincaré. Having participated in a very late autopsy, I would like to describe some of the findings.[7]

What the renowned mathematician Henri Poincaré diagnosed was that classical systems with a given degree of complexity, due to the non-linear interactions present among their parts, give rise to very complicated motion. Today we have arrived at calling this kind of motion — which he first encountered — 'chaotic.' In the case of Poincaré, the system at hand was the celebrated 'three-body problem' within the setting of classical Newtonian gravity. Poincaré's investigations inspired another famous mathematician of those days, Jacques Salomon Hadamard to study a more general setting for this phenomenon.

Hadamard probably was the first to articulate what we now call 'sensitive dependence on initial conditions' or 'the butterfly effect' — that hallmark of chaos. Indeed, it was in the year 1898, almost twenty years before the dawn of quantum mechanics, that Jacques Hadamard published his work on the motion of particles in surfaces with negative curvature, demonstrating that this motion is everywhere unstable.[8]

---

1. Bohr founded Quantum Mechanics proposing the 'Complementarity Principle'. As Freeman Dyson puts it in his review of the book by Gino Segrè, *Faust in Copenhagen: A Struggle for the Soul of Physics* (New York: Viking, 2007) ("The New York Review of Books," Vol. 54, No 16, Oct. 25th, 2007): "... Two descriptions of nature are said to be complementary when they are both true but cannot both be seen in the same experiment. ...". For an in-depth discussion of this principle and its far reaching implications in science and culture one might consult the book by Robert Nadeau and Menas Kafatos *The Non-Local Universe: The New Physics and Matters of Mind* (Oxford: Oxford University Press, 1999).

In order to deal with the discoveries of Poincaré, Hadamard had to transcend the limitations of the mathematics of his era and invent a novel method. He utilized a simple description of all the possible sequences, induced by the motion on the geodesics of surfaces with negative curvature. His idea was to project this motion onto partitions upon the surfaces in the regions and examine all possible trajectories of the visiting particle. By constructing a finite set of forbidden pairs of 'symbols' associated with each region of the partitioned surface, he subsequently showed that the possible sequences are exactly the ones which do not contain the forbidden pairs. Actually, he was the first to introduce the new and powerful tool we now call 'symbolic dynamics' into the fundamental notions of discrete probability. That was to serve as a spring board for what later became information theory.

Although quite mathematical for the physicists of his time, this work proved to be rather fertile. It was later taken up by George David Birkhoff and John von Neumann in their work during the early 1910s, on the so called 'ergodic hypothesis.' The ergodic hypothesis is a key working hypothesis in statistics where it is — explicitly or implicitly — assumed that the average of a process parameter over time and the average over the statistical ensemble are the same. Which means that to observe a process for a sufficiently long time is equivalent to observing a sample of many independent realizations of the same process.

Further decisive progress came again through Henri Poincaré. He was concerned with the instability and integrability problems of dynamical systems and provided a celebrated result which further increased his fame even more by winning an important prize put forth by King Oscar II of Sweden and Norway. This contest consisted of several questions, one of them formulated by Karl Weierstrass concerning "our understanding of the solar system," in other words the 'three-body problem': the Sun, Moon and Earth, attract each other thanks to Newton's gravitation law. Could a solution be found in a closed form, or just a form, manifesting in a converging series? Poincaré won, although his celebrated result is a negative one, because he managed to show that this particular motion does not have any conserved quantity and thus is non-integrable.[2] In his own creative way he made explicit the limits of classical determinism. Nevertheless, highlighting these limits, Poincaré's work opened up an area of research that enabled us to deepen our understanding of the solar system — exactly as that competition demanded. It also enabled us to deal with a wide class of systems with unstable motions. Poincaré based his approach on geometry and provided us with a wealth of techniques and concepts which are widely used today in chaotic dynamics. He is thus considered as the founding father of the theory of Nonlinear Dynamical Systems.

The work of Birkoff, Poincaré, and others was almost equaled by Aleksandr Mikhailovich Lyapunov and his celebrated "Russian School" in dynamical systems. Later on, Aleksandr Aleksandrovich Andronov, in his work on nonlinear oscillators, formalized and deepened the understanding of the particular class of planar dynamical systems and prepared the ground for the interpretation of the experimental results of Lord Rayleigh III, laid out in his famous treatise "Theory of Sound", as well as those the Dutch physicist Balthasar van der Pol and the German engineer Georg Duffing on forced oscillators with friction. These latter works were later taken up by Lady Mary Lucy Cartwright and John Edensor Littlewood. While Andronov was leading his group in Russia, in the other parts of Europe this area of study was almost halted. The theory of Relativity and Quantum Mechanics were attracting almost all the attention.

Yet, although the 1910–1950 period was generally stagnant in the area of nonlinear dynamics, some work paved the way to a renaissance in the field during the mid sixties. In a series of papers starting from 1921, Marston Morse presented a scheme for the enumeration of orbits in the class of systems considered by Hadamard. This body of work motivated the studies of Emil Artin, Gustav Arnold Hedlund, and Heinz Hopf, which finally proved that motion of a ball on a surface of constant negative curvature was ergodic. One of the first physicists to realize the importance of these results was Nikolai Sergeevitch Krylov. He argued that a physical

---

2. Actually what Poincaré showed is that what is called the Bernoulli technique of finding a conserved quantity cannot yield any conserved quantity reducible to the momenta and positions of the bodies. Curiously enough, a Finnish mathematician named Sundman was later able to find a series of the type for which Weierstrass had asked. But Sundman's technique, though constructive, is useless for any calculation. So it remains undeservingly forgotten.

billiard ball is a system with negative curvature along the lines of collision. Later, Yakov Grigorevich Sinai showed that a physical billiard ball can be ergodic (the well studied 'Sinai billiards').

After more than a century of development, today we come to appreciate a 'billiard' — or a pinball, in modern terms — as a typical example of a chaotic system.[9] Figure 1 illustrates the complexity of such a seemingly simple system. In describing the sequence of the trajectory of a test-particle visiting each disk here, complexity enters through the nonlinear relationship (the curved surfaces of disks) that develops among its parts (the disks). It is this aspect that renders the dynamics of such a system chaotic. If the reflecting surfaces were flat (*i.e.* rectangular boxes instead of disks) the system would be complicated but not complex — the parts would uniquely define the whole as their linear superposition. Not so in complex systems. There the whole is more than its parts because of the intricate, non-linear, interrelations among parts and whole. Thus emerging properties are attributed to such systems.

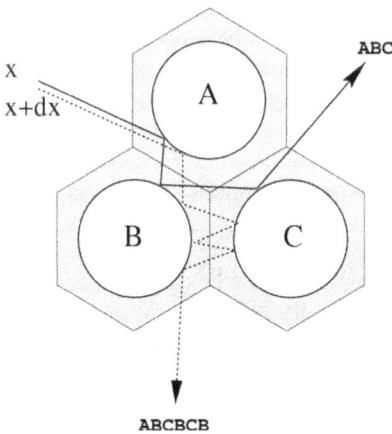

Figure 1. Motion of a test particle in 'pinball' serves as a simple, representative, and very descriptive model for chaotic/complex systems. Complexity gives rise to chaos on account of the strong nonlinear relations among its parts. Here two initial points differing only by the slightest follow very different courses of evolution. One hitting the disks ABC; the other bouncing around ABCBCB and going totally in the other way. This is the 'sensitive dependence on initial conditions' or 'butterfly effect'.[7, 9, 11]

4 Coming of the Age of Complexity

The connection between deterministic causality and the stability so typical of classical systems did not escape, even in earlier days, the penetrating genius of James Clark Maxwell. Reflecting on the roots of causality, he wrote:

> It is a metaphysical doctrine that from the same antecedents follow the same consequents. No one can gainsay this. . . . It is not of

much use in a world like this, in which the same antecedents never again concur, and nothing ever happens twice . . . The physical axiom which has a somewhat similar aspect [with this doctrine] is "that from like antecedents follow like consequents".[10]

Chaos and complexity studies have shown that the classical belief in determinism as a reliable source of prediction represents no more than a fantasy. This fantasy stems from the Newtonian/Laplacian paradigm. As a matter of fact, it embodies something more than even a fantasy. It embodies a persistent fallacy in scientific and philosophical thought, which has lasted for over three hundred years. Pierre Simon Laplace's all-knowing daemon, the god of naïve reductionism, is symbolized in one of his most famous proclamations which appeared in his classic treatise *Essai philosophique sur les probabilités* (published in Paris in 1825):

... *if* we can imagine a consciousness great enough to know the exact locations and velocities of all the objects in the universe at the present instant, as well as all forces, then there could be no secrets for this consciousness. It could calculate anything about past or future from the laws of cause and effect.

A relevant discussion about the Newtonian/Laplacian doctrine and modern developments of chaos theory can be found in [11] (pp. 9–14). This Laplace's daemon prevailed as a paradigmatic bias which was overthrown only by Werner Heisenberg's uncertainty principle. What is of interest here regarding this principle is that on a different level, it speaks of complex systems as well. So let us follow Heisenberg's line of thinking. He states that:

In the strict formulation of causality — "When we know the present precisely, we can calculate the future" — it is not the final clause, but rather the premise, that is false. We cannot know the present in all its deterministic details. Therefore, all perception is a selection from an abundance of possibilities and a limitation of future possibilities.[11]

This is true for quantum mechanics on account of its ontologically probabilistic nature. But is it not also true of complex dynamics? Even if we think of them as ontologically deterministic, could we ever hope to know in perfect detail their precise initial conditions? If we ascribe to the fact that initial conditions are represented by the continuum of real numbers, can we pin down with infinite precision real numbers? How can one pinpoint an infinitely small point without using an infinite amount of information?

For the mind of the Laplacian god of naïve reductionistic mechanics, that would be definitely true. However, in any act of projection, such as measuring or specifying the initial conditions that we poor humans need to work with, we necessarily lose all absolute certainty, ending up with probabilities. We must stress, once again, that the above is unavoidable even if the laws are deterministic and our theories stipulating these laws turn out impeccably.

Definitely the vivid discussions over causality, determinism, and quantum mechanics — and relativity, to some extent — dealt with what chaos and complexity studies were whispering until the sixties and seventies. With the appearance of fractals, self-organization, emergent pattern-forming systems, and the realization that seemingly simple, deterministic yet non-linear, dynamical systems (which are, by the way, fully transparent to rigorous mathematical investigations) give rise to chaos, we now have entered a new frontier in science.

Actually, it is not uncommon for scientific ideas to follow meandering pathways in the course of time, sometimes re-surfacing and sometimes immersing back into the collective consciousness and behavior, for a multitude of reasons. Social, societal, competition for available resources among scientific communities, the appearance of influential scientific leaders, pressing technological demands, and the like all contribute to determining what emphasis will be assigned to a given scientific quest at a given time. This is not an issue touching on the post-modern simplistic discussions about truth being a construction and the small-minded denial of the existence or not of objective truth. It is more an issue of "the truth about what in the service of what?" as the philosopher Isabelle Stengers so radically puts it. [Quoted from the review of her book *The Invention of Modern Science* (Minneapolis, MN: University of Minnesota Press,

2000), "Theory out of Bounds Series," Vol. 19, which appeared in *TechDirections*, cited on <http://www.upress.umn.edu/Books/S/stengers_science.html>]. The history of science provides a plethora of such instances.[3]

Moreover these are not the only filters that are in play in the quest of truth, scientific or otherwise. Naturally personal bias, preconceived mental frameworks, emotional preferences, and metaphysical conditioning, all paint decisively our picture of reality. Scientific endeavor is no foreigner to this fact; Francis Bacon called attention to what he called the various 'idola' ('idola' or 'idols', are illusions grouped in four categories: common to the tribe, particular to individual, due to language constraints or misuse, and due to abuse of authority). In this encounter with our 'idols' it is science that, according to Bacon's conception, will liberate us from their grip. Four hundred years after Bacon we come today to realize that this is due to a fundamental faculty of our consciousness. We filter out our findings; we group and process them in order to carve out a place for us to be. As it is far more easy to see the biases of others, than our own (we see the speck in the eye of our brother but fail to see the plank in our own, as the parable puts it) it is far more difficult to practice a science that reflects upon its own foundations. Today Emilios Bouratinos' treatment of "self-locking versus self-releasing objectification" ([12, 13], also his entry in this book) serves exactly this purpose. By proposing a method of developing science rather than yet another actual science, it awakens us to our own biases. This cannot but broaden and deepen our understanding of our place within the greater reality that hosts us.

The lessons we are learning from this new era of emerging complexity studies are numerous and still continuing. One that we shall focus on is that we must be fully aware of what kind of objects we are dealing with. We looked through the microscope of quantum mechanics and we discovered an ever-changing reality of dancing entities; we looked through the telescope of relativity and we saw a plenum universe of energy fields. Now that we are looking at the complex cosmos around us, we might need nei-

---

3. Here is a curious anecdotal instance from antiquity: *Hero of Alexandria* and *Ctesibius* actually invented the prototype of the steam engine, but their contemporary administrators worried about the impact on labor. If engines were used to irrigate fields and for production, what would the slaves do? We do not need another Spartacus, was the counter argument of the politician to the scientist of the era. *The Forgotten Revolution: How Science Was Born in 300 BC and Why It Had to Be Reborn*, by Lucio Russo, trans. Silvio Levy (Berlin: Springer, 2004).

ther microscope nor telescope. Nevertheless, we need to be aware of the color of the glasses on our eyes, especially if these glasses filter out and obscure the fact that this complex cosmos around us is ablaze with life.

5 The Complex and the Living

Τό πᾶν ἀλλ' ἐστι τι τό ὅλον παρά τά μόρια
(The Whole is different from its parts.)
ARISTOTLE, METAPHYSICS 1045A

Along with the Newtonian/Laplacian determinism, another bias which has prevailed was the dogma that animals, and for that matter that all living beings, are machines. The echo of the notorious Cartesian treatment of the animals as automata still remains with us, alienating the human race from the surrounding life. Indeed a mere mechanical conception of nature leaves no place for life. And the inadequacy to deal with the fundamental question "what is life?" has been haunting physical sciences ever since.

It is well known that many early workers exploring the foundations of quantum mechanics, like Wolfgang Pauli and Ervin Schrödinger, were preoccupied with the question "what is life?" Niels Bohr was the first to point out that a generalized complementarity principle, which he proposed in the framework of quantum mechanics, could be at work in the case of living systems. Indeed living systems are the most profound of complex dynamical entities. Ever changing in time, yet keeping a distinct sense of wholeness and identity, dynamically adjusting themselves, equipped with vast yet undermined information processes, they stand out on the highest levels of the hierarchies for both structural and dynamic complexity. Non-living complex systems could provide a stepping stone towards a renewed, richer, and deeper understanding of the phenomenon of life. The one condition for this to happen is for us to avoid at all costs the strait-jackets imposed by pre-ordained paradigmatic thinking.

Revisiting Aristotle, though daring, may prove helpful in this respect. Aristotle maintained that plants are animals compared with rocks, but are rocks compared with animals. Something similar applies to complex systems and their emerging properties. As Leibniz essentially suggested, the complexity[4] of a living being is infinite, while that of any man-made machine cannot be but finite. The parts of an organism are made of other parts and these of other parts *ad infinitum*, whereas the parts of a part of a machine reach a point where there are no more parts in them. Machines are just made up by concrete objects, organisms are not, Leibniz reasoned. Indeed complex systems can be seen as more 'alive' compared to machines, but still complex systems viewed partially and in a reductionistic fashion remain sophisticated machines compared to living systems. Actually, nowadays we come to understand that the complexity of living process goes as far down as the macromolecular level and that quantum processes play essential roles in life's molecules interactions. We know today that the basic biochemical processes of life, such as ligand binding, enzyme recognition, photosynthesis, and metabolism, are partially but essentially determined by quantum mechanical processes. Thus, we understand that the complexity of the living organisms has to be, for sure, infinite. Moving from the naïve mechanistic logic of hard objects towards the sophisticated logic of living organisms, one should not be surprised if one finds oneself going through a further logic — that of complementarity, self-reference, and paradox. The case of quantum mechanics suggests as much.

The idea that complementarity can be useful not only in physics but in other areas as well — particularly in biology (see [14], p. 87) — was familiar not only to Bohr, but to other early thinkers in the field as well. As Walter Elsasser remarked as early as 1968:

> L. Brillouin has gathered a great many illustrative examples to show how in problems of classical physics any initial uncertainty increases with time. His work is clearly related to the fact that since the advent of quantum mechanics there have been the two schools of thought: those who tried to return to classical determinism and those who found in quantum theory a challenge for investigating all possible ramifications or generalizations of indeterminacy which may be part of physical description and prediction.[15]

---

4. Actually the term in his "Monadology", §64, of the year 1714, where this thought appears for the first time was closer to the word 'intricacy'. The word 'complexity' was not widely used during this time.

Brillouin's work belongs to the second category; so does Elsasser's, who had already investigated the implications of the generalized complementarity principle in the fields of statistical mechanics and biology.[15, 16]

Since the discovery of the double helix of DNA and the genes carried within, biology's main dogma, the so-called 'Central Dogma,' was that everything emanates from the genetic code. The fact that there are other mechanisms at work which control gene expression and influence even the genetic material by catalytic actions, the so-called 'epigenetic networks' of biochemical reactions, has only recently resurfaced. Their complexity and fundamental role in biology led modern biology to revise the domain of validity of its central dogma. And, when it comes to modern thinking in biology, no-one has expressed the urgent need for a radical change more eloquently (and convincingly) than Richard Strohman.[17] Beginning in the mid-90s he had anticipated the "surprising results" of the genome project, which became public knowledge around 2001. Building on the ideas of Goodwin[6] and others on the role of self-organization, nonlinearity, and dynamic complexity in systems biology, Strohman developed a sound argument about the profound implications of complex systems studies for epigenetic networks. His main point was to challenge the underlying naïve reductionist view of modern biology that "everything is in the genes." Indeed, he explained why no further understanding of molecular biological systems could rely "on genes alone."

Strohman realized that the nonlinear interrelations involved in gene expression necessitate a change in perspective that will influence the entire area of investigations. This radical change will help scientists move from an object-mediated view of biological systems to a system-wide understanding of dynamical processes. After the "surprises" generated by the conclusion of the genome project (when 'mainstream' biology was stunned to learn that humans have far fewer genes than expected in comparison to other simpler life forms), we now realize that a gene represents a functional unit acting in relation to a whole, and not an agent operating on its own in the DNA.

As Strohman put it when he introduced a collection of state-of-the-art publications dedicated to the topic:

Human disease phenotypes are controlled not only by genes, but by lawful self-organizing networks that display system-wide dynamics. These networks range from metabolic pathways to signalling pathways that regulate hormone action. When perturbed, networks alter their output of matter and energy which, depending on the environmental context, can produce either a pathological or a normal phenotype. Study of the dynamics of these networks by approaches such as metabolic control analysis may provide new insights into the pathogenesis and treatment of complex diseases.[18]

In the above quotation we would like to underline particularly the concepts of self-organization, system-wide dynamics and network structure. These concepts rely heavily on the presence of non-linear interrelations within a complex whole. They reveal the fundamental relevance of the recent advances in complexity and statistical mechanics, which result from the seminal work of Albert-László Barabási and co-workers.[19] Although a deeper dynamical system's perspective is absent from these investigations of 'life's complexity pyramid,' as they call it, the authors themselves (as well as many others) maintain that such a step has to be taken — eventually.

How this will be accomplished and where it will take our understanding of complexity, entropy, information, and life remains, of course, to be seen. Nevertheless, it is certain that we can expect not just interesting theoretical breakthroughs in biology. We can also expect some fundamental questions to be raised about the logic and mode of thinking that permeates such investigations — like those raised by Walter Elsasser.

To return to Niels Bohr and his epistemological reflections:

no experience is definable without a logical frame. Any apparent disharmony [among observed phenomena or levels of phenomena] can be removed only by appropriately widening the conceptual framework.

It means that we must take on board the notion of Emilios Bouratinos that there is a need to investigate the pre-epistemological level of conceptualization. As he writes,

... modern science is constantly broadening, deepening and differentiating the world image. But if the world image is being constantly enriched, so must our ways of knowing it ... [12, 13]

See also his entry in this book.

6 Pre-Epistemology: The Complex and the Subjective

The sciences of complexity and the entire field of complex systems studies reject the notion of a monolithic paradigmatic description. They call instead for a creative interplay beyond and above paradigms. The challenge is to find appropriate levels of description to express any underlying hidden universalities.

This redefinition of the objectification scheme required for understanding any complex system is not a question of just choosing the best model available. The situation calls for something radically different. We must find a way for articulating the fact that both the deterministic description and the probabilistic description of a given reality reveal aspects of its truth. Moreover, such nonlinear thinking makes us aware of the extent to which these partial objectifications can be considered as reflecting the system's realities.

Whatever the benefits of a paradigmatic conceptualization, it also brings limitations. Complexity forces us to reflect on our objectification scheme. Regardless of the kind of thinking this scheme arises out of (reductionistic, holistic, mechanistic, probabilistic, dualistic, or metaphysical), any description filters and thus reflects only partial aspects of the unified picture of a complex system — and it does so only on one level of the abstracting structure required for portraying it.

One of the great twentieth century's mathematicians working on probability, Bernard Osgood Koopman, maintained that "knowledge is possible, while certainty is not"! As he wrote in 1940, "both in its meaning and in the laws it obeys, probability derives directly from ... intuition and is prior to objective experience".[20] As a result of Koopman's work, intuition and subjectivity can now be rehabilitated theoretically. But there is a condition: they must be practiced openly, knowingly, and honestly (see also [12, 13]).

Furthermore we shall be able to cope with the lighting of intuition, not to shun away from it but bravely to embrace it. Since intuition strikes at rare moments when our conceptual veils and mental filters suddenly cease to obscure the deepest nature of reality, its communication to others through language or paradigmatic thinking makes it seem a very subjective experience. Only a disciplined inquiry conscious of the rationalization process itself can produce convincing verification. Intuition, insight, instinct all might refer to the same faculty of our consciousness of occasionally lifting barriers obscuring comprehension. The ability to pass — on the basis of clues, pointers, and bits and parts of given facts — from the unknown to the known, in Sufi parlance is 'firâsa.' Interestingly enough, 'firâsa' also means the instrument of conjectural knowledge. A conjectural knowledge, nevertheless, fully aware of its own conjectures.

Daniel Robinson, a distinguished professor of philosophy, is hosting and moderates a heated, ongoing, dialogue among neuroscientists about brain/mind studies, and he has chosen these words to stress the need of self-reflection in scientific practice when dealing with the complex realities of neuroscience:

> The cosmos is ablaze with facts, the great plurality of them beyond our senses and even our ken. Out of that fierce and brilliant fire, we pull a few bits — the visible or nearly visible ones — and begin to weave a story. On rare occasions, the story is so systematic, so true to the bits in hand, that other stories flow from the first, and then others, and soon we are possessed of utterly prophetic powers as to which ones will come out next. It is the philosopher, however, who must put the brakes on the enthusiasms of the story tellers, for left to their own devices, they might conjure a future that vindicates only our current confusions.[21]

It follows that the crucial question confronting us is: To what extent can we experience reality without being blinded by our preconceived ideas about it? How can we be free from our own projections if we deny their very existence?

Outlook

The sciences dealing with complexity find themselves at a crossroads. According to some skeptics, the very notion of complexity is ambiguous. Furthermore, the skeptics believe that it has given rise to a very ambitious project. They insist that its basic concept is far too all-embracing, holistic, and blurred to ever become the subject of a proper scientific investigation. It is needless to add that similar skeptical reservations had been raised in the past against the study of Time and Space, Entropy and Information, Cognition and Consciousness. Skeptics in science frequently want to fit reality into their static vision of science. But the real challenge for investigators would be to fit their vision of science into the dynamics of reality. We shouldn't allow our concepts to fashion the picture of the world. Rather we should allow the essence of the world to fashion the nature of our concepts.

Scientific thinking today has reached a stage which doesn't compare with that of any other in its history. The feeling is that Complexity and Emergence, Time and Space, Entropy and Information, Cognition and Consciousness are now at the forefront of fundamental research in the physical sciences. Despite that, these realities cannot be defined in exclusively objective and quantitative terms. The reason is simple: they also constitute the ultimate prerequisites for the observations carried out in their name. You need to have emerged into complexity to become aware of its operation; you need to be in time and space to observe their function, or even their occasional absence; you need to be experiencing entropy to sense it; you need to be properly informed to be in a position to assess information; you need to be cognizant to cognize; and finally you need to be conscious to know the significance — and operations — of consciousness.

In our times the very foundations of what we perceive as a properly established epistemological ethos have been cast in doubt. This calls for a radically new kind of science — one that can reflect on its own foundations. It also calls for a new kind of scientists. They need to be aware not only of their limitations, but of their objectifications. In addition, they need to be familiar with the relative merits of different, complementary, or even seemingly contradictory approaches to their subject-matter.

206 Complexity, Interdependence, and Objectification

Never before has the need for qualitative change in science been so apparent and pressing. The importance of complexity studies lies in that it has made such a radical change not just possible, but imperative. It can only directly inform and inspire the struggle for introducing self-reflection into the practice — and the understanding — of science.

Acknowledgments

I would like to express my gratitude Robert G. Jahn, Brenda Dunne, and Emilios Bouratinos, for inspiring discussions, sharing ideas and very fruitful comments. This chapter is widely based on the author's previous work.[22]

References

1. D'Arcy Wentworth Thompson. *On Growth and Form*. Cambridge: Cambridge University Press, 1942.
2. Albert-László Barabási. *Linked: The New Science of Networks*. Cambridge, Mass: Perseus Books Group, 2002.
3. Steven Henry Strogatz. *Sync: The Emerging Science of Spontaneous Order*. New York: Hyperion, 2003.
4. Hermann Haken. *Synergetics: Introduction and Advanced Topics*. Berlin: Springer-Verlag (reprinted edition), 2004.
5. Grégoire Nicolis and Ilya Prigogine. *Exploring Complexity: An Introduction*. New York: W. H. Freeman, 1989; see also Grégoire Nicolis and Ilya Prigogine. *Self-Organization in Nonequilibrium Systems: From Dissipative Structures to Order through Fluctuations*. New York: John Wiley & Sons, 1977.
6. Brian C. Goodwin. *How the Leopard Changed Its Spots: The Evolution of Complexity*. Princeton, NJ: Princeton University Press, 2001.
7. John C. Sommerer. "The end of classical determinism." *Johns Hopkins APL Technical Digest, 16*, No. 4 (1995). pp. 333–347.
8. Jacques Salomon Hadamard. "Les surfaces à courbures opposées et leurs lignes géodésiques." *Journal de Mathematiques Pures et Appliquée, 4*, No. 1 (1898). pp. 27–73.
9. Predrag Cvitanović, Roberto Artuso, Ronnie Mainieri, Gregor Tanner, and Gábor Vattay. *Chaos: Classical and Quantum*. Copenhagen: Niels Bohr Institute, 2005. Available on http://www.ChaosBook.org. (Open Access).
10. Basil Mahon. *The Man Who Changed Everything: The Life of James Clerk Maxwell*. New York: John Wiley & Sons, 2003.

11. Heinz-Otto Peitgen, Hartmut Jürgens, and Dietmar Saupe. *Chaos and Fractals: New Frontiers of Science.* New York-Berlin: Springer-Verlag, 1992.
12. Emilios Bouratinos. "A new conceptual framework for physics." In Rosolino Buccheri, Avshalom Elitzur, and Metod Saniga, eds., *Endophysics, Time, Quantum and the Subjective: Proceedings of the ZiF Interdisciplinary Research Workshop, Bielefeld, Germany, 17–22 January 2005.* Singapore: World Scientific Publishing, 2005.
13. Vasileios Basios and Emilios Bouratinos. *Gödel's Imperative for a Selfreflective Science.* Collegium Logicum, 9. Vienna: Kurt Gödel Society, 2006.
14. Max Jammer. *The Philosophy of Quantum Mechanics: The Interpretations of Quantum Mechanics in Historical Perspective.* New York: John Wiley & Sons, 1974.
15. Walter M. Elsasser. *Theory of quantum-mechanical description.* Proceedings of the National Academy of Sciences (USA), *59*, No. 1 (1968). pp. 738–744.
16. ———. "On quantum measurements and the role of the uncertainty relations in statistical mechanics." *Physical Review, 52*, No. 1 (1937). pp. 987–999.
17. Richard C. Strohman. "The coming Kuhnian revolution in biology." *Nature Biotechnology, 15*, No. 3 (1997). pp. 194–200.
18. ———. "Maneuvering in the complex path from genotype to phenotype." *Science, 296*, No. 5568 (2002). pp. 701–703.
19. Zoltan Nagy Oltvai and Albert-László Barabási. "Life's complexity pyramid." *Science, 298*, No. 5594 (2002). pp. 763–764; and also, among many, Reka Albert and Albert-László Barabási. "Statistical mechanics of complex networks." *Reviews of Modern Physics, 74*, No. 1 (2002). pp. 47–97.
20. Bernard Osgood Koopman. "The axioms and algebra of intuitive probability." *Annals of Mathematics, 41*, No. 2 (1940). pp. 269–292.
21. Daniel Robinson. *Neuroscience and Philosophy: Brain, Mind, and Language.* New York: Columbia University Press, 2007. Conclusion.
22. Vasileios Basios. "Encountering complexity: In need of a self-reflecting epistemology." In Rosolino Buccheri, Avshalom Elitzur, and Metod Saniga, eds., *Endophysics, Time, Quantum and the Subjective: Proceedings of the ZiF Interdisciplinary Research Workshop, Bielefeld, Germany, 17–22 January 2005.* Singapore: World Scientific Publishing, 2005.

The Human Shape of Cosmological Structure: Topological Association of Quantum Mechanics and Consciousness

ZACHARY JONES
Tempe, Arizona

ƐIAƐ

The most profound distances are never geographical.
— JOHN FOWLES

Introduction

There continues a time-worn debate on whether patterns within the flows of the universe have an objective existence. Do these patterns appear because of our human eyes? Do dogs or fish see a different cosmos? Or, does the natural order demonstrate the same patterns to all beings?

Regardless of the outcome of that debate, certain human-recognizable forms are closely knit with awareness and information. So closely knit that attention to them offers the most effective means of rendering aspects of the 'natural order' into wisdom, especially that aspect of wisdom that is capable of being sustained across the evolution of culture.

Scale is paramount to this process, as we come to realize that there exist larger and smaller things than the naked senses of our body can observe. Tools and models facilitate awareness beyond the dimensions of our body, and in so doing influence the language of observation and cognition that we use to organize our experiences. Consequently, models become the governors of our reality.

All models systematize and mediate awareness, organizing the sensory information that is increasingly distant, both physically and perceptually, from the body. As developed in this paper, things of small and large scale have a *symmetry* that allows them to be considered together as a set, comprising an 'envelope' of scale, rather than necessarily being regarded as independent concepts.

This evokes the alchemical realization of "as above so below," which over numerous translations has been generally stated[1] as:

> What is below is like that which is above, and what is above is like that which is below, to accomplish the miracles of one thing.

Whether a most-passionate reader shall prefer Davis' translation of Kriegsmann's infamous text,[2] the root of this alchemical principle drove the formulation of the high arts, and the resultant science that we have today. When the archetypal opposites are brought into conjunction, the result bears the identity of a divine channel for creating a new whole. Such wholeness presents itself as the foundation upon which greater works may come.

The wholeness of each envelope, comprised of symmetrical great and small, happens at many intervals of scale. These discrete points within the continuum of scale create context for the models respective to each. As cognition allows the context to form a network of perceptual and cognitive linkages that integrate our knowledge from various perspectives to create a more comprehensive understanding.

Taking each model as an element of language[3] we may infer that there exists a 'grammar' to consciousness. Such a deeply rooted structure would predicate how we see and communicate about the world. By developing a clearer understanding of this structure we are better able to utilize it, rather than blindly bumping into its walls.

Integral to realizing this structure is the idea of a 'Macroscope,' a conceptual device that allows one to look outward to see greater range detail in context, rather than inward toward the separation of one thing from another. In juxtaposition, looking past context to view the nuances

---

1. "Hermes Trismegistus. Emerald Tablet." In Julius Ruska, *Tabula Smaragdina: ein Beitrag zur Geschichte der hermetischen Literatur.* Heidelberg: Carl Winter's Universitätsbuchhandlung, 1926. p. 2.
2. "These things below with those above, and those with these join forces again so that they produce a single thing the most wonderful of all. And as the whole universe was brought forth from one by the word of one god, so also all things are regenerated perpetually from this one according to the disposition of nature." Tenney L. Davis. "The Emerald Tablet of Hermes Trismegistus: Three Latin versions which were current among later Alchemists." *Journal of Chemical Education, 3,* No. 8 (1926). pp. 863–75.
3. semiotic, or more specifically semasiological

of detail is the function of a microscope or telescope. The two, in fact, bear an intimate relationship. Microscopes and telescopes operate on a reductionistic model of isolated observation bounded by the capacities of their resolutions. A macroscope, on the other hand, would permit the appreciation of a wider context at a smaller scale, and derive forms of iteration and interaction that derive from integration and conjugation.

Numerous semi-orchestrated aspects of our technology already provide the elementary components of a macroscope. By peeking through these embryonic macroscopes, we can comprehend the very large or the very small relative to our own human scale. Yet, despite our ability to view the cosmological or sub-atomic dimensions of the world, we are still unable to comprehend their relationships to each other.

As is the case when we approach any measurement of the sub-atomic, or the cosmic,[4] the limitations of our perceptual tools unavoidably propagate a degree of uncertainty that is based in our current investigative methodologies. Through the processes of reduction and disregard for context, we have limited our ability to perceive relationships and the cooperative essence of wholeness.

Uncertainty is bound together with superposition and other quantum mechanical principles — perhaps unnecessarily so. 'Quantized' phenomena, *i.e.* things that are defined as functional units — are components of all complex and dynamical systems, and their models use statistical or stochastic measurements to characterize their apparent ambiguity. Such phenomena include bifurcations, emergence phase transitions, stress precipitation, and other spatio-temporal forms.

From the perspective of the macroscope, quantum mechanics relates to a discrete range of functioning *based upon the discrimination and orientation of our senses*, and may thus be thought of as the fuzzy 'shape' of our perceptual system. The quantum 'scale' would thereby apply universally, invariant of scale. It would represent a measure of precision relative to our perception, both innate and technological, and operate at any degree of smallness or largeness.

---

4. The cosmic, we may argue, has a lesser degree of 'corruption' from context isolation, particular with the development of accessible parallel processing, and ambitious data projects like COBE and WMAP.

Using approaches consistent with ancient practices and latent human capacities, we may endeavor to encode knowledge that has been made available only recently *via* modern tools and technologies.

Scale and Metaphor

In order to define and understand notions of scale, let us review the common metric (base-10) system, but mixed with a concept of symmetry. The first several orders of scale will show a correlation with the senses of the human body. Thereafter, prominent 'milestones' in the orders of scale will reveal their own wholeness, and will do so in proportion again to the human body. Ultimately this continues, to the extent of our natural observations.

In scientific measurement, scale is composed by powers of 10. (Many may recall the *Powers of Ten* animation by Demetrios.[5]) Symmetry is the concept of *similarity*; and means that things move, or are structured, in the same way.

The central unit in this system is the meter. Our first understanding of scale, the human body, also holds this base unit. Though when born we are just more than half this size, and as adults we can grow to more than 2 meters, the adult torso — the majority of our mass — generally holds the range of 1 meter, or 3 feet. In a scientific form, 1 meter is written as 10^0, where the raised '0' can be any number, and represents the number of zeros to follow the '1'. Thus $10^0 = 1$, and $10^2 = 100$, and $10^4 = 10,000$.

A series of envelopes emerges in this way, each envelope of scale as an exponent of the previous envelope, originating from the base 'unit' of our body. That is also to say that no matter how large or small a thing we experience, our understanding of it is based on our perception of the 'unit' of our body.

However, the base-10 scale may not originate arbitrarily from anthropocentrism. The natural dimensions of the physical cosmos may predicate the human scale, or our scale may influence what we have the capacity to perceive. As developed in this paper, the largest and smallest scales we

5. *Powers of Ten*. Prod. IBM. Dir. Charles and Ray Eames. Perf. Philip Morrison. Videocasette. IBM, 1977.

observe are 32 orders of magnitude different from the human body. The size of our body may have naturally occurred by being the center of this range.

If we reduce this scale by an order of magnitude to 10^{-1} (1/10th of a meter, ~4 inches), we have measurements on the scale of the human hand. If we go up in scale to 10^1 (10 meters, ~30 ft) we have measurements on the scale of a house. Every power of 10 represents more than an order of scale, it represents a filter. It sets and choreographs our perception of nature.

Both of these scales, 10^1 and 10^{-1}, are intimately relevant to our human experience, as the things we design at one scale have a reciprocal relationship to the other. Most tools, or parts thereof, that we use with our hands are designed on the scale of 10^{-1}. Paper, dinnerware, books, *etc.* all are on this scale. As well, most fruit and leaves have this scale — perhaps in no small part because of their long history of being plucked by hands and mouths.

Most buildings, or spaces of human habitation and interaction are constructed on the scale of 10^1 because this is a comfortable envelope of experience.[6] Houses, dining and dancing halls, courtyards, gardens, street intersections, *etc.* are all on this scale — a comfortable distance for interacting with the personal space of others. In wild nature we also find this scale present in ponds and in any given line of sight portion of streams and trees — many of which grow to a scale of 30–60 feet (10–20 meters). It is perhaps no coincidence that most houses are also built at this scale, but it does indicate how so many aspects of our lives are influenced by patterns in nature.

The symmetry of these scales can be seen in the relationships between objects within each. For example, light switches, door knobs, window latches, thermostats and handles, all 10^{-1}, are the mechanisms that we use to operate the 10^1 scale of the building — such as a home. As well, each sub-division of the house has a distinct set of hand-sized objects, *e.g.*, kitchen utensils, lamps, yard/garden implements, office supplies, bathroom toiletries, *etc.* We may see this in nature, too, where fish, frogs, rocks, most fruits and vegetables, grasses, and insects are the 10^{-1} pieces that make a

6. Christopher Alexander. *The Nature of Order.* Vol. 1–4. Berkeley, CA: CES, 2004.

10^1 pond. Let us call this symmetry between 10^1 and 10^{-1} an *envelope*.

Our interaction with each envelope is perceptually 'framed,' or filtered, through a model. Each model formulates an awareness of our relationship to both scales of a given envelope, those envelopes that may precede it, and those that are subsequent. Thus, our experiences at any scale are filtered through the series of models for each envelope beyond the body. These models also constrain the dimensions of our awareness, however, as they set the structure and boundaries by which our innate faculties know the world. Complementarily, that structure is the *affordance* of a model — that which grants its capacities.

At the next envelope of experience we have the scale of 10^{-2} (1/100 of a meter, or about half an inch), measurements just relating to the fingertips, or other similar sizes. Things of this size include jewelry elements, the width of pencils and other small hand tools, and buttons (on our clothes or to operate our technology). Much of our smallest food (above ground granules) is on this scale: peas, beans, seeds, grains, *etc*. This is the scale

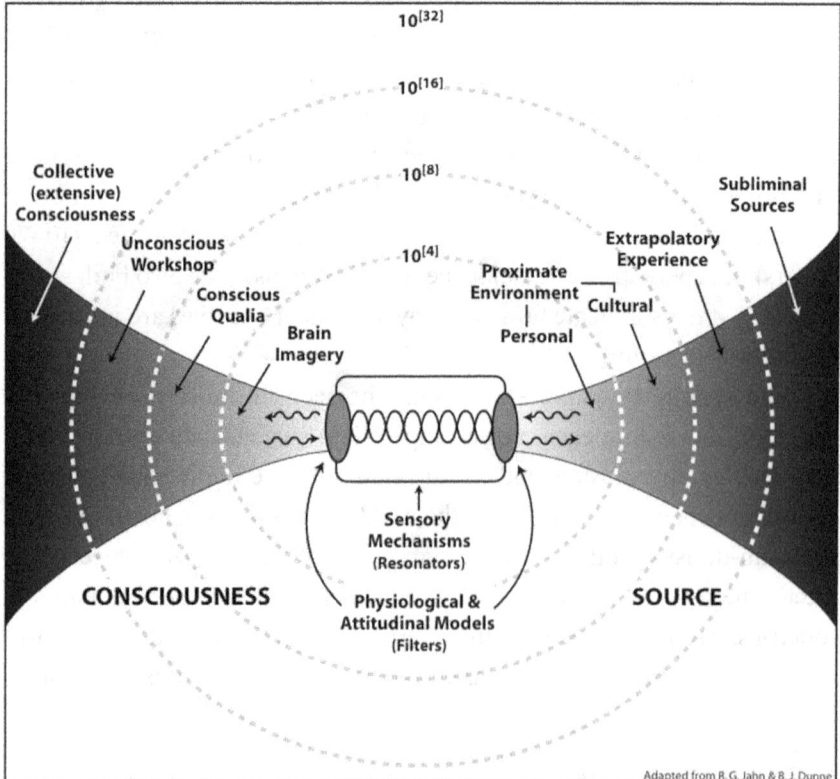

Adapted from R. G. Jahn & B. J. Dunne

of 'delicacy,' and more attention and carefulness tends to be paid to this scale than to a hand-scale.

At 10^2 meters (100 meters, ~300 ft) we have a scale of human experience where rules are used to mediate interaction. This is the scale of arenas, fields, factories, ships, *etc.* Each of these venues requires rules — a model — in order to guide experience. Games/sports are played in arenas, crops are systematically planted (and fairs are held) in fields, buildings have floor plans, and there is an order of operations to factories, ships, or airplanes.

In wild nature this scale is represented by minor lakes or rivers, or large trees like giant sequoias. Rivers and lakes, in particular, or coastal harbors, are often vital elements in the organization of human social activity at the scale of villages and towns. Towns also have a close connection with the small scale of this envelope. Jewelry and ornamentation (10^{-2}) denote social standing and role within a community (10^2). Pencils and marking tools record resources and financial records. Beans and seeds have their greatest value in multitude, where they can feed a community.

Both 'directions' of scale at the second envelope require some model, or set of rules, to understand our interactions and relationships. Without these conventions, the interactions of people in this scale of space can become chaotic, as in a *mob*, or other hive-like mentality. If beans are not in sacks, buttons not in drawers, accounts not carefully recorded, gemstones left unpolished, *etc.* (all things 10^{-2} in scale), they are regarded as 'clutter.'[7]

At the next envelope we have 10^{-3}, which represents the approximate diameter of a grain of sand. Operation at this scale can be closer linked with its inverse 10^3 — 1 kilometer or 3000 feet. A material can be ground into sand or granules, but doing so requires the labor of many people, and is an operation that usually benefits an even larger number. Involving this number of people, the scale of interaction is often the size of a village, or other community that has begun to organize its land by residence, commerce, and the like. These structures have a scale in the thousands of feet; nearly a mile. Appropriately, at this scale unorganized human interaction can become a *riot*, or worse, similar to how scattered sands can become a sandstorm.

---

7. contemporarily: "MOOP." Matter Out Of Place.

At the next envelope we have 10^{-4} meters — the diameter of a hair, a thread, or plant fibers. Our sense of touch can be trained to feel the difference between subtle thickness differences in hair, *etc.* Arguably though, sensory measurements at this scale become increasingly difficult, usually requiring the assistance of precision tools, pre-processing, or bulk measurements.

Its inverse, 10^4 meters (10 kilometers, or 30,000 feet), is a scale at which coordinated planning is required to distinguish it from the previous village scale envelope. This scale may be associated with a town, small city, the district of a larger city, or similar political unit. A cessation of organization at this scale could be related to community disputes and other matters that, like a cancer, take on an inferior form of sub-organization, incapable of organizing itself with others into a greater whole. Such is the case of cults and like groups.

There may be some value to the developing perspective to consider that there are five classical senses, and that each one can be well-associated to one of the first five (0–4) envelopes. The tactile sense ('touch') is the base scale, that of the body. The sense of taste is that which we can put in our hand or mouth, the first envelope. The sense of smell is the second envelope; few people can smell more than 300 ft without a wind, hunger, or other augmentation — and few things smaller than one-half inch, by themselves, emit an odor discernible to humans at a distance of 300 ft. The sense of sound correlates with the third envelope, as only a small range of sounds commonly travel farther than 3000 ft, and granule-sized things produce discernible sounds only in limited ways. Our sense of sight generally has difficultly observing the details of things as small as a single hair or as far as 30,000 feet. We see the sheen and body of a head of hair, not an individual strand; we see waves of grain and the life of a hamlet, not the constituents.

Additionally we may consider that to perceive a thing beyond the normal envelop of awareness demands an abnormally largely quantity of it, and the result is an altered consciousness. When so much rotting and decay occurs that it can be smelled from greater than 300 ft it's not just unpleasant — it's frightening. When so many people are happy that it's apparent from farther than any individual's happiness could be perceived, it's not just joyous — it's grand. This concept will be revisited once after further elaboration.

For consciousness, each envelope is a filter: in its symmetry of scales, correlation with a sensory organ, and physical morphology. The words 'envelope' and 'filter' can be used interchangeably throughout — though we use the term 'envelope' for its conventional ease in conveying a concept of nesting.[8]

Beyond the Basic Senses

Through to this point, we've seen the first four envelopes of scale beyond the human body, and seen their composition of symmetrically small and large things. From here, the next four envelopes of scale, 5th–8th, will show a similar pattern of relationship from one envelope to the next. The 'four-scale-unit' will appear throughout our explorations of scale, which shall become increasingly brief beyond the 8th. A fractal pattern will emerge, as 4-scale units make a whole 8-scale unit, two 8-scale units make a whole 16-scale unit, and as well with the 32nd scale.

The fifth power is the first scale in which perception occurs almost entirely *via* an abstract model: 10^{-5}, 1/100th of a millimeter, is a cellular scale. Tissues and organs of the body can be differentiated by their constituents and layers, but without the aid of technology such as lens optics or chemical analyses, perception and measurement of phenomena of this scale can be understood only in terms of aggregates.

Inversely, 10^5 is 100 kilometers or 60 miles. This is the scale of a large city region, or a geo-political unit. Both require a model or organizational structure in order to conceive or represent their wholeness. The city scale is comparable to the cellular scale of the body; constituents exist but they cannot survive independently of their system. This is the first appearance of climatological zones such as forests, deserts, or jungles.

At the sixth order we cross another envelope: 10^{-6} is 1 micron, a sub-cellular scale, which references the size of cellular components and the length of a DNA strand. Energy associated with this wavelength is referred to as being in the Near Infrared, and we experience it as heat,

---

8. It should be noted that hierarchical nesting is not the only topology for the relationship between filters. Physical scales may not truly take a nested structure, despite the commonality of expressing it that way — and this paper encourages that *gedanken* experiment.

particularly in the sense of body temperature. Optical magnification of this scale is only marginally effective — energy dynamics, such as light scattering, must be employed to 'magnify' micron-scale events.

The scale of 10^6 is 1000 kilometers, or 600 miles and encompasses entire regions, islands, or small nations. For humans, statehood occurs at this scale, as a more complex organizational unit than that of a typical city, and models for human interaction increasingly involve representational government and mediation. Our models on the small scale, for units of organismic functioning, match closely to those of governmental units at the large scale. Major issues for 10^6 scale 'organisms' are connected to individual health that is driven by illness at 10^{-6} scale. At the scale of 10^6 we encounter phenomena such as climatological zones that form regional weather patterns.

The scale of 10^{-7} is 1/10 of a micron, and is populated by viruses and complete protein components. In all their varied 'species' and configurations, proteins build sub-cellular components, while viruses work to infect or corrupt them. Regardless of how they make up the bigger organism, healthy or sick, these are the building blocks for living systems. Cancerous mutations occur at this scale, in large part due to malformed or corrupted proteins.

When we move to the envelope of 10^7, that being 10,000 kilometers or 6000 miles, we are dealing with the scale of continents. For human organization, this is the dimension of large nations, or a council of smaller nations. Complementary to the preceding envelope, health trends become epidemics and interactions between sub-national groups, and inter-nationally, are increasingly complex. In nature, continental weather conveyors emerge out of such regional patterns.

10^{-8} is 1/100th of a micron, or 10 nanometers, which is the size of the regularity in a crystal lattice and basic protein structures. Molecular principles of this scale give rise to the concept of nanotechnology. The 10^{-8} scale delimits the wavelength of ultraviolet light, which it used to a vast array of effects by activity of this scale.

10^8 is 100,000 kilometers, or 60,000 miles. The primary reference we have to this scale is the circumference of the Earth (40,000 kilometers)[9].

---

9.   The average planetary circumference in our solar system is 157,000 kilometers.

Our models spanning the whole Earth are in their infancy, encompass human rights, cultural memory, and ecological interactions, and will require an international effort to address patterns of polar weather migration, earthquake dynamics, and oceanic changes, as well as global warming and cooling cycles.

Of note here is the correlation between the 4th and 8th envelopes, the 4th envelope being the extents of sensory perceptions by an individual and the 8th envelope being the extents of direct perception by a large community or a global organism. In a complementary fashion, the organization of the |5|–|8| envelopes follows the same pattern as the |1|–|4| envelopes.[10] As individuals gather their home, community, and neighbors and become a county[11] — so do these counties gather together as regions, states, and countries to form the whole planet. We say that envelopes |1|–|4| are thus *homeomorphic* to |5|–|8| (meaning they have the same pattern) and together form a *unit identity* that we see develop into the next set of envelopes.

"One Small Step ..."

The next envelope of scale is the 9th power. 10^{-9} is one nanometer. This is the scale at which atomic structure directly translates into the most elementary molecules: the base pairs of DNA and other crystal formations. Wavelengths of this scale are x-rays, which are most often used to perform measurements here.

10^9 is 1 million kilometers, and almost 1 million miles. This is the orbital 'distance' the Moon travels around the Earth. This 'distance' generally can be thought of as a circumferential measure. Humans have no strong bureaucratic models for this scale, although we have rough accords that cover space law and an international/planetary reserve.[12]

This scale begins the threshold where mythological models hold equal or greater weight to people worldwide than scientific or bureaucratic frameworks. As the moon is our closest celestial object, and a satellite,

---

10. We shall also write an envelope number with vertical bars, as |1|, in the same way absolute values are written in mathematics.

11. borough, prefecture, *etc.*

12. "Rudimentary provisions for space law based on the Antarctica Treaty." Lowry Burgess. *The Toronto Manifesto*. Toronto: Carnegie Mellon University, 2001.

these mythological models include stories which encompass cyclical information and generally govern human ritual. Like the small scale of the ninth envelope, our models here are almost entirely representational. The mythological framework used to represent each large and small scale of this envelope is often the same. Recent technological developments have also created a beautiful symmetry between scales at this envelope: increasing proficiency over the nano-scale is yielding models of carbon nanotubes that suggest themselves to be critical in our move to orbital space, such as the concept of a Space Elevator.

The scale-symmetry within an envelope shows itself here again in the similarity of form and dynamics between the nucleus and electron of an atom, and planet/moon orbitals of a planetary system. Moreover, the geometric boundary of orbit helps us to see that objects and phenomena at each scale are best defined through a boundary, rather than a length or distance. As an example of how the large scale may tell us about the symmetrically small, we may find that atoms bonded as a molecule experience their neighbors as though they were in motion due to the atom's own internal dynamics.

Figure 2. Atom and electron shells

The tenth envelope of scale incorporates 10^{-10}. This measure is also known as an Angstrom, and is the size of an atom, including its electron layers. Using electron microscopes we can measure whole atoms with reasonable precision. Beyond 10^{-10}, as we subdivide the atomic size and attempt to assert electron shell size and shape, our visualizations presume our models to create graphical or pictorial representations. Coincidentally, as the scale we measure continues to get smaller, our apparatuses for measuring get larger — accelerators, cyclotrons, colliders, other novel mechanisms, and the systems needed to operate them.

10^{10} is a distance of 10 million kilometers, or 6 million miles. It is the scale of measure between planetary orbital radii in the inner solar system (Mercury, Venus, and Mars). The general accessibility and relevance of our models becomes increasingly skewed toward the mythological, as various systems of metaphor begin to arise based on the movement of planets in the night sky. Precise measure, of position, *etc.*, is overshadowed by multi-body problems.

The eleventh envelope begins the first significant gaps for the small scale. 10^{-11} is comparable to the outer of three general electron orbital distances (from the nucleus of the atom). Our scientific models are further representational, based on the aspects of crystal formations. Matter composed of atoms bearing this scale are generally metals, and often are radioactive.

10^{11} is referred to as 1 Astronomical Unit (AU), since it is the distance between the Earth and the Sun. This is also the rough scale of distance between the Earth and any of the other planets in the inner solar system.

10^{-12} is called a picometer, and is the scale of the inner electron orbitals. Matter composed of these atoms can be metal or mineral. 10^{12} is 10 AU, is a scale for measuring Jupiter's orbital distance from the Sun. This is the first scale to represent the outer solar system. As with the identity relationship formed by the coupling of envelope sets $|1|$–$|4|$ and $|5|$–$|8|$, the scales of Jupiter also form part of an identity relationship of scale in the solar system. In this identity we see Jupiter as a boundary. Scientifically we know it to be so as well, as its gravity governs and protects the inner solar system, and is hypothesized to create conditions for a fertile Earth. Mythologically, Jupiter/Zeus is the ruler of the gods and governor over all the Earth.

$10^{|12|}$ is a special scale. Like $10^{|4|}$, which is the edge of the larger world of $10^{|5|}$–$10^{|8|}$, $10^{|12|}$ is the edge of what comes beyond it. For us, the 13th–16th envelopes are the outer solar system, and the range of other stars. Formally, we call the relationship of ($10^{|1|}$–$10^{|4|}$) and ($10^{|5|}$–$10^{|8|}$) a unit identity. What we are exploring here beyond $10^{|8|}$ is that a similar unit identity exists from ($10^{|9|}$–$10^{|12|}$) to ($10^{|13|}$–$10^{|16|}$). These scales will briefly be covered.

10^{-13} is the scale of the inner electron 'shell' of the atomic nucleus.[13] Materials arising from this scale are minerals and non-metal elements, which are the building blocks of organic life. These characterize the earliest stage of cosmic development, when hydrogen-burning stars make basic elements.

10^{13} is 100 AU, and is the distance from the Sun to a sheath of material known as the Heliosphere. The heliosphere is a 'shell' of stellar material produced by our solar system that buffers us from the interstellar medium.

---

13. More specifically, it's the Compton wavelength; the orbital measure of the fundamental electron shell around the atom nucleus.

In the symmetry between large and small scales we may compare the cloudy structure of cosmic nebulae, and the electron cloud density.

10^{-14} is a scale represented by the nucleus within each atom. The large scale of this envelope, 10^{14}, is 1000 AU. Many comets have orbits that span this distance. Trivially, a special place exists for comets in mythological models, naming them the heralds of great change — understandable even today, considering that they travel outside of our solar system and return.

10^{-15} is called a femtometer, and is the classical size of an electron, proton, or neutron,[14] though at this scale all effects in the domain of 'quantum' are most commonly measured in terms of energy, and not size. 10^{15} is 10,000 AU, and is the longest orbital distance of any comet we know. It is almost the distance to the nearest star.

The common trend of symmetry between the scales remains through the 9th to 15th envelope. Particle physics (the small) increasingly becomes a matter of astrophysical observation (the large), wherein we watch the dynamics of celestial events in order to deduce the inter-particle forces that underlay them. The power that deities are assigned is over a realm that is as fundamental as atomic and sub-atomic forces. That is, were forces of the scales 10^{-9} to 10^{-15} to suddenly operate differently, the macroscopic effect to the human mind would be extremely mythological. It becomes increasingly clear that the large and the small scales of a given order are formulary envelopes. The mythologies are no less intertwined. Pantheistic forces are commonly identified with stellar structures of 10^9–10^{15} scale. 10^{15} is the threshold for what is the size of a solar system.

"... One Giant Leap ..."

What lies beyond this envelope of scale? On the small scale there are but few subatomic particles dotting landscape seen mostly through mathematical calculation. After the electron at 10^{-15} we have the lepton, calculated to be no larger than 10^{-18} in size. Neutrinos have been estimated around 10^{-30} in diameter — a debated measurement.[15] By proposition, somewhere smaller than all of this is a vacuum state, of which little is known.

---

14. John Baez (http://math.ucr.edu/home/baez/physics/General/open_questions.html).
15. J. L. Lucio, A. Rosado, and A. Zepeda. "Characteristic size for the neutrino." *Physical Review D, 31*, No. 5 (1985). pp. 1091–1096.

On the large scale we know only slightly more. We can see structures at this scale, but the things they're made of cannot be seen clearly given our technologies. Notably, the 10^{16} scale is the distance from our star to other stars. 10^{21} is the radius of the Milky Way. At 10^{22} we have the diameter of our Milky Way galaxy, which hold all of the stars that we can see with the naked eye. Among the models for this scale, most accessible to the mind are stories about the constellations and their movement.

Beyond our galaxy, at 10^{22}, we have the distance to the Andromeda Galaxy, our closest galactic neighbor. In fact, 10^{22} is the average measure of separation between all galaxies. 10^{24}, or 100 million light years, is a rough scale between our solar system and the center of the Universe. Following our pattern of identity, $10^{|24|}$ is a 'unit identity,' and again we see a scale-pattern of center to edge/boundary. Beyond this, in the range of 10^{30}, is the most recent estimates for the diameter of the universe.

Let us consider a metaphorical relationship of the symmetry between smallest and largest scale. Within the universe there appears a great axis around which all things move. In the night sky from the Earth this axis is drawn through the constellations Sextans and Aquilla.[16] The axis is called a 'cosmological anisotropy,' and reveals itself in light and other electromagnetic waves like a needle-orientation of a cosmic compass.[17] By the way we measure this axis, we are left with a single plausible reason for its existence, that it is a property to the electromagnetic vacuum.[18] Here again we see a bridge of symmetry between what looks like things in the range of 10^{32} and 10^{-32} — yielding the envelope $10^{|32|}$.

The largest and smallest computable scales that we have to deal with are on the order of 10^{32} and 10^{-32}, respectively. The proposition being

16. The constellation *Sextans* represents the sextant, the ancient navigational instrument by which seafarers would orient themselves. *Aquila* is the messenger from Heaven — the mythological Eagle leading souls on their journey. Their association *via* the 'poles' of the cosmic anisotropy 'axis' are metaphorical analogs of our scientific knowledge, as the 'axis' orients light and all electromagnetic waves.

17. An axis around which the polarization plane of electromagnetic radiation becomes the most twisted as it journeys across the fabric of space.

18. Since the polarization rotation we observe has such a systematic dependence on the direction of travel of the radiation, it is posed as implausible that it is generated by anything other than a vacuum property [Borge Nodland and John P. Ralston. "Indication of anisotropy in electromagnetic propagation over cosmological distances." *Physical Review Letters*, 78 (1997), 3043–3046. <http://xxx.lanl.gov/abs/astro-ph/9704196>].

made, in light of such scientific data, is that structure of the largest scale we can measure arises directly with that of the smallest scale that we can envision. A "spin" in the vacuum, like a whirling, brings an image of a vortex. This same shape has been proposed as the "shape"[19] of the cosmos. This irrevocable connectedness between large things and small things, the above and the below, the world within and the world beyond, is rendered by the alchemical realization of "as above, so below."

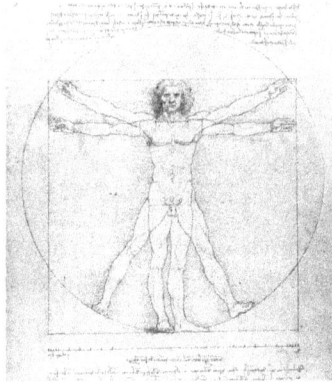

Photo Luc Viator

Beyond the Quantum

Once we recognize the symmetry of scale present throughout nature, we may begin to understand the role of consciousness in it. Let us begin again from the base scale of the human body. From this, each envelope of scale is an order of the previous envelope[20] originating from the base 'unit' of our body.

It is no small statement to say that we experience envelopes because of their physical structure. This would mean that physical reality has these dimensions — rather than the more casual notion that we see this structure because it matches our own dimensions (anthropomorphism). Such a notion calls into question the origin of complementary pairs: which

---

19. *Topology*, more precisely. [Ralf Aurich, Sven Lustig, Frank Steiner, and Holger Then. "Hyperbolic universes with a horned topology and the cosmic microwave background anisotropy." *Classical and Quantum Gravity, 21* (2004). pp. 4901–4925] and [Ralf Aurich, Sven Lustig, Frank Steiner, and Holger Then. "Can one hear the shape of the universe?" *Physical Review Letters, 94* (2005) 021301].
20. like eigenfunction

came first? With reference to the filters concept of Jahn and Dunne,[21] any model acts as a filter in this regard. Each physically real thing, and the perception of it, directly affects every other. A model's bias or neutrality to information is the discrimination of our mind.

These models are like sensory organs, in this way. Considering models as discrete modes, we may reflect upon their consonance with the concept of filters. The structure, of a model/filter when employed directly by an individual is correlated with their apperception of phenomena. Without filters, the source stimulus is an unintelligible chaos — yet, at the moment of apperception, the degrees of freedom to that chaos are those afforded by one's model/filter.

Consider that the models and the 1st–4th envelopes (including the 0th, the body) are experienced in tandem with the basic senses, and thus require no abstract 'cognitive modeling.' They are a direct transduction of the environment. At the fifth envelope none of our base senses suffice to experience the world directly, and we must rely upon models for perception and interaction.

Cultures have chosen to approach this initial 'envelope of the envelopes' in various ways. Material methods, as in the case with a lens, are most often applied when addressing the small scale; *i.e.* tools are constructed based on models of light, heat, or other energy. These tools allow the 'small' to be 'enlarged' — all self-consistent with the models that gave rise to them.

Systems of medicine also can be applied to conceive of the small scales, and reciprocally define the demographics of the large scale. Bacterial and virulent disease, genetic variations: these small-scale differences make up the population demographics that represent the large scale. In this light, the fifth envelope can be seen as the *cellular* threshold of technology.

Each model, giving rise to a measurement tool, is based on a biological sense. Tools transduce measurements into the biological range, from the direct source at envelopes removed and distant from the human body. The transmission of information from the source, albeit whole, does not

21. Robert G. Jahn and Brenda J. Dunne. "Sensors, filters and the Source of reality." *Journal of Scientific Exploration, 18*, No. 4 (2004). pp. 547–570.

come absolute. Our sensation has been structured — *rectified* — by the model used to build a given tool. Structuring the source into a 'signal' has the potential to make the 'signal' look mostly like the model, consciousness itself, rather than revealing inherent structure of the source.[22]

Our awareness of information from the first five envelopes is multifaceted, in as much a degree as we have trained our senses. Yet, the way we construct a model to transduce information from envelopes beyond the first five generally focuses upon visual information, and occasionally auditory. We do not commonly use metaphors, let alone technology, that communicate smell or taste.[23] For instance, we smell the health or rot of food, the way our body reacts when it is ill, and sense that things 'may not taste right.' These are measures of cellular activity. Only in metaphor do we say that something 'smells funny' in the affairs of politics (10^5–10^8).[24] Our models usually convey information on visual or acoustic bases.

When using a tool or instrument, the reduction of information *via* the tool's model bears a direct dimensional relationship to the uncertainty in our measurement. As our sensation becomes increasingly mediated through models, our uncertainty grows. Our experience in these situations can open to creativity, association, imagination, and metaphor. These, rather than being *baseless* mystery, may in fact be observations of phenomena that have *circumvented mediation* in the same envelope.

Consider viewing something smaller than the eye can see. Often we use light expanded through the glass lens of a microscope, making it cover enough area for the eye to see. In this case, we are limited to the precision that our model specifies for the lens material and the properties of the light. More generally speaking, when the model (*e.g. light dispersion*) is used to create a tool (*e.g. a microscope*), observation may reach the tool's limit (*energy density, absorption, refraction, etc.*) to conduct sensory information. That is, the limits of the model govern the information density of a tool.

---

22. In one regard this stymies total immediate knowing, allowing at best fragmentary images or prophetically broad awareness; on another it speaks to multi-dimensional observation as the method of rendering insight.

23. Smell-o-vision failed, though odor has become a component of branding at the beginning of the 21st century.

24. George Lakoff and Mark Johnson. *Metaphors We Live By.* Chicago: University of Chicago Press, 1980.

As the scale between models of material and energy approaches equivalence we reach a boundary. The diminishing difference in scale between matter and energy has a direct relationship to the diminution of the certainty of our measurements. We extrapolate our models to the edge of the atomic scale, where we reach the classical threshold of quantum mechanical operation. The quantum mechanical uncertainty inherent in the data of this scale, however, is integral to the model we have conceived — it is integral with our state of consciousness. Thus, the characteristics[25] of a model's uncertainty are those of consciousness itself.

With this, we can consider the 'quantum scale,' and the uncertainty inherent in it, to be a measure of precision relative to our perception, both innate and technological. As such, it would be a discrete range of functioning *only relative to the discrimination and orientation of our senses* — our filters, or the 'shape' of our own perception. Some aspects of quantum mechanics may therefore be relevant to scales of smallness and largeness. In actuality, any 'quantized mechanics' may operate invariant of scale, or at certain intervals of scale. If these systems truly have similarities, they will exhibit homeomorphism — though they look different, they operate on the same rules set[26] — and quantum mechanics would thus be isomorphic to them.

The interdependence of quantum mechanics and uncertainty may be a characteristic of any system in which a sufficient threshold of information is indistinguishable, disallowing discrete awareness. The operations and boundaries of quantum mechanics would hold true for systems that are 'large' to the atomic, even human or galactic, and those mechanisms of astronomic scale would be equally true for the miniscule scale. The quantum and the non-linear, originating together from the configuration of our consciousness, could each be used to create models for studying the other.

The notion presented here, and in the work of Jahn and Dunne, is that quantum states may occur over personal and social dimensions. Models at the quantum mechanical scale begin to take on a new light in the interaction of consciousness with phenomena or concepts relating to any scale.

---

25. dimensional and topological
26. topology

Models of particular interest would include observation-based wave functions, dimensional properties of state change, and other aspects that are difficult to realize when dealing with phenomena that are confounded by the models we have instrumented. At large scale, we still have model limitations, namely the collection of sufficient data. Rather than not being able to collect enough (or requiring exotic energies to do so), however, we face *achievable* methodologies of sensor nets, and other distributed data collection.

From the consideration of large-scale quantum domains we may re-consider our 'envelope' model. As photo-electric wave functions are mod-eled as sub-divisions of the atomic domain space, so may the envelopes presented through our perception be sub-divisions within consciousness. We may even consider the 4th, 8th, 16th, and 32nd envelopes as meta-phorical corollaries to electron orbital shells.[27] Given the established im-pact of observation upon wave function, we may, humbly, consider the role of consciousness — and its filters — in the realization of physical envelopes of scale.

Conclusions, and the Conceptual Macroscope

The main point of this paper is the proposition that all models serve the purpose of systematizing awareness, and data derived from them are, ir-revocably, to some degree the constructions of consciousness. As models are contextualized in relation to other models, the overlaps and differenc-es create a map for navigating our state of awareness and communicat-ing with others and with our environment. The contextualization process increases the significance of measure, without which measured data re-main orphaned. The reason for this significance lies with the synergistic emergence, wherein the many ways in which we learn create the basis for more comprehensive understanding. Upon such a foundation of many cornerstones can occur true accord and traversal of the source.

---

27. Jahn and Dunne proposed an 'atomic' model for quantizing consciousness and physical complementarity, which has significant congruence with this paper. To note, the symmetry between scales and perception outlined in this paper may serve well as the *a priori* distance property sought within their model (p. 755). Developing the association fully is beyond the scope of this essay. [Robert G. Jahn and Brenda J. Dunne. "On the quantum mechanics of consciousness, with application to anomalous phenomena." *Foundations of Physics*, *16*, No. 8 (1996). pp. 721–772.]

Association, *broad scope*, and *discrimination* are paramount to any systemic exploration of natural phenomena. The development of modern instrumentation has focused heavily upon increasing resolution in order to discriminate details more precisely. As the demand for resolution has increased, the size of the instrument also has increased. Without context, the measured details ever lose association to the environment that more richly informs them. As that association is lost, so is our ability to model them, and thus arises uncertainty — along with quantum mechanics. As constructions of consciousness, these mechanics may be operative at any scale, given sufficient context.

The functionality of a macroscope, perhaps like the mind itself, allows a smooth contextual ramp for exploring new areas of knowledge, as bridges are built between varied perspectives based on their symmetry. The structure of this model would allow us to navigate through the lesser known domains and toward realms of new insight.

Metaphor and mythology are representations of the structure in this space. Metaphor is an inevitable facet of human consciousness that represents an increasing absence of articulation *at the given scale*. We may consider again that metaphor delivers data from beyond a specific model in order to create a more integrated perception at the given scale. Far from being irrelevant, the mythological maps the terrain of general awareness, *i.e.* 'the big picture.' Such a *broad domain*, shedding light on the characteristics of complex systems, is the hallmark of a macroscope. Systems modeling, risk management, political planning, and other attempts at a comprehensive investigation gain extended 'reach' through the use of macroscopic perception.

In addition, by framing the structure of our knowledge across scales we gain the advantage of being able to describe it mathematically. Generalizing the properties of physical occurrences allows for symbolic representation of the relationships between them. The collected wisdom of stories becomes a valuable source for understanding more deeply the directions of human growth and structural relationships.

Considering that the relationships in these stories emerge from natural observation, they have the capacity to encode phenomenological functions that cross scales, existing as they do beyond the ways we have become used to looking at the world. The nature of many mythological identities is chimeric, multi-faceted, and multi-dimensional.[28] Plainly, these identities represent that which is unlike our usual sense of human-ness and unlike our customary envelopes or filters. Yet, these stories have emerged from our experiential world, and therefore they hold important keys for its understanding.

As we encounter a growing array of scientific anomalies and insta-bilities in our global system, we need new approaches for our future. The potential for articulating the 'anomalous' offers one method of providing continuity to the PEAR (now ICRL) work that gave birth to "Sensors, Fil-ters and the Source of Reality" for a new generation. The use of metaphor as a research tool for explorations across the scales of human activity en-hances our ability to articulate the anomalies and subtle patterns that hold the keys to our growing understanding of nature and ourselves.

> *We are measuring not nature itself, but nature exposed*
> *to our methods of inquiry.*
> — WERNER HEISENBERG

---

28. David Carrasco. "The Tezcatlipoca Ixiptla: To change place." *To Change Place: Aztec Ceremonial Landscapes*. David Carrasco, ed. Niwot, CO: University Press of Colorado, 1991. pp. 31–57.

A Retrocausal Model of Life

ANTONELLA VANNINI AND ULISSE DI CORPO
Rome, Italy

1 Introduction

In 1977 Ulisse Di Corpo developed a Vital Needs Model which required an independent property, symmetrical to entropy, which is here identified as "syntropy". According to this model, syntropy could not be a product of the laws of the macroscopic world, as all the laws of the macrocosm are dependent on entropy. For this reason the authors searched for evidence of the property of syntropy at other levels, finding, at the quantum mechanic level, equations that always yield a positive solution, which moves forward in time, and a negative solution that moves backward in time. For example, Klein and Gordon's wave equation has two solutions: a positive one which describes diverging waves (retarded waves), governed by the law of entropy, and a negative one which describes converging waves (advanced waves), governed by the symmetrical law of syntropy. In 1941 the mathematician Luigi Fantappié demonstrated that the advanced waves concentrate energy, produce differentiation and structures, and show qualities which are identical to those which can be observed in living systems. In this way, Fantappié arrived at the conclusion that living systems are a response to causes originating in the future (retrocausality).

In this paper the authors argue that:

- Life reacts both to causality and retrocausality, and that sensory exchanges can therefore take place in both directions:
  o in the form of information, for causality;
  o in the form of feelings, for retrocausality.
- Retrocausality displays anomalous properties, such as non-locality, which could help to explain anomalous sensory experiences.

Whereas stimuli coming from the past can easily be detected by our five senses and understood and processed by our brain, stimuli coming from the future are more difficult to understand and process as they are experienced in the form of feelings. Often, these feelings are experienced in the form of anticipation: something which is going to happen, but about which we do not have any information. As a consequence people usually follow what the five senses suggest, since this information seems to be more certain and reassuring.

2 Advanced Waves, Syntropy, and Living Systems

In the Copenhagen Interpretation of quantum mechanics, the collapse of the state vector (the collapse of a wave into a particle) occurs at the same time at all positions in space. This collapse would seem to require faster-than-light propagation of information, violating in this way the limit of the speed of light posed by Special Relativity in the propagation of causality. This was Einstein's original objection to quantum mechanics, which was later formulated into the Einstein/Podolsky/Rosen (EPR) paradox.

Analyzing the EPR paradox, Schrödinger concluded that the problem lies in the way time is used in quantum mechanics. The Schrödinger wave equation, which was the focus of most of the discussion surrounding EPR, is not relativistically invariant and treats time in an essentially classical way. For example, it assumes that there can be a well-defined "before" and "after" in the collapse description.

The relativistically invariant version of the wave equation was produced by Klein and Gordon in 1926. In order to convert the Schrödinger wave equation into a relativistically invariant relation, Klein and Gordon had to insert the energy/momentum/mass relation:

$$E^2 = c^2p^2 + m^2c^4$$

(where E is the total energy of an object, p the momentum, m the mass, and c the speed of light), which has a positive and a negative solution, arriving to what is now known as the d'Alambert operator.

The d'Alambert operator depends on a square root, and thus allows a dual wave solution: retarded waves (which propagate forward in time) and advanced waves (which propagate backward in time). The Schrödinger wave equation has, in contrast, only the retarded wave solution.

The advanced wave solution of the d'Alambert operator usually has been ignored because it was considered to be not physical. But, as proposed in Cramer's Transactional Interpretation (Cramer, 1986), and in Costa de Beauregard's Advanced-Action Interpretation (Costa de Beauregard, 1953), the EPR paradox disappears if the advanced waves are considered to be real physical entities.

The same conclusion was reached, in December 1941, by one of the major Italian mathematicians, Luigi Fantappié. While working on quantum mechanics and Special Relativity equations, he noted that the retarded waves (retarded potentials) are governed by the law of entropy, while the advanced waves (advanced potentials) are governed by a symmetrical law that he named "syntropy."

The following letter, written by Fantappié to a friend, describes the implications of the law of syntropy:

> I have no doubts about the date when I discovered the law of syntropy. It was in the days just before Christmas 1941, when, as a consequence of conversations with two colleagues, a physicist and a biologist, I was suddenly projected in a new panorama, which radically changed the vision of science and of the Universe which I had inherited from my teachers, and which I had always considered the strong and certain ground on which to base my scientific investigations. Suddenly I saw the possibility of interpreting a wide range of solutions (the anticipated potentials) of the wave equation which can be considered the fundamental law of the Universe. These solutions had been always rejected as "impossible", but suddenly they appeared "possible", and they explained a new category of phenomena which I later named "syntropic", totally different from the entropic ones, of the mechanical, physical and chemical laws, which obey only the principle of classical causation and the law of entropy. Syntropic phenomena, which are instead represented by those strange solutions of the "anticipated potentials", should obey two opposite principles of finality (moved by a final cause placed in the future,

and not by a cause which is placed in the past): differentiation and non-causable in a laboratory. This last characteristic explained why this type of phenomena had never been reproduced in a laboratory, and its finalistic properties justified the refusal among scientists, who accepted without any doubt the assumption that finalism is a "metaphysical" principle, outside Science and Nature. This assumption obstructed the way to a calm investigation of the real existence of this second type of phenomena; an investigation which I accepted to carry out, even though I felt as if I were falling in an abyss, with incredible consequences and conclusions. It suddenly seemed as if the sky were falling apart, or at least the certainties on which mechanical science had based its assumptions. It appeared to me clear that these "syntropic," finalistic phenomena which lead to differentiation and could not be reproduced in a laboratory, were real, and existed in nature, as I could recognize them in the living systems. The properties of this new law, opened consequences which were just incredible and which could deeply change the biological, medical, psychological, and social sciences.

3 The Vital Needs Model

The vital needs model is based on two considerations:

- That at the macrocosm level entropy prevails.
- That at the quantum level entropy and syntropy are balanced and syntropic processes can take place.

Albert Szent-Györgyi stated "It is impossible to explain the qualities of organization and order of living systems starting from the entropic laws of the macrocosm". This is one of the paradoxes of modern biology: living systems show properties opposite to the law of entropy which governs the macrocosm.

The hypothesis on which the vital needs model is based is that life originates at the quantum level. But, when life structures grow beyond the quantum level and enter into the macrocosm level, where entropy prevails, life starts conflicting with entropy.

The conflict between life and entropy is well known and has been discussed continuously by biologists and physicists. Schrödinger, answering the question about what permits life to contrast entropy, concluded that life feeds on *negative entropy* (Schrödinger, 1988, 74). The same conclusion was reached by Albert Szent-Györgyi when he used the term *syntropy* in order to describe the qualities of negative entropy as the main property of living systems (Szent-Györgyi, 1977).

This hypothesis, of a basic conflict between life (syntropy) and the environment (entropy), leads to the conclusion that living systems need to satisfy three vital conditions:

- Acquire syntropy from the microcosm;
- Combat the dissipative effects of entropy;
- Solve the conflict between entropy and syntropy.

3.1 Combat the dissipative effects of entropy: material needs

In order to combat the dissipative effects of entropy, living systems need to acquire energy from outside and protect themselves from the dissipative effects of entropy. These conditions are now referred to as **material needs**, and include:

- In order to combat the dissipative effect of entropy: the need to acquire energy from outside, for example with food; and the need to reduce the dissipation of energy, for example with shelter (housing) and clothes.
- In order to combat the continuous production of waste, which is the consequence of the destruction of structures under the effect of entropy: the need for hygienic and sanitary standards and waste disposal.

When these needs are partially unsatisfied, pain is experienced in the forms of hunger, thirst, and sickness; and when they are totally unsatisfied, death is the consequence. The total satisfaction of material needs leads to a state of well being, which is characterized by the absence of pain linked to material needs.

3.2 Acquire syntropy from the microcosm: the need for love

Satisfying material needs does not stop entropy from destroying the structures of the living systems: cells die, and structures are destroyed; the living system is therefore continuously called to repair the damages associated with entropy. In order to mend these damages the living system needs to feed on syntropy, which is the only property which allows one to create order and organization, and to counterbalance the destructive effects of entropy.

Experiments on retrocausality suggest that the autonomic nervous system, which supports the vital functions of the living system, would be the neuro-physiological structure which acquires syntropy (–E, negative energy) from the microcosm (Radin, 2006), supplying the vital functions and the regenerative processes. Negative energy behaves as an absorber of energy, therefore:

- When a good connection with –E is established, energy converges in the autonomic nervous system (mainly in the thorax region) producing feelings of warmth and well being, signaling the acquisition of syntropy. These feelings match what is now generally described with the word *love*;
- When the link to –E is insufficient, energy diverges, causing feelings of chill and emptiness in the autonomic nervous system (thorax) associated with suffering, caused by the dissatisfaction of the need to acquire syntropy. This suffering coincides with what is now usually named anxiety and can take the form of fear, panic, and neuro-vegetative symptoms such as nausea, vertigo, and feelings of suffocation.

Therefore, the need to feed on syntropy would be felt as need for love. When this need is not satisfied, feelings of pain would be experienced in the form of anxiety and discomfort in the thorax area. When this need is totally unsatisfied, the living system is unable to feed the regenerative processes and repair the damages produced by entropy, and death will occur.

Thus, a role for love in healing is to be expected, given the assertions that love is felt when the link to syntropy is strong and that syntropy is the property which rebuilds and heals what entropy destroys. This last statement might seem contradictory. According to the vital needs model, love is a consequence of *retrocausality*, so how can love also *cause* healing? It is important to note that, in the entropy/syntropy model, life is the meeting point of causality (macro level) and retrocausality (quantum level) giving way to a new type of causality, which Chris King named supercausality (King, 2003). Love, with its resonant loops of causality and retrocausality, is here considered to be the most important form of supercausality.

3.3 Solve the conflict between entropy and syntropy: the need for meaning

In order to satisfy material needs, living systems have developed cortical systems which reach their highest complexity in human beings. These cortical systems produce representations of the environment which permit the comparison of the living system with the environment. This process initiates the conflict between entropy and syntropy: while entropy has inflated the universe towards infinite (diverging waves), syntropy (converging waves) forces living systems to be finite and localized. Comparing the infinite of the environment (entropy) and finite of the living system (syntropy) produces a result which tends to zero.

$$\frac{1}{\infty} \rightarrow 0$$

In this equation 1 symbolizes the living system which is finite (syntropy), while *Infinite* symbolizes the environment (entropy). The comparison between the living system (1, finite) and the environment (infinite) tends to zero. In other words, comparing ourselves with the environment which is infinite we become aware of the fact that we are equal to nothing. But to be equal to nothing is equivalent to death, a fact which is incompatible with the feeling of life. It is therefore necessary to solve this conflict between being (1) and not being (0), a conflict which consumes energy and increases entropy. This conflict is generally felt as the ***need to give a meaning to life***, for example:

- increasing our own value (through richness, power, achievement, *etc.*);
- finding a purpose in life, a finality (through ideologies, religion, *etc.*).

In living beings with highly complex cortical systems this need is vital because, when it is not solved, it leads to the dissipation of energy, and in the most serious cases to death. The existential crisis associated with this conflict is accompanied by feelings of being useless, purposeless, reduction of energy (dissipation of energy, entropy), usually named depression, felt in the cortical area in the form of tension, and usually strongly correlated with anxiety and feelings of pain in the thorax. This strong correlation between depression and anxiety is suggested by the fact that, from a mathematical point of view, the conflict between being and not being is solved when:

$$\frac{1 \times \infty}{\infty} = 1$$

where the operator $\times$ coincides with union, which is the property of syntropy, love (converging waves, $-E$). In other words, when we unite ourselves (1) to the environment, comparing ourselves to the environment, we find our identity (= 1).

This last equation indicates that:

- when the need to create meaning is addressed by increasing the value of the numerator (power, richness, achievement), the identity conflict remains unsolved — because whatever the finite value of the numerator compared to an infinite, the result tends to zero;
- perfect correlation between anxiety and depression must be observed, because when the unity ($\times$) is weak, anxiety increases along with the identity conflict and depression;
- only through love we can solve the identity conflict between being and not being, and experience the meaning of life. Uniting ourselves with the universe is a property of syntropy, converging waves.

4 Causality, Retrocausality, and Consciousness

Wheeler, Feynman (1949) and Fantappié (1942) showed that advanced waves behave as absorbers whereas retarded waves behave as emitters. In 1941 Fantappié discovered that, according to the law of syntropy, living systems are a consequence of advanced waves and would behave as energy absorbers; he then arrived at the conclusion that the energy balance of living systems should, therefore, always be positive, in favour of absorption. The assertion that living systems absorb energy is consistent with the realization that nearly all the energy used by humanity derives from biological masses: wood, coal, petrol, gas, and bio-fuels.

This distinction between absorbers and emitters provides an interesting insight into one other basic property of life: the "feeling of life." According to Kant "the feeling of life is the essence of life itself". Likewise, Fantappié asserts that "advanced waves are the essence of life itself." If both Kant and Fantappié are right, it would follow that the feeling of life is a direct consequence of advanced waves, since life itself is, according to the law of syntropy, a consequence of advanced waves. A more intuitive understanding of advanced waves may come when considering the "feeling of life" as a consequence of converging waves/absorbers, rather than a consequence of diverging waves/emitters (retarded waves). The equivalence "feeling of life = advance waves" leads to the conclusion that systems based on the positive energy solution (entropy), as for example machines and computers, would never show a "feeling of life" independently from their complexity, while systems based on the negative energy solution (syntropy), as for example life itself, should always have a "feeling of life", independently from their complexity.

The distinction between absorbers and emitters was used by Chris King (King, 2003) in order to explain free will, another basic property of life. Chris King states that living systems are constantly faced with bifurcations between information coming from the past (retarded waves) and information coming from the future (advanced waves), and that they are in a constant state of choice. This constant state of choice would be common to all the levels and structures of life, from molecules to macrostructures, up to organisms and in the most complex systems would take the form of free will. Free choices and free will would cause chaotic dynamics which would explain why life is organized in fractal structures, another important property of living systems.

According to this retrocausal model of life, living systems would constantly receive:

- Stimuli from the past, in the form of information received by the five senses: sight, hearing, smell, taste, and touch;

- Stimuli from the future in the form of feelings mediated by the autonomic nervous system.

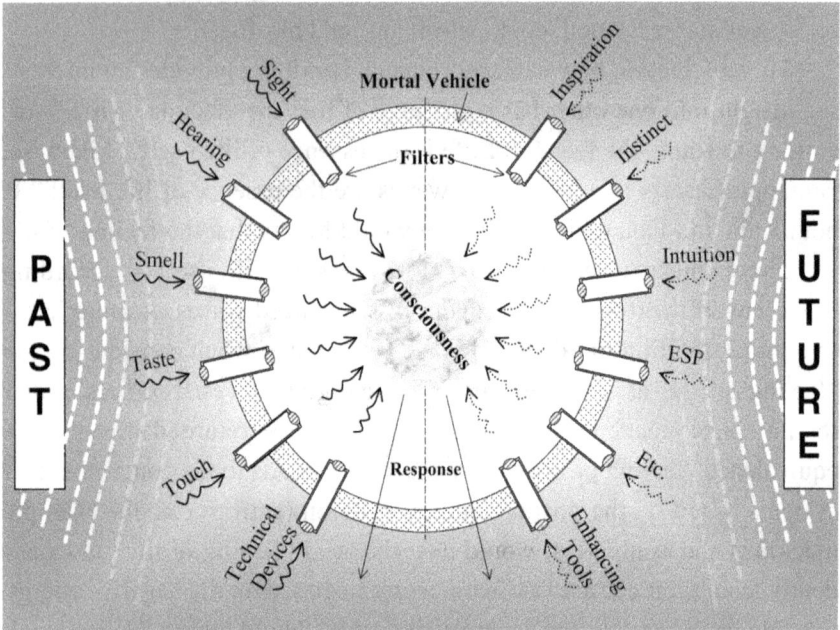

Figure 1: Stimuli coming from the past would be received using the five traditional senses: sight, hearing, smell, taste and touch, and mediated by the brain, while stimuli coming from the future would be received by the autonomic nervous system, and generally described as feelings of the heart. These two types of stimuli would then meet, giving place to free will and consciousness.

The diagram used by Robert Jahn and Brenda Dunne in their paper "Sensors, Filters and the Source of Reality" can therefore be changed in order more clearly to accommodate stimuli from the future (figure 1).

5 Evidence

It is important to note that it appears to be impossible to test the existence of advanced waves in a physics laboratory:

- According to Fantappié, anticipated waves do not obey classical causation, therefore they cannot be studied with experiments which obey the classical experimental method (Fantappié, 1942).

- According to Wheeler's and Feynman's electrodynamics, emitters co-incide with retarded fields, which propagate into the future, while absorbers coincide with advanced fields, which propagate backward in time. This time-symmetric model leads to predictions identical with those of conventional electrodynamics. For this reason it is impossible to distinguish between time-symmetric results and conventional results (Wheeler and Feynman, 1949).
- In his "Transactional interpretations of quantum mechanics," Cramer states that "Nature, in a very subtle way, may be engaging in backwards-in-time handshaking. But the use of this mechanism is not available to experimental investigators even at the microscopic level. The completed transaction erases all advanced effects, so that no advanced wave signalling is possible. The future can effect the past only very indirectly, by offering possibilities for transactions" (Cramer, 1986).

Nevertheless, living systems constantly seem to be engaged in anticipation, and show behaviours which cannot be explained by classical causation or studied in classical laboratory settings.

According to Fantappié, living systems should be a direct consequence of anticipated waves and backwards causality (law of syntropy), therefore it should be possible to test retrocausality using living systems. For example, in the field of psychology, various empirical evidences show the existence of retrocausality and anticipatory effects:

- *Pre-stimuli heart rate differences*: In their article "Heart rate differences between targets and nontargets in intuitive tasks" Tressoldi *et al.* reported the results of two experiments, aimed at investigating pre-stimuli heart rate changes. In the first experiment a statistical significance of $p = 0.015$ was obtained, while in the second experiment p reached 0.001. These results support the hypothesis that the heart rate reacts before the stimulus takes place (Tressoldi *et al.*, 2005).
- *Anticipatory reaction of skin conductance*: In 2003 Spottiswoode and May of the Cognitive Science Laboratory replicated Bierman and Radin's 1997 experiments, which demonstrated an increase in skin conductance 2–3 seconds before emotional stimuli were presented.

Spottiswoode and May replicated these results with a statistical significance of $p = 0.0005$, and included controls to exclude all possible artifacts and alternative explanations. These results further support the hypothesis that the autonomic nervous system reacts prior to the presentation of the stimuli (Spottiswoode and May, 2003).

- *Retrocausality in REG (random event generator) experiments*: The Princeton Engineering Anomalies Research (PEAR) laboratory, established in 1979, carried out extensive studies of anomalous mind/machine interactions using microelectronic random event generators (REGs). In unattended calibration, these REG systems produced precise Gaussian distributions, but when a human operator attempted to distort these distributions only by the expression of intentionality, highly significant statistical deviations were observed. Even more fascinating is that those distributions generated *before* the operators' expressions of intentionality showed an amplified effect. The statistical significance of these "retrocausal" amplifications was $p < 0.000000001$ (Jahn and Dunne, 2005). It is important to note that these effects were amplified when the operators reported experiencing a feeling of emotional "resonance" with the devices. Other REG experiments, referred to as "FieldREG," were carried out in environments that reflected strong group resonances, such as spiritual rituals or theatrical performances. In these studies there was no specific intention expressed, only a marked enhancement of collective group consciousness. Control studies were carried out in non-resonant environments, and the differences observed between the resonant and non-resonant settings showed a statistical significance of $p < 3.2 \times 10^{10}$ ($p < 0.00000000032$). These FieldReg experiments demonstrated that emotions play an important role in anomalous mind/machine interactions. Therefore, according to the authors, it would be more accurate to speak of these interactions as "anomalous heart/machine interactions."

6 Conclusion: Choosing Between the Brain and the Heart

It is common experience that whilst stimuli coming from the past can easily be detected by our five senses and understood and processed by our brain, stimuli coming from the future are more difficult to understand and process since they are experienced in the form of feelings, such as anxiety, pain in the chest, happiness, love, and heat in the thorax region, but with no information associated with them. Often these feelings are experienced in the form of anticipation, either positive or negative, of something that is going to happen, but of which we have no information. As a consequence of this constant sensing of stimuli coming from the past and stimuli coming from the future, we are faced with bifurcations, comprised of the following two components:

1. That which is known and certain: *e.g.*, coded information, or memory, coming from the past, that tells us what to choose (brain);
2. That which is unknown and uncertain: *e.g.*, feelings of attraction or avoidance coming from the future, that suggest what to choose (heart).

It is common experience that what is suggested by the brain generally does not coincide with what is suggested by the heart. Usually people choose what the brain suggests, since it is based on information which is known and relatively certain, and therefore appears to be more reassuring. But in doing so, they restrict their lives to cause and effect–based, or entropic logic, which usually is incompatible with the syntropic nature of life and frequently results in dissatisfaction and suffering. This process of suffering has led a significant number of people to suspect that it might be wiser to follow what the heart suggests. As a consequence, a growing number are now interested in learning how to listen and understand what their hearts tell them.

Many strategies are available to help enhance the perception and the understanding of the feelings of the heart. Generally these strategies are based on a simple consideration: making choices that decrease entropy and increase syntropy, favour the perception of the heart, and enhance sensitivity to feelings of anticipation. In any moment of our lives we are faced with choices: the way we eat, we work, we live, we consume, we socialize. When we follow the less entropic choices and/or increase the syntropic alternatives, we enhance our ability to feel and understand the heart — thereby enhancing our ability to use, in a constructive and positive way, the feelings of anticipation and attraction that come from the future.

References

Dick J. Bierman and Dean I. Radin "Anomalous anticipatory response on randomized future conditions." *Perceptual and Motor Skills, 84* (1997). pp. 689–690.

Olivier Costa de Beauregard. "Une réponse à l'argument dirigé par Einstein, Podolsky et Rosen contre l'interprétation Bohrienne des phénomènes quantiques." *Comptes Rendus de l'Académie des Sciences, 236* (1953). pp. 1632–1634.

John G. Cramer. "The transactional interpretation of quantum mechanics." *Reviews of Modern Physics, 58,* No. 3 (1986). pp. 647–688.

Luigi Fantappié. *Teoria Unitaria del Mondo Fisico e Biologico.* Roma: Di Renzo Editore, 1991. (Originally published in 1942.)

Robert G. Jahn and Brenda J. Dunne. "The PEAR proposition." *Journal of Scientific Exploration, 19,* No. 2 (2005), 195–245.

Immanuel Kant. (AA.VV.) *Rassegna di Scienze Filosofiche.* Palermo: Editrice Astrea, 1970.

Chris King. "Chaos, quantum-transactions and consciousness: A biophysical model of the intentional mind." *NeuroQuantology, 1,* No. 1 (2003). pp. 129–162.

Dean Radin. *Entangled Minds: Extrasensory Experiences in a Quantum Reality.* New York: Paraview Books, 2006.

Erwin Schrödinger. *Che Cos'è la Vita.* Firenze: Sansoni, 1988.

S. James P. Spottiswoode and Edwin C. May. "Skin conductance prestimulus response: Analyses, artifacts and a pilot study." *Journal of Scientific Exploration, 17,* No. 4 (2003). pp. 617–641.

Albert von Szent-Györgyi. "Drive in living matter to perfect itself." *Synthesis 1, 1,* No. 1 (1977). pp. 14–26.

Patrizio E. Tressoldi, Massimiliano Martinelli, Stefano Massacessi, and Luisa Sartori. "Heart rate differences between targets and nontargets in intuitive tasks." *Human Physiology, 31,* No. 6 (2005). pp. 646–650.

John Archibald Wheeler and Richard Phillips Feynman. "Classical electrodynamics in terms of direct interparticle action." *Reviews of Modern Physics, 21,* No. 3 (1949). pp. 425–433.

Acoustical Resonance Iteration Filtering: The Children's Version

THOMAS ANDERSON
ICRL Acoustics Laboratory
Nashville, Tennessee

Introduction

Using the proper "filter" in one's perception, one may come to see almost all consciousness processes in terms of filters. Each style of filter-process observed yields new insights, serving as a metaphor and a template for further exploration and understanding. One such ubiquitous filter-process is filtration by iterated acoustical resonance. A great woman once said, "If it cannot be explained to children, it is not worth explaining." Since the acoustical resonance iteration process is certainly worth explaining, here we explain in a way children can understand. For those readers who are a bit more advanced in their graphical interpretation skills, we also provide a visual explanation for adults.

ARIF: The Children's Version

Sound is made out of invisible waves in the air. These waves are much like waves in the water. They travel around, bouncing here and there, crossing each other and moving things that they hit. When sound waves are stuck in a box, on a string, or anywhere where they can bounce back and forth, over and over, a very special thing happens. This special thing is called *resonance*.

Resonance means something like this: when sound waves bounce around inside something, the shape of the thing in which they are bouncing affects the way they bounce. Because of the way it is shaped, some of the sound bounces away very quickly and some of the sound stays around and bounces for a while. The sound that stays around for a while is like a special song that this place likes to sing, or you might call it a special *chord* that this place likes to play on its very own musical instrument. A *chord* is a bunch of notes, like the sounds of the keys on a piano, played at the same time. The notes that bounce around for a while are called *resonant notes* and when they are bouncing around, it is called *resonance.*

Now we can use this place, this resonator where certain resonant notes like to bounce around, to do a funny thing. We can play *white noise* into the resonator; white noise is a sound which is made out of pretty much every-note-in-the-whole-world, all added up together. It sounds kind of like a fan or a waterfall. When the white noise, made of pretty much every-note-in-the-whole-world, is played into the resonator, most of the notes bounce away quickly, but the resonant notes stay around for a while.

After we have played white noise into the resonator and there is sound bouncing around inside which is mostly made out of the resonant notes, we can record the sound. Now we have a recording of a sound which has a just a little bit of every-note-in-the-whole-world, but a whole lot of the resonant notes of the resonator. Here's where the really funny part starts: Now we will play this recorded sound, which is a little bit of every-note-in-the-whole-world mixed with a lot of the resonant notes, into the resonator. We record this new sound as it is played inside the resonator, just like the first time.

The new recording is a lot like the first one except that it has even less of every-note-in-the-whole-world and even more of the resonant notes. Now we play this new sound and record it, just like the last time. In fact, we will keep playing each new recorded sound into the resonator and recording it again. Every time we repeat this process, the new recording will have more of the resonant notes and less of all-the-notes-in-the-whole-world. And we will finally stop repeating this record/play process when the new recording has pretty much only the resonant notes and pretty much none of the rest of all-the-notes-in the-whole-world.

This whole process of starting with every-note-in-the-whole-world, playing them into a resonator, and then being left with only the resonant notes, has a funny name: *Acoustical Resonance Iteration Filtering*. That sounds tricky, but the name is actually simple and helps us remember how it works. *Acoustical* means "anything that has to do with sound." *Resonance* means "waves bouncing around, back and forth, in a shape for a while." *Iteration* means "doing the same thing over and over." *Filtering* means "to take a mixture, full of a bunch of stuff, and take out only some of the stuff that you want." This is kind of like filtering coffee, where you take out the good coffee-drink but leave the wet coffee-grounds (which you definitely do not want to drink!). So the fancy name, *Acoustical Resonance Iteration Filtering*, just means "filtering sound by bouncing it around in something over and over." Because the name can be hard to say fast, sometimes we just say the initials: *ARIF*.

Now that we have done the ARIF, we have a recording of a very special sound. This sound is the resonant chord of the resonator. It is a sound made up of the resonator's favorite sounds, the sounds that like to stay in the resonator while all the other sounds leave. But now you might wonder why we would want a recording of the resonant chord of this resonator. We want it for the same reasons that we might want a map or a picture. A map tells us a lot about a place without having to actually go there. A picture shows us what something or someone looks like, even when they are not around. In very much the same way, the resonant chord that the ARIF records tells us a lot about the resonator, especially its shape. We might say that the ARIF gives us the name for the shape in a universal language of sound and resonance.

But why would we want to know the sound of some certain shape? There are many reasons, but one is my favorite: Every sound that we hear gives us a certain feeling. Sometimes that feeling is good (like the feeling we get from hearing a beautiful song played on a flute). Sometimes that feeling is bad (like the feeling we get from hearing a terrible song played on a flute). And as the ARIF shows us, every shape around us has a sound; the rooms that we live and work in have a sound. Just like the flute, the shape's sound may be good or bad. But unlike the flute's sound, the shape's sound is so quiet that we usually cannot hear it. That's why we need the ARIF. The ARIF makes it possible to hear the sound of a shape. Once we hear this sound, we might think it's beautiful and decide we like the shape even better; or sometimes we might realize that the shape makes a bad sound and decide to change the shape. For instance, we could find out what sound your bedroom makes while you sleep, and if it's good, we will leave it the same. But if it is bad, we might change the shape of the room to make it good. This might even give you better dreams.

We know that every shape has a sound, and each shape can be used to filter out its own special sound from a mixture of every-sound-in-the-whole-world. This process is called ARIF: Acoustical Resonance Iteration Filtering. Using ARIF, we can make the quiet sound of shape loud enough to hear and that once we can hear it, we may feel like it's a good or bad sound. If it's a good sound, we may want to use that shape more often; if it's a bad sound, we may want to change the shape or use a new shape. Although this is great reason to use ARIF, I hope that you think of many more and find yourself in beautiful world of sound and shapes dancing and singing.

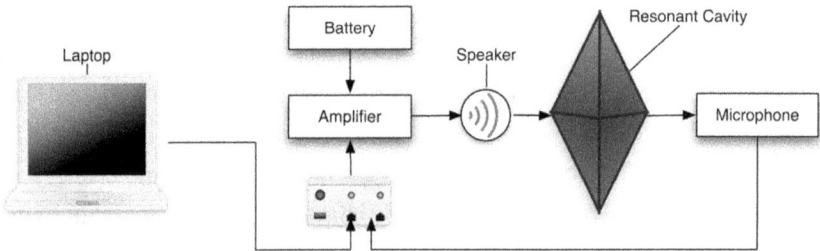

Diagram and Sequential Iteration Graphs for the Acoustics of an Octahedral Cavity

The ARIF: The Adult's Version

The above diagram shows the basic setup for acoustical resonance iteration. The computer generates a white noise signal which is amplified and directed into the resonant cavity. The white noise is recorded back into the computer by means of the microphone after having

ARIF Using an Octahedral Resonance Cavity

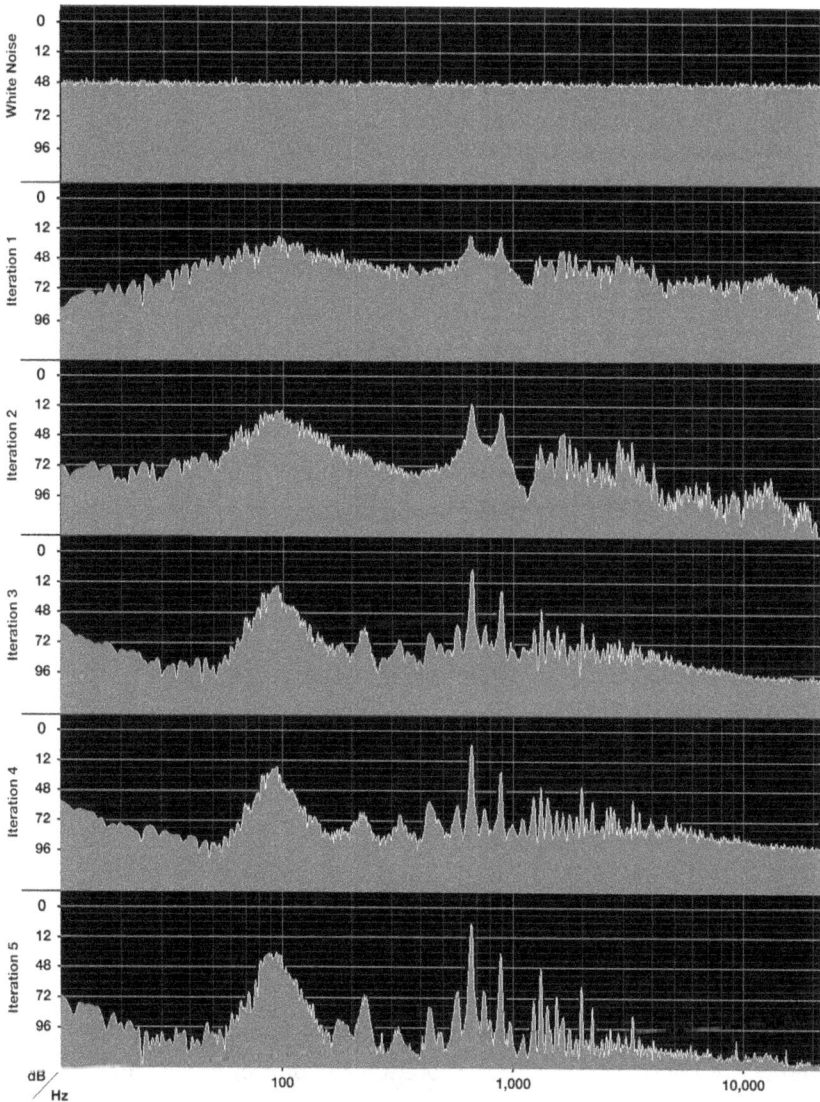

passed through the cavity. As the noise passes through the cavity, the resonant frequencies are relatively boosted. Next, the new recorded sound is played back through the cavity and recorded again. The resonant frequencies are further relatively boosted. This process is iterated until the non-resonant frequencies are sufficiently filtered out.

The graphs below display this process visually over five iterations with an octahedral resonance cavity, with the horizontal axes representing the frequency and the vertical axis representing the amplitude. The top graph shows the original white noise signal as generated by the computer and played into the cavity. Notice the even frequency composition; all frequencies are equal in amplitude.

The second graph, labeled *Iteration 1*, shows the composition of the recorded sound when the white noise is reverberated within the cavity. Here the frequency composition is no longer even and peaks are forming. These peaks are the resonant frequencies of the cavity. This new sound, containing the accentuated resonant frequencies, is played back into the cavity and recorded again. The composition of this recording is shown as *Iteration 2*. Notice that the resonant frequencies are further accentuated. When this process is repeated with further iterations, the non-resonant frequencies are progressively filtered down, leaving us with a sound that is composed primarily of the resonant frequencies of the cavity. As we further iterate this process, we approach the true sound of the cavity ... the acoustical "signature" of the cavity in the pure language of vibration.

Conclusion

We live in a world of shapes and vibrations where resonance is occurring everywhere in everything. Every *thing* is imposed upon by external sources of energy. Everything is singing its resonant song in response and dissipating the rest. Everything is filtering through resonance.

Likewise, our perception is filtering through resonance. We perceive only what resonates with our sense organs and information processors. Can we find any process anywhere which does not involve resonance filtering? Thus far, I know of none, and therefore suggest that this topic invites a great deal of further exploration and deeper understanding.

You'll Never Get There from Here: REG Experiments and Conventional Assumptions about Reality

JOHN VALENTINO
Psyleron, Inc.
Princeton, New Jersey

Introduction

I stumbled across the PEAR lab as a high school student, when I was reading through physics forums on the internet. After contacting the lab, I became a volunteer and then took a year off from school to work full-time as an intern. During this time, in addition to participating as an operator in several of the experiments, I built REG hardware and software, analyzed data in novel ways, and ultimately designed and conducted several experiments of my own. The results and implications of what I found excited me in a profound way, but my continued involvement with the lab led me to believe that attempting to understand and explain the nature of the REG phenomena using only the conventional scientific or philosophical filters would never lead us to any comprehensive understanding of the effects.

As an experimenter, hardware designer, and data analyst, I had come to develop a deep appreciation of the "hard" or "objective" side of the experimental process. I found myself convinced that the ability of intention to affect a random event generator was indeed a real effect, but also realized that these effects were strange and did not seem to respond to the kinds of factors that a traditional engineer might expect. On the other hand, as a participant in many random event generator (REG) experiments, and the kind of person who would use the REG for hours on weekends, I found myself convinced that there was indeed a structure to the effect. Watching others participate in experiments, speaking with them, and seeing how some efforts were successful and others were not, I came to believe that the phenomena we were studying were as much related to issues of meaning, subjectivity, and the mental states of operators as they were to the physical hardware.

As a result, a dilemma arose in that our scientific method seemed fundamentally limited when it came to addressing an effect that expressed itself in physical terms, but whose primary mode of stimulation might actually exist in the domain of human subjectivity. In any given situation as an experimenter, it was almost as if we would have to choose between a stiflingly controlled experiment which might fail to elicit an operator-driven response, or a series of anecdotal experiences and data points which could very well constitute an effect but might also be due to self-delusion or misinformed data-selection.

My personal remedy to this problem was to take a new path. Rather than aspiring to become a researcher in the traditional sense, I went "off the radar" and carried out personal experiments while in college. I founded an organization called Psyleron, whose goal was to make it possible for others to conduct and carry out their own explorations more easily, and I thought deeply about the limits of our scientific method and how they related to the nature of the effect we were finding. I eventually came to realize that the problems with studying these phenomena are based not in their inability to be broached through scientific inquiry, but rather in the kinds of basic assumptions that many people, particularly scientists, make about the nature of the world around them when constructing hypotheses and interpreting data.

This paper could attempt to highlight those assumptions and systematically assess their strengths, weaknesses, origins, and implications; but many others have already done this. Philosophers have long contemplated the kinds of epistemological issues that are often ignored by scientists working in an applied setting, and the so-called "mind-body problem" is an ongoing topic of heated debate. In modern physics there are massive, well-established bodies of data and theories that bring into question the assumption that all interactions in the universe are inherently causal and exist in the kind of time-linear fashion that most of us take for granted *via* our "common sense." Simply put, empirical facts and observations in everything from relativity to quantum mechanics show that the universe is more fundamentally complex than it appears to be on the surface.

Instead, this paper will deal only with the empirical data and results that I know well, and point out what I consider to be some of the misleading notions in traditional science to the extent that doing so is necessary to convey certain relevant points about REG experiments and mind-matter interactions. My hope is that by drawing on my own experiences working with other researchers, operators, and the general public, it might be possible to create a more comprehensive picture of how different filters affect and are affected by the phenomena in question. By speaking to both the objective and subjective nature of the experiments, I hope not only to provide an intellectual perspective on REG research, but also to shed some insight into why it matters, and why it is important that all phenomena in nature be considered through many different filters.

Part I — The Objective: REG Experiments in a Scientific Lab

PEAR Background, The Experimental Method, and REG Data — Why an REG?

When an undergraduate student first proposed a project assessing the effect of human consciousness on random event generators as an independent research project to Princeton's Dean of Engineering in 1976, his first response was that it sounded a bit crazy. His second response was that he would allow such a project on the basis of open intellectual inquiry — but only if the student could convince him that such a project could be carried out in a way that was firmly rooted in real science.

But what does the term "real science" mean in the context of the crazy idea that a human being can affect the world with the mind? For Bob Jahn and this student, it meant that the experiment should be conducted in accordance with the scientific method that attempts to explain and understand the world in a systematic way by stating a hypothesis and then collecting data to test its validity. In the usual process, an experimenter begins with a specific question and then seeks to make observations under controlled conditions, testing one variable at a time. These observations are then subjected to some form of quantitative analysis that can determine the probable likelihood that the original hypothesis should be accepted or rejected.

Luckily, random event generators are extremely well suited for this purpose. Unlike other devices or processes that might also be influenced by human intention through physical means, an REG is a form of electronic device which produces its outputs in a way that is, in principle, completely independent from any environmental or human influences. The apparatus is designed to be shielded from the effects of stress, heat, physical vibration, electromagnetic radiation, and just about any conventional factor that could be said to influence their output.

At the same time, according to modern physics, the outputs of an REG are microscopically unknowable yet statistically predictable. Whereas it is impossible for any person or process to predict what the next sequential output of the REG will be without actually observing it, calibration tests and the theoretical expectation of the devices allow us to know that the outputs will conform to specific statistical distributions when left unattended. This creates an experimental control condition, which then can be compared to the case where an operator attempts to influence the performance of the device using only his or her intention. The experiment is further controlled by having the data process recorded electronically, leaving little room for unintentional human error. Furthermore, because data can be generated at speeds of hundreds or thousands of bits per second, the output distributions comprise hundreds of thousands of data points per operator session, assuring that the distributions are sufficiently large for reliable statistical evaluation.

Under these conditions, it is possible to use the standard scientific method to test the hypothesis that operators might be able to affect the output using only their intention. By specifying in advance the number of trials to be accumulated, and asking the operators to alternate their intentions on different trials to eliminate the possibility of any unanticipated environmental artifacts, it becomes possible to develop a compilation of data where the only factor that varies is the stated intention of the operator. Under the null hypothesis, the intention of the operator should have no effect on the output of the REG, and straightforward statistical tests can be applied to determine whether any changes in the output distributions are attributable to chance.

Over millions of trials with hundreds of operators, the REG experiments at PEAR showed something very exciting. When the operators intended that the output of the REG devices go "high," the results tended to come out higher than expected, and when they attempted to make it go "low" the reverse tended to happen. The differences between these "high" and "low" results would be almost impossible to attribute to chance, and both datasets differed significantly from the theoretical and calibration expectations. On the other hand, the baseline intention, essentially a null or control condition, behaved in accordance with theoretical expectations. Thus, by applying the traditional scientific method, it was possible to demonstrate that the mind does seem to interact with the physical world in an inexplicable way, and to do so in a manner that confirmed their scientific validity.

That is the good news — and it is approximately what I already knew when I first went to work at the PEAR Lab.

Assumptions / Interpreting the Data

The bad news is that when most scientists who accept these results attempt to explain them, they immediately tend to invoke certain traditional assumptions. In an almost implicit and subconscious way, they begin to think in terms of a process in which some object (*e.g.* the mind, brain, or some variant thereof) acts on another object (*e.g.* the REG, electrons, the computer) through some kind of known or unknown force in order to produce a result correlated with intention. Under this model, many new experimenters begin by asking questions that presume such a causal relationship, asking questions along the lines of "How much data must I generate to see a significant effect?" or "Which part of the device is it, exactly, that is susceptible to the influence of intention?"

Thus, without even necessarily realizing it, these scientists are starting out with hypotheses that are predicated on a particular model of the physical universe. This filter assumes that the observed data are driven by a direct object-to-object force, that the space in which the interaction takes place is what we usually experience as our physical one, and that all information about the experiment is contained in its physical makeup. The focus is put on factors such as bit rate, the number of operators in an experiment, and other issues of that nature.

While this makes a great deal of sense given the way that other experiments in the physical sciences have produced results in the past, and while nearly every person educated in the sciences finds himself approaching the phenomena through this filter, it is not completely compatible with many of the more subtle findings in REG experiments. In fact, the majority of our experimental results seem to suggest that the effect of intention on random processes is *not* mediated by the kinds of variables that conventional science might suggest.

Empirical Results

To begin, there is the issue of the physical noise source or REG itself. The traditional engineering perspective defines a system in terms of its parts, and then asks which of the parts is being influenced to produce the observed output. In the case of the REGs, it is very difficult to identify any particular "part" of the process that seems to be susceptible to intention. To the contrary, we find that the same kinds of effects seem to emerge even when the parts of the physical system are changed or made quite differently. At PEAR, operators were able to produce the same kinds of results using an REG-driven robot as they were on a microscopic electronic noise with feedback on a computer screen, or with a macroscopic ten-foot-high mechanical device that dropped 9000 polystyrene balls into a distribution of collecting bins. At Psyleron, we have found little or no difference in the nature of anomalous effects obtained using various different physical noise sources and processing methods.

This suggests that the effect has less to do with the physical makeup of the device and more to do with the fact that the consciousness of the human operator seems capable of interacting directly with processes that are intrinsically probabilistic or have their roots in physical uncertainty. Even when this concept is understood, the traditional scientist's next effort is typically to attempt to quantify the extent to which a person can influence the probabilistic process. This often leads to attempts to enhance the experimental results by changing the noise source, or by creating larger databases, and/or using faster data generation and processing rates.

In the case of most conventional physical effects, or in a situation where the operator is able to mechanistically influence a particular component of the physical process, this would make perfect sense. With the REG experimental results, however, there are clear indications that changing the classical correlates does not seem to enhance the effects or make them more reliable. There are instances where experiments with relatively small amounts of data will yield levels of statistical significance comparable to that of larger datasets and often, in the case of the larger data sets, operator data will appear to hover at the level of some arbitrary significance criterion. As more data are accumulated, it is almost as if the effects adjust to maintain a relatively constant level statistical significance. This result is totally inconsistent with the null hypothesis that stipulates no effect, but it also appears to be nothing like the rules that govern other physical processes.

To complicate matters further, there is almost no question that different operators, different experimenters, and different operator-experimenter combinations can create different experimental results relative to one another. In most other areas of science, it is expected that every person will create the same results every time that the same physical process is followed, but the REG data tell a very different story. In fact, one of the most widely recognized issues in the field of anomalies research, and a major reason why the results are frequently greeted with skepticism (or outright rejected) by many mainstream scientists, is that different experimenters tend to obtain different results, apparently depending upon their personal styles, beliefs, and ways of relating to data (*i.e.* their filters). Worse yet, experimenters in the same laboratory will frequently find different results when using the same objective experimental methods.

A classic example of this is the so-called "Series Position Effect," where operators often generate extremely significant results in their initial studies, only to find that the effect disappears in the next series, and then reappears in a more modest way in subsequent efforts. Across a wide variety of different experiments, even those operators and experimenters who are usually successful often find that periods of positive-going statistical significance may be followed by periods of backwards-going results. This can sometimes lead to an average bottom line result suggesting a greatly diminished or even null overall effect, but the very process by which the data end up "nowhere" is quite anomalous in itself. This kind of structure seems to pervade experiments at many different levels and is frequently reported by experimenters and REG users, but it is difficult to capture if experimenters are not aware of these structures or capable of looking for trends in their data that they were not expecting. In this way, even the most open-minded and successful experimenters are likely to be constrained by the limitations of the filters they unconsciously apply.

Finally, perhaps the most difficult element of the experimental results for a person deeply steeped n traditional assumptions to accept is the idea of distance and time independence. In many REG experiments, it would appear that operators can produce the same kinds of intention-driven effects at distances up to several thousand miles as they produce in a lab. In other cases, which are sometimes referred to as "off-time" experiments, operators seem to be able to create intention-correlated effects in data that was already generated, or which will be generated at some future point in time. In the former case, data is generated by an unattended REG or computer and kept completely unknown, until an operator then states an intention and attempts to influence that same data as it is presented to them in real time. In the latter case, operators state and apply their intention sometime before the REG device is run at some future date. In both cases, researchers have found indications of the same kinds of consciousness effects that we find in standard experiments.

These concepts are disturbing when considered within a conventional belief system wherein our entire worldview is predicated on the idea that events and causality flow in a forward and time-linear way. What we seem to be finding here is a class of phenomena where our standard notions of causality break down, where experimenters cannot be fully separated from their experiments, and where our traditional ideas of the relevance of physical variables hardly matter. At the same time, numerous experimenters have been able to replicate and find similar results, and there do appear to be indications of a consistent structure in the objective empirical data.

It may thus be that without understanding the fundamental nature of these effects and by depending on habitual filters to interpret them, experimenters do not even realize what it is that they are actually testing or finding.

Part II — The REG Experience:
The Operator's Perspective

The empirical findings of anomalous human/machine interactions may be counterintuitive to many people, but I would contend that this is an artifact of the ingrained assumptions, or filters, that are so often used to think about the world. This section will speak to the softer and less known side of the REG experiments — the way that the mind of the operator, experimental environment, and other subjective elements, such as the role of the experimenter, seem to come together to shape the experience of working with an REG.

To do this, we need to re-orient our perspective from that of the objective properties of the physical world that were discussed in the previous section. Now, instead of looking at the world as being composed of compartmentalized, reducible, and causal-mechanistic physical processes, we should begin with the concept of subjective experience. This means that we must acknowledge that all information about the physical world, including our empirical observations and consistent physical laws, come through the filters of our own consciousness. It is a logic akin to that of Descartes when he spoke of a deceiving demon — the entire world around him could be falsified, or a mere illusion created by a demon, but of his own ability to observe that world he could be certain.

For an REG experiment, this means looking beyond its physical aspects and considering the mind and perspective of the operator. In objective coordinates we might define the operator and his or her mind in terms of the brain, physiological measurements, and the kinds of information that are objectively conveyed to us by them. Here, however, we concern ourselves with something much more ineffable — the feelings, ideas, and perceptions of the operator and his relationship to his environment. This part of the world is inherently subjective, but from the ultra-skeptical perspective of Descartes' deceptive demon, it is equally valid. More practically speaking, in light of the epistemological constraints and seemingly perplexing objective results described previously, the subjective approach may be more effective in shedding insight into our empirical results.

Intention

When new operators approach an experiment, one of the first questions that they ask the experimenter is "How do I do it?" This question has broad implications and vastly different meanings to different people, but the value of the issue should be appreciated. The answer that is usually given, both for lack of a better one and the desire not to bias the operators' own experience tends to be "intend that output goes where you want it to!" Or, as some of the early PEAR experimenters were fond of saying, "Do it how you can!" This does little good for most people, but it raises the essential question: What exactly is this "intention" that seems to be able to shape the output of physical devices in the first place?

Given the subjective nature of intention and the constraints of language, I don't think it is possible to provide a comprehensive answer, yet a number of issues do become clear to the experienced operator. First, he or she realizes that stating an arbitrarily chosen desire, such as "I want to make the random event generator produce an excess of positive cumulative binary outcomes" may not actually be equivalent to having that intention at the level of consciousness that is necessary to produce the kinds of effects desired.

Instead, the kind of intention necessary to create an effect seems to come from a much deeper source in the operator's psyche. Whereas academic and cognitively stated intention is useful for objectively indexing an operator's dataset, "real" intention may have more to do with a person's feelings and the relevance of what they are doing to the broader context of their life, purpose, and identity. So, for example, when operators would visit the PEAR lab for the sake of a personally relevant goal, such as generating data for a student project, or using the experiences for self-exploration, they seemed to create effects that were, on average, larger than those of the general population.

Also, in a sharp contrast to the conventional and somewhat dubious notions of "psychic powers" and the need for some kind of special skill to produce results, some of the best results seemed to have everyday stories behind them. A young woman excited about the lab might bring along her disinterested new boyfriend, who would then produce extreme results that would win her admiration or regain her attention as she spoke with lab staff. In other cases, people anxious to prove the efficacy of their new meditation technique or technological device performed much better using their techniques or devices than without; but there is little evidence that their techniques or products work for other operators! Similarly, the principals of Psyleron would sometimes generate data to demonstrate a point in some theoretical debate. These types of experiments frequently produced extreme effects, often in support of the individual experimenter's position!

Frequently the best results manifest when outcomes are meaningful and relevant to operators. Even the most successful operators, when reporting boredom or loss of interest in the results, tend not to do very well. There are even situations where true intention might go directly against the stated intention. For example, an operator known for producing excellent results might become angry or frustrated with the experimenters and then produce data that are still extremely significant from a statistical standpoint, but in the direction opposite to intention. Others, believing in the phenomenon but convinced that they have bad luck might do the same thing. Yet all claim that they were intending to produce positive-going results!

In this sense, intention in an REG experiment becomes a very multifaceted and elusive human-oriented matter that can only be captured indirectly in objective terms. On the one hand, the stated intention of the operator is necessary to drive the experimental results in a desired direction. On the other, the very nature and design of an experiment, or the environmental factors at both subjective and objective levels may dramatically influence the operator's experience and deeper intention. This says a great deal about both how experiments must be assessed, and how they should be conducted.

When it comes to assessing results, the standard checklist of physical parameters is no longer sufficient. One needs to look at more subjective factors and begin to ask questions such as: Do they really care about the experiment? Is it fun for them? Why are they trying to get good results in the first place? What are the personal implications if the results manifest one way or another? What are the implications for the experimenter(s)? How do these people relate to success or failure? What do they expect to happen? How do the implications of the experiment relate to their dominant belief system? The list is long and complicated by the fact that the personalities and circumstances that shape the experimental dynamic cannot usually be directly modified or consciously controlled. Worse yet, these factors may be susceptible or even likely to change for any variety of unpredictable reasons!

As such, experimenters and operators must ask themselves many questions about the experimental process and then hope to establish an environment that will be most conducive to addressing their relevant hypotheses. This is an art of sorts, and it requires a cooperative effort between experimenters and operators that goes beyond the needs of a traditional scientific endeavor. It requires that experimenters create an environment and conditions conducive to operator success, and that operators approach the task with at least a rudimentary level of self-awareness and a personal interest in succeeding. Without this, any experimental effort is essentially a waste of time because the requisite operator intention may not be present, leading to an experiment where the experimenter is not even testing the stated hypothesis!

Attention

After the intention hurdle, the next question that is frequently asked is how, if these effects are real, the "thoughts" and "intentions" of so many different people in the world are kept from "interfering" with the experiment. This concern is especially relevant when viewed in light of the claim that we are working with an effect that is said to be both distance- and time-independent. If this were really the case, how can we be sure that people in the other room, or even halfway around the world, are not influencing my experiment as I, the operator, attempt to create a particular experimental outcome?

Whereas most of objective physical science lends itself to the ideas of distance, mass, and time that underlie the aforementioned concerns, the subjective world can be thought of in a very different way. Where conventional assumptions postulate that all objects and phenomena exist everywhere around us at all times, subjective experience defines a much more narrowly scoped space. In this space, everything that exists for us does so through the movement of our attention, and the way that we associate one piece of information to the next will define the entirety of our experience as conscious beings.

To give an example, you can probably realize that at any given moment there are thousands, if not millions, of elements in the world around you that you are not currently observing or relating to. In the course of reading this paper, you are probably not consciously aware of the chair that you are sitting on or the movement of an ant on the floor 10 meters away. At the same time, if I were to ask you what you are sitting on, you might seamlessly shift your attention to it and respond by saying that it is a chair or a couch. That very action of shifting your attention might then lead you to notice something else, such as the fact that the chair is dirty or uncomfortable.

Objectively, we assume that this chair must have been dirty and uncomfortable all along, but it is actually impossible to know that this is the case. Furthermore, our traditional notions of reality often cause us to postulate a form of causality that does not necessarily exist in subjective space. If I call my mother on the phone and ask her what she has been doing, she will give me a long detailed sequence of events. It is assumed that these events took place sometime in the past and in parallel to what I was doing; yet I have no way of knowing that directly. Simply put, *all* information that I can conceivably develop about reality arrives through a process of attention; and my experience is a sum of observations and their associations to other concepts.

This kind of logic also has something to say about the role of other participants in my subjective reality. Even though I might be in the same physical vicinity as another person, the two of us might well be placing our respective attention on fundamentally different elements of the world, and sharing little or no information with one another. In a way, we might be thought of as existing in separate realities. The same goes for the countless billions of individuals, events, and circumstances that "I" will never encounter. In fact, the only real difference between the non-interactive person who is in the same room as I and an unknown child in some distant nation is that it has already come to my attention that I am in the same room as this first person.

The relevance of this notion to REG experiments is that the nature and movement of this subjective attention may offer much more explanatory power with regard to the empirical data than do standard ideas about physical proximity. Given that our experiments show idiosyncratic differences among operators, effects attributable to experimenters, and very little in the way of the influence of uninvolved bystanders, it would seem impossible to treat all of these participants as equal. In my own way of thinking about the results, this is because the operator has a unique vantage point in an experiment that allows him the maximum level of attention to the experimental situation.

In the typical experimental protocol used by most experimenters in this field, the operator is the only person capable of paying attention to every single experimental outcome, receiving feedback on that outcome, and then reacting to it. The operator usually controls the timing of the experiments, writes in the logbooks, and determines any secondary configurations of the experiment. The objective results of what the operator does will ultimately be conveyed to the experimenters second hand, through the data that were generated and any other recorded information, but only the operator knows the entire subjective experience of the data-generation process.

From the standpoint of a reality constituted only by associative information that is transferred between people, this effectively creates a sort of "isolated" or selective state of reality. Prior information conveyed by the physical environment, experimenters, or other experimental participants will have a channel into the data through the operator's tendency to relate to them, but an unknown and unrelated bystander will not. In this sense, the "affectors" of a data-generation process should not be defined by their stated goal of thinking about the experiment, but rather by the extent to which they have associative links to the experimental processes and outcomes.

Attention also has vast implications for the operator's personal experience while generating data. When a given REG output is brought to the operator's attention, he or she will have a tendency to react to it. The sight of a positive result could lead the operator into a deeper level of enthusiasm or excitement, or it might cause a fear of loss of future positive results. For some people, the very appearance of an effect can create a state of cognitive dissonance and cause them to back away from the experiment and/or reverse intention. Thus, the way that an operator relates to the activity of the REG not only has to do with paying attention to it, but where his attention is led as the result of personality, expectations, beliefs, and prior knowledge or experience.

This applies not only to a single segment of data, but even that of an entire experimental session, series, or to an experiment as a whole. To address this issue, rather than concerning our analyses with some block of objectively quantifiable data (such as 5 minutes worth of data collection; 2,000 bits; 500 trials; or some other arbitrary amount), it may make sense to talk about a *unit of meaning*. A unit of meaning relates to the way that an operator's attention shifts and moves over the course of a given experimental session or number of experiments.

For example, after having generated 1,438 trials worth of data, an operator might be told that she now has a significant effect and that her results are quite important. If this information is meaningful to the operator and affects the way in which she relates to that dataset (an inherently subjective concept), then we can define her first 1,438 trials as being a part of a particular unit of meaning. Since the information conveyed to her might easily influence the operator's attitude and expectations toward future trials, the generation of any subsequent data will be part of a new unit of meaning. If approached in a naïve way, this concept could be confounded by data selection problems, but where it is possible to analyze data in accordance with particular and pre-specified units of meaning, effects can be observed that may be considerably more informative than those that would be captured if subjective information were not included.

Issues such as distance and time independence, series position effects, experimenter influences, and co-operator results can also be addressed through the concept of attention and subjective association. It is beyond the scope of this paper to go into technical detail about how experiments can be modeled in terms of subjective attention, but suffice it to say that understanding the full implications of REG data is severely limited without information about the operator's attention.

Micro-Psychology and Resonance

Micro-psychology is a term intended to capture the way in which intention and attention — two important components in an operator's relationship with an REG — interact to create a continuous experience. Whereas intention and attention suggest static concepts, micro-psychology addresses the way the mind of an operator goes through a multitude of dynamic movements on a moment-to-moment basis. These movements are cyclical in nature: the operator affects the REG, and the feedback and results from the REG affect the operator. Intention and attention can thus change rapidly over a very short time-scale, and it becomes increasingly difficult to talk about causality in any classical sense.

Often, operators who have been able to achieve the best measures of objective success in REG experiments will describe their successful experiences in terms like "resonance," "being in the flow," or "becoming one with this process." They frequently comment that focusing on the separation from themselves and the REG, or becoming too analytically oriented during the process will disrupt their ability to produce meaningful effects. As they develop the ability to hold a focus without being too swayed or affected by the feedback presented to them, their success rates improve.

This kind of skill can improve dramatically with practice and even seems to create positive benefits in the lives of those who are able to develop them. In other cases, however, these micro-psychological perturbations may limit the ability to succeed or continuously produce positive results. Examples would include situations where a person's self-regard changes due to some external life circumstance, or where learning of extremely successful results midway through a dataset might result in a reversal in data trends.

At Psyleron, we have seen some very specific examples of this phenomenon and have even defined a phrase called "boundary aversion" to deal with one of the more frequent micro-psychological movements. To give an example, one extremely prolific operator with over 300 hours of data had reported not being able to break through the "barrier" of achieving a Z-score (measure of statistical significance) of four or more at any point during his runs. He would note an internal response as the data got close to this score, and though many local results came very close to this range, none ever achieved this desired outcome. When one of our programmers created a new feedback intended to excite the operator and encourage significant results but to conceal the actual score, we saw a change. On his first day of data generation using the new feedback, the operator achieved a Z-score greater than four for the first time in over two years of data generation up to that point.

If this and similar anecdotes provide any insight into the nature of the actual effect and the mind of the operator, it has severe implications for experimental results. What appears to be a straightforward objective effect, such as a bit-per-bit mean shift, may actually be the averaging of countless micro-psychological fluctuations that take place within a given dataset. Put another way, such fluctuations in the operators' subjective states may be responsible for some of the inexplicable, but highly prevalent characteristics of the objective data, such as inverted correlations with intention, series position effects, and idiosyncratic operator signatures.

Taking these fluctuations into consideration in the design of new experiments could result not only in effect sizes considerably larger than those reported in the past, but also shed new insights into the true nature and source of these effects. At the very least, experiences such as those described above can provide insight into the inner workings of operators' consciousnesses and help individuals to come to a deeper understanding of the subjective processes and boundaries within their own minds.

Conclusion

One way to summarize this paper is to say that it talks about two sides of reality: the objective, which can be concretely quantified and conveyed through empirical data; and the subjective, which is ineffable and exists in the domain of the human mind. My claim is that these two sides of reality are not separate, but complementary, and we cannot continue to separate them if we truly hope to understand our experience of the universe. We will need to develop new and more comprehensive filters, perhaps even one that is capable of addressing filters themselves, if we hope to construct a fuller picture of reality.

The REGs, which are simple devices based on known physical principles, are not special because of their physical makeup or properties, but because of the way that they can help us to understand the relationship between the subjective and objective realms, a relationship we might otherwise miss or mistakenly attribute to other factors. Where reductionism and dualism lend themselves to statements like "Everything will make perfect sense once we understand all of the properties of all of the parts," or "Science will never be able to explain the more ineffable elements of mind," the movement towards a more holistic and integrated science gives us a new way of conceptualizing our universe.

This is particularly obvious when one realizes that the REG phenomena do not speak so much to some kind of special "supernatural force" or "psychic power," but rather to the nature of reality itself. If our objective data and subjective experiences tell us anything, it is that even the most natural and common-place elements of human consciousness seem to be capable of driving mind-matter effects that otherwise appear to be anomalous. The meaning that people find in life, the way that they shift their attention around, and their beliefs and expectations may all be drivers of the subtle subjective effects that we just happen to able to capture using an REG as an objective tool.

Rather than being a specialized force that is exerted by a specialized few in some kind of anomalous way, the interaction between consciousness and the physical world may be so ubiquitous in life that we cannot help but miss it. It is possible that the effect is a stabilizer and something that leads to consistency in our probabilistic processes and allows the universe to evolve in a more ordered form. The true "anomaly" in anomalies experiments may be not that we are dealing with an "anomalous" effect, but rather that by using it to produce results that violate our conventional expectations, we are uncovering a hidden, deep-seated process of the universe.

With this in mind, it is also important to realize that as difficult as the phenomena are for some people to accept, there is no reason to believe that they are in any way at odds with established bodies of scientific data. The REG phenomena imply no contradictions of traditional physical processes, nor do they necessarily violate ideas such as the conservation of energy or thermodynamics. Rather, they may indicate that in some particular instances, specifically those involving physical uncertainty and probability, consciousness can intervene and somehow play a role in shaping the physical. This understanding, and others derived from REG experiments may provide us with a glimpse of properties of the universe that were once considered inaccessible to scientific inquiry.

If we must insist that the phenomena do not make sense nor fit into conventional science, this probably has much more to do with our assumptions about the world — and about the nature of science — than it does with any possible flaws in the empirical data. Our fixation on concepts such as linear and forward-flowing time, traditional causality, and a singular block universe may lead to an inability of science to move forward when addressing more human-oriented domains. Just as quantum mechanics surpassed classical mechanics and determinism when dealing with the small scale, as did relativity at the large scale, we now need to invoke new models and methods of science that can deal with those processes involving uncertainty and subjective meaning.

These effects may be particularly relevant when dealing with processes in biology and the social sciences. Well known but little understood phenomena such as placebo effects, spontaneous remission, and the influence of attitude on physical well-being appear to have characteristics very similar to those of REG effects. In anthropological contexts that involve cultures or people who use different filters, or in academic situations where researchers in the social sciences accumulate quantifiable data on subjective parameters, we might develop a deeper understanding of why certain outcomes turn out to reflect the attitudes and expectations of the experimenters.

In the longer-term, ongoing debates on issues such as creationism and evolution will begin to look silly in light of perspectives that require neither and both, and traditional philosophical approaches to issues such as the "mind-body problem" will be judged in light of a science that can incorporate subjective meaning, and we could develop new ways to engineer subjective-objective processes for creating practical benefits. Early adopters of Psyleron's REG devices are already reporting enhanced emotional intelligence, mental well-being, and improved personal and business capabilities.

Indeed, if there is anything real about these effects, the next level of science may be as much about understanding ourselves as it is about understanding the external world.

Nought But Everything

JEFF DUNNE
Systems Engineer
Eldersburg, Maryland

Franklin Samuel Davenport III was nearly eleven years old when his age was taken from him for a very good reason, a not-so-good reason, and absolutely no reason whatsoever. He was sitting calmly, nearly bored, listening to his father talk about football and cricket and how they could be considered complementary sports that truly defined the breadth of the British spirit. It was a pleasant kind of afternoon, in a tedious sort of way, because he was always happy when he could spend time with good old FSD II, but this was the first time he had ever dropped through existence to land heavily and unceremoniously on the backstage of reality's set. Four out of five dentists agree that it was rather unexpected.

This essay shares Sam's experiences as he confronts Od, Po, and Dwinkle, the big squishy scintillating glob that the gnomes call Everything, unpredictable and insubstantial drywall of seemingly random translocation, and markedly unsettling eyewear. It would be lovely to say that it ends happily ever after, and as we seek, so it is. But F. Sam Davenport III, like everything else, never gets to go back home.

"You see," Sam's father was explaining, "both require discipline. Discipline is the key. You see that, right?"

Sam nodded methodically, because that was better than being asked again.

"That is what draws them together. It's why they are complementary in their own fashion ..."

Thump. Push. Wiggle. Ding.

"... and why they are so important for young boys to learn. Football will give you an instinctive degree of coordination, and is very important for developing the left side of the brain."

"Why the left side?" asked Sam. It seemed like a good question. His dad hadn't really talked about it yet, so he wouldn't sound like he hadn't been paying attention, and it was a question likely to occupy him for long enough to allow Sam to come up with a way of turning things from talking about games to actually playing them.

Squish. Slide. Spin.

"Well, consider the physiology of the brain, Sam. You learned in school how your thinking is a consequence of neural firing patterns. The legs being in constant movement will ..."

Hum. Twist.

"... produce greater brain activity in the ..."

Oops.

It was an unusual sensation to be sure, one that Sam had most certainly never experienced before. The maple cabinetry, the glass table, the picture of him in his school uniform, they seemed to vanish in the whiteness that filled his eyes. His father's rolling baritone had been completely washed away by the static hiss, and everything he had and had not smelled evoked his past and future memories. Not that he could tell what they were, all jumbled together and in no order.

After several disorienting minutes, Sam's ears were the first to explore his new surroundings.

"It's okay. No harm done, of course."

"Maybe you should stand over there."

Ding.

"No sense pushing the little sprout too hard, I say."

"Me too."

"And me."

Pause.

Ding.

"Should we push that back?"

"Only if it bothers you."

"Leave it. Maybe it will grow."

The light faded, though Sam was unable to tell whether it faded in or out. He stood near the edge of a large room of irregular shape, defined by what appeared to be untreated drywall and supported by wooden beams and braces. In the center of the chamber was a round and polished marble stand — grey shot with streaks of green, red, and blue. Above the stand, and touching it only occasionally, floated an enormous amorphous blob. Well, not so much amorphous as "enormous amorphous" sounds silly, because it was mostly spherical, looked wonderfully soft, and yet deformed readily like a giant squooshy ball with not quite enough pudding inside to fill it out completely. Nearly six metres in diameter, it would have made a splendidly comfortable piece of furniture were it not for the frequent prodding of the gnomes.

Two of the creatures, one slightly shorter than the other, were moving about the pulsating blob in erratic and unpredictable ways. The shorter one wore more green than any other colour, a dark but friendly shade, and held a triangle in his left hand and a small silver rod in his right. The taller one, who held nothing in his hands, wore nearly every colour in equal proportion, as if he had been physically accosted by a gang of malicious rainbows.

Sam watched for what seemed several minutes, attempting to surmise their actions. They had stopped speaking (for Sam was certain that it must have been they who had spoken before), and with the exception of the occasional ringing of the triangle, the room had become so hushed that he could hear the padding of their feet stepping one way and then another as they moved about the marble dais. At times the taller gnome would push the glob gently, causing it to deform around his hand, or encourage it to spin with both hands placed just so.

The more Sam watched, the more he became convinced that their movements and actions could be nothing but random. Then he saw the third gnome. Standing nearly against the wall far off to the right, this one was taller than either of the other two, and was wrapped in what could best be described as a big, blue, flour tortilla. With sleeves. It was immediately clear to Sam that this one was directing the other two, for it (it was difficult to tell whether it was male or female) would make very similar movements as the others as it pointed at each of them in turn. Mostly, but not always, the motions were in perfect unison with its cohorts.

The gnomes seemed wholly unconcerned with the boy's presence, apparently prepared to go about their activities indefinitely. Sam, who was unwilling to wait that long, approached the directing gnome and tapped it on the shoulder. The tortilla was rough but not abrasive.

"Excuse me, sir, but what are you?"

Like a conductor forced to turn from his score, the tortilla'd creature twisted about to face the boy but glanced back regularly and continued to motion with one arm. "We're gnomes," it said, not unkindly.

"Gnomes," Sam repeated, his brow furrowed slightly as he thought about the answer. "Well, *who* are you, then?"

"I am called Dwinkle. He," Dwinkle pointed to the rainbow-garbed gnome, "is called Od, and she is called Po."

Sam turned to look at Po, who he had been quite certain was male, then to Od, and finally back to Dwinkle. "Po is a woman?"

"Of course," Dwinkle responded with a giggle. "And Od is male."

"And what about you? Are you a male or a female?"

The gnome seemed almost surprised for a moment. "You see!" Dwinkle then declared with a smile, and laughed again.

Sam knew that his conversational partner was joking, not intentionally being difficult, but wasn't sure if it would be considered impolite to ask the question again. Instead, he thought he might be able to figure it out for himself if he could just figure out what traits gave away gender for gnomes, and so asked, "How can you tell that Po is a woman?"

Dwinkle looked closely at Sam, as if to tell whether he was serious. Deciding that he was, Dwinkle replied, "There are lots of ways to tell, but I suppose the easiest is that she has the triangle."

"Why does that matter?" Sam asked.

"Of course it does."

"Okay, but why?"

"But *what*?" Dwinkle asked quizzically after a short pause.

"Why?"

Sam waited patiently, and so did Dwinkle. Eventually both of them assumed that the other had decided not to continue the conversation. Dwinkle returned to its movements, and Sam walked over to Od.

Od had been motionless for nearly a minute, and Sam figured that he must be taking a rest.

"I'm Sam," the boy introduced himself.

"It is nice to meet you." Od's voice was high and squeaky, but not unpleasant.

"What is that?" asked Sam, pointing to the floating glob.

"That's Everything," the gnome replied in a matter-of-fact tone.

"Everything?"

"Everything."

Sam squinted his eyes, a habit of his when he felt confused. "That's everything?"

"Everything," Od repeated.

"Why is that everything?" the boy asked with a suspicious and doubting voice.

"Yes," Od said slowly, as if to a dim-witted and unplugged toaster. "Everything."

"Why?" Sam asked, but received no reply. Soon thereafter Od began pacing widdershins around the Everything and Sam walked away, stopping near the wall where he had first appeared. He was not accustomed to such oddly stilted conversations, but could not bring himself to feel hurt. There was no malice in these gnomes, and he thought they looked as confused by the conversations as he felt. He leaned back against the wall to think.

JUNCTION

Franklin S. Davenport III stood by the side of county highway 83. All around him was scenery, but that didn't really matter. Somehow he knew that. What caught his attention first was the man in the denim jacket.

He had features, colours, and postures, but they didn't matter anymore than the scenery. But Sam watched, intensely, as he closed the hood of a Buick sedan and walked around to the driver's side door. He continued to stare as the man got in, closed the door, and inserted the key into the ignition. The engine started with the usual muffled roar.

As Sam watched the car drive down the highway, he blinked. And then again, for he had not done so since appearing by the highway. His hand rose to his face, intent on rubbing his dry eyes, and that was when he realized that he was wearing glasses.

Sam removed the spectacles and studied them. Like a device to be found on the table of a 20th-century ophthalmologist who had been transported back in time a few centuries, they comprised perhaps thirty or forty lenses, fifteen or twenty per eye. Each lens was shaded a different hue, had its own unique shape and thickness, and could be rotated about the optical axis. And as if that were not sufficiently complex, each lens could be combined with any other by flipping them up or down before the eyes. What was most surprising about them, however, were the hemispherical domes attached to the back ends of the arms so as to cover the ears. A finely crafted set of rods, levers, and gears ran along the arms of the glasses to connect the earphones with the lens.

The boy looked up, only then noticing that everything had gone white. He could hear nothing above the static white-noise hiss.

Sam replaced the device on his face, and twitched his head in confusion and wonder as the country lane came back into focus. A dusty trace from the Buick could just be seen in the distance. The boy knew that any reasonable, clear-headed adult would suggest that he should walk down the road until he found someone who could help him find his way back home. So he did what came naturally to him and flipped a new set of lenses into place.

The murmur of the crowd could be heard through the locker room doorway, but it was a distant, irrelevant thing. The pre-game hustle and bustle of opening and closing lockers, slaps and jests, and thrown uniforms were there to capture Sam's attention, but they didn't. Instead, he gazed steadily at the 6′9″ frame of Izar Elman. The point guard recruited from Alabama State was sitting on a low, metal bench as he laced his hightops with intense, almost reverent concentration.

When he had finished he stood, rocked back and forth, and then hopped a few times. He shifted his right foot counterclockwise in final adjustment, and then joined his teammates as they walked and trotted out towards the stadium.

Basketball was not as popular in Bradford, England, as it was in Birmingham, Alabama, and Sam found himself thoroughly unimpressed with the whole experience. So he made another adjustment to the glasses, just in time to see a man in dark blue trousers and a freshly pressed white linen shirt sit down at his desk.

The black-haired executive reached across to the monitor and hit the power button. The other hand loosened a red silk tie. Then he waited.

"Oh, this is getting very exciting now," Sam mumbled to himself in utter boredom. Yet he continued to watch as the man typed in his user name and password. The screen changed, and the man selected an icon.

Sam shifted the glasses.

The green room. Actors donning costumes, assistants applying make-up …

Shift.

Center city construction site, a man strapping on his tool belt …

Shift.

A riverbed. An otter holding a shell in its mouth picks up a rock …

Sam removed the glasses again, and the nothingness returned.

Up until now, he had always shifted the lenses one pair at a time. "Boring," he said aloud, although he could not hear himself. At random, Sam flipped several lenses into place, gave each an arbitrary twist for good measure, and then slapped them back onto his head.

His surroundings were like nothing he had ever seen before. There was no ground, for example, and this disturbed him. When he noticed that he had no feet, this disturbed him more. But all of this was a by-the-way thing, for his attention was primarily focused on the shape before him. It was oblong and perhaps as large as he thought himself to be, with long tendrils that waved and swayed in the current. Its surface was a mottled off-white, with individual spots of brown and mauve, and Sam began to wonder if it weren't some huge amoeba or biological cell. And then it twisted, and he knew that that wasn't it, for on the other side was a structured pattern of blinking lights and what looked like a dial of some kind.

The shape turned again, and stretched along its minor axis, passing through spherical-ness as it elongated in this new direction. Soon it was nearly tubular, and began to bend its ends towards each other to form a loop. As it bent, the space that could increasingly be considered "on the inside" began to darken to a deep blue, while the region immediately on the exterior faded towards a lime green. When the ends of the shape finally touched, there appeared in the center of the loop a black cube. From the center of each face of the device a short silver cord undulated slowly as if from a gentle breeze.

The shape gradually unbent itself, returning to its original oblong form. Those tendrils of the shape nearest to the box reached out and laced themselves around it, drawing it closer. As the cube and the shape neared each other, the edges of each between them began to blur. The two began to merge. Within moments they had combined in entirety, and what hovered before Sam was a complex geometric form with the mottled off-white colouration of the original shape, but with hard, sharp angles and faces. The dial could not be seen, and the coloured lights had been redistributed. Sam could not be sure if there were the same number as had once been there.

Almost immediately after the transformation was complete, a soft ringing sound started to emerge from the construct, and it began to pulsate with a soft, yellow light.

Sam watched for a while longer, but when it became clear that no further developments were forthcoming, he removed the glasses. The whiteness, the omnipresent hiss, even the coated, clotty feeling in his mouth were almost welcome changes from what he had just perceived, if only because they were, in some sense, familiar. Directing his attention to the spectacles, he turned them over in his hands, felt their weight.

"I wonder," he mused, and lifted all the lenses away from the optical path. As the last one was removed, the earphones flipped up. With a questioning look, he placed them back on his head.

No change. The whiteness remained.

He took them off again, and tried to remember which lenses were in place when they had first appeared upon his head. Focused on the coloured discs, he did not notice that the whiteness had begun to fade until his attention was caught by a distinct and familiar sound.

Ding.

He looked up. It was hard to make out, but as the lights adjusted ("is it becoming lighter or darker?" he wondered) Sam realized that he had returned to the irregular-shaped room where the gnomes danced around the Everything.

"Dwinkle," he called as he walked over to the gnome. "Do you know what these ..." Sam stopped, for the glasses were gone. He looked down, then back, felt his pockets although he knew he had not put even his hands in them all afternoon.

"Do I know what?" asked the gnome as he slowly danced through a series of seemingly uncorrelated movements.

"I had a pair of glasses a moment ago, but I seem to have lost them."

"You're wearing your glasses," Dwinkle replied unexpectedly.

Sam reached up to his face, but the spectacles were not there.

"What did you say?"

"You are wearing your glasses," the gnome repeated.

"No, I'm not."

"Suit yourself," it shrugged. And then, with a smug look, "but you *are* wearing them."

Sam nodded his head slowly, as one does when being told something by someone whom you know better than to believe, and backed away several paces. His movements brought him towards the center of the room, where the Everything floated above the marble base. Od and Po were still circling the floating glob, occasionally pushing it, pinching it, twisting it. Sam thought he could hear a faint rhythmic pulsing, a sound he had not noticed before. As he strained to hear it, the sound grew louder, and now he could make out a more complex beat underlying a simple but beautiful set of interwoven melodies. He could not tell from what instruments the sounds would have been generated, but it seemed to emanate from the floating glob. Sam walked several steps closer, but the music did not grow any louder.

His approach brought him nearer to Po, who smiled at him as she struck the triangle once again. "Hello Franklin Samuel Davenport III."

Samuel smiled weakly back at her. "Hello, Po."

"You are distressed. I am sorry."

"Well, yes. I must confess that I am rather confused. It is odd enough just being here ... Why are you laughing?"

"Yes. I find it amusing that you see it as strange to be here, as if there is an alternative."

Sam did not know what to make of her comment. "But what I find so strange is what happened just a few minutes ago."

"Tell me what you find strange. Perhaps I can help," Po offered, and so he did. The gnome remained silent as the boy spoke, except for the occasional *ding* from the triangle. When he finished describing his experiences, she was silent for only a moment longer before saying, "You speak so strangely. I apologize, for I cannot give you the help you are seeking. Perhaps you should seek the source of your experiences."

Sam was not sure what she meant by this. As a guess he offered, "It all started when I leaned against that wall."

"What wall?" she asked.

"That wall." Sam pointed to the drywall panel upon which he had leaned his back.

"I do not understand what you say. There are no walls here."

"Of course there are," Sam retorted, his voice rising. She was either joking or teasing, he knew, and this was the time for neither. "This whole room is surrounded by them. There, there, there, there ..." he pointed around the chamber.

Po shook her head. "I am sorry, Franklin. There are neither walls nor a 'room'."

Sam was nearly shaking with frustration now. He ran to the nearest sheet of drywall. "No walls?" he shouted out to the gnome. "Then what is this?" he cried as he knocked his hand against the board.

EXCHANGE

Sam stood patiently in line, next after the fat lady dressed in red. Above the unshuttered window was a blue and white sign that read "Department of Assessments and Taxation."

He listened for a time as the man behind the window explained in a calm voice that it was an accepted, standard policy to pay taxes throughout the year, and that just because the tax forms were filed in the spring did not mean that that was when the money was due. The lady in red seemed genuinely confused and concerned, and once again explained why she felt that someone should have explained this to her before assessing penalties.

The glasses had returned. Sam knew this even before his fingers felt the warm metal. He lifted the device up high enough to peak out beneath the bottom of the lenses, saw only white, returned the glasses to his nose.

"I wonder," he mused to himself, and ever so slightly twisted the right lens clockwise. The scene before him blurred, and he immediately readjusted it. Sam noticed that the left lens had twisted with the right, and he wondered what would happen if he could twist only one.

Gripping the right lens firmly, he twisted the left. It was connected to the other rigidly, with only the barest amount of play in the mechanism. With the lenses misadjusted in this slight way, he looked out through the spectacles.

In some ways it was like having his eyes crossed such that each sees from a slightly differing angle, but it was more than that, for each eye now saw not just a different perspective, but a subtly altered scene. Adding to the disorientation, each ear was hearing a different dialog.

Sam closed his left eye. Once again he could see the lady in red, her hands wringing as she spoke with the man. She was getting nowhere, and had clearly begun to appreciate the futility of her situation.

Sam switched eyes. The woman was still there, and still wore the same red dress. She still wrung her hands nervously, but the conversation had become very one sided.

"Check," the man said. Sam could not tell whether it was a request or a question. From somewhere else, Sam heard a frustrated sigh.

The woman said nothing. After a moment she adjusted something on the counter between them. A moment later she did so again.

"Check," the man repeated, more sternly this time. From Sam's left ear he could hear an alternate conversation, voices the same but not coinciding with the movements of the people he could see. *"I am sorry, Ms. Brinzberg, but these are state regulations, and it is your responsibility as an independent contractor to be familiar with them."*

The woman was silent as she shook her head slowly from side to side. From the other scene he could hear, *"Well, it's not right and I am simply not going to pay it."* The voice was unsteady, incongruent with the harsh conviction of the words.

"Checkmate," said the man behind the counter. As if from a ghost, Sam could hear his unseen counterpart reply, *"Ma'am, you can do whatever you like, but don't be surprised when, not if, the authorities seize your assets. Next!"*

Sam released the right lens, and his vision focused in the usual manner. The man behind the counter was replacing the chess pieces. When he finished he looked out and saw the boy in front of him. His eyebrows raised in surprise, and he leaned over the board to speak with Sam. "Are you here to play chess, young man?"

Sam hesitated before replying, "No, sir. I am just watching."

"Well, you can do that just as well from over there. There are people behind you waiting to play."

F. Samuel Davenport nodded. "Sorry," he said as he backed out of line. Tripping over the cloth rope that separated his line from the next, he reached out blindly for support, but found none. He hit the ground hard, his head knocked against a metal post.

Sam rubbed his head where it had struck the tree. There was no blood, although he felt bruised. The glasses had transferred much of the shock to the bridge of his nose.

Putting his hands down into the grass to steady himself, he looked up and across the meadow. Two young boys were throwing a ball between them.

A slight twist of the lenses … Two young girls were playing with dolls in a playground.

A bigger twist … Two kittens chased each other around a log.

TWIST.

Strings of light, crosswise and intertwined. The one pushed the other, but not in any way that could be seen. Nearby across the known universe another strand of light was bent in response, and its crosswise partner responded. And another, and another. As Sam watched, his field of vision grew, and soon he saw that they were not separate strings at all, but one long, long strand of light that circled back to itself, twisted crosswise and interwoven as only Möbius or Escher might have imagined, and then only while taking hallucinogens. The light shot through a single globe, and its opposite globe that looked identical. And there were more globes, and there was only one. Each line of light was unique and separate just as it was connected to all of the others. The globes were constructs of the light. There was no light, only holes in the darkness. Each band of darkness-lack was an infinite connection of globes, touching end to end.

Those globes were light, that light was a lack of darkness constructed of smaller globes. The smaller the globes, the thicker the light …

Whiteness.

Sam held the spectacles in one hand, while his other grasped at his eyes. He was panting and sweating, and far too distraught to notice that there was neither air to breathe nor moisture coming from his skin.

The hiss was upsetting to him for some reason, and once his eyes felt almost normal he wasted no time flipping a different pair of lenses in place and putting them back upon his nose — an uninjured nose, but that went unnoticed.

Sam had long wished that he lived in the future, in the days of ultimate technology and everyday space flight. As he stared out of the large force-fielded window, a broad grin spread across his face. Beyond the shimmering was an enormous space frigate, moored to the space dock by pulsing tractor beams. He watched in wonder as smaller vessels shuttled back and forth between the ship and station, loading or unloading goods of some kind.

After a time, the shuttles stopped their commuting and returned to the ship. One by one the mooring beams ceased pulsing, faded into the black backdrop of space. The vessel began to move. Sam expected some kind of rumble or vibration when the behemoth craft departed, but there was nothing. It moved slowly, gradually becoming smaller and smaller against the starscape. Sam found it impossible to gauge its speed as he watched it dwindle to a pinprick, and then to nothing.

Unlike with the other scenes that he had witnessed, Sam was loath to leave. He knew, somehow, that there was nothing left to witness, but he had so long desired to live in a time like this that he decided to explore. But as he walked the station, he could not escape the sense that there was nothing truly *real* about the things he saw. He had felt this way in the other scenes as well, but it had not struck him as sharply as it did now.

He lifted the glasses ever so slightly, saw the edge of stark whiteness below the rims. With a sigh, Sam flipped down another set of lenses at random.

Before him was a scene out of his biology textbook, but huge and dynamic. To his left was some kind of cell, and to his right another.

Between them he could see a flow of comparatively small, ragged objects that slowly emerged from one of the cells that seemed to contain a lot of them inside of it. Once they were free of the first cell, they would drift to the second, which had very few, and slowly penetrate its outer surface.

Sam flipped a few sets of lenses in front of his face this time. He never cared much for biology, and felt no great need to study osmosis in this much detail.

A misty haze of violet hung before his eyes, pulsing, swirling. Above it hung a small, quiescent cloud of blue, and beneath it a similar one of red. The violet mist suddenly became aware of Sam, though the boy could not say how he knew this, and it pulsed violently, pushing blueness into the upper reservoir as it took upon itself a harsher, menacing magenta.

The boy and the fog faced off in stillness and silence, neither so much as shifting. After three long minutes, the magenta fog apparently decided that Sam was not a threat, and drew some blue into itself to return to its original colour. Then it did it again, and again, now a deep azure with almost no red visible. The blue haze was nearly gone, and the red seemed larger. Without warning, the azure mist extended itself towards the boy.

While Sam had no doubt that it meant well, the suddenness of the movement startled him. He jumped back and threw down a whole fistful of lenses.

The world was dark and obscure with so many lenses in place. He was in a nursery of some kind, surrounded by infants that he could not quite see. Overlaid underneath the room was a backdrop of a subway station scene, the figures moving in sharp jumps separated by periods of motionlessness.

"Luh!" The sound came from behind him, and the subway travelers jerked.

Sam spun around in time to see a group of long, complicated vocalizations gathered around a newborn consonant. They fussed and grinned, and patted each other on the back. It was a joyous time.

"Aahh." The sound came from the other end of the room, and was accompanied by another twitch in the scenery. More elated parents gathered around their newborn vowel.

Sam walked slowly through the room, gazing this way and that at all of the newborn sounds snuggled in blankets, wiggling in cribs.

He came upon another group of complex noises gathered together. One motioned towards a sound waiting by a button on the wall, the message somehow very clear: "Give the people a push. We can't wait all day."

The scene jolted again. "SssT!". All the sounds waved about, jumping and gleeful.

Sam found the scene disturbing. It made him feel mechanistic, hollow. Used. He took off the glasses, and sat down upon nothing in the whiteness.

"How many lenses are there?" he wondered aloud, although as before he could not hear himself above the hiss. When he had first looked at the glasses he had thought that there were, at most, two dozen pairs, but there were clearly more. He began to count, his fingers inching forward along the lenses. When he reached thirty he assessed how far through the set he was, and it was not much.

Ding.

"Enter the gnomes," he chuckled to himself without looking up. He counted another thirty pairs, and he was still not noticeably through the lenses.

Ding.

Sam looked up, and what he saw surprised him. In addition to Od, Po, and Dwinkle, another person was in the room. She was a slender woman, perhaps a little older than his mother, who looked around as if she were trying to find a trail through a forest. She did not seem to see him.

Sam walked around some yellow that was moving out from the Everything to try to get in front of her, but she turned to her right and took a few steps. She ducked her head slightly to avoid a ringing sound that drifted lazily around at shoulder height, took several more steps. Sam waved to Dwinkle, who was watching him, and moved forward again until he was next to the woman.

"I have not seen you here before," he said. "I'm Sam."

The woman jumped back, startled. "Did you just say something?" she asked.

"Yes. I said that my name is Sam. Are you lost?"

"As a matter of fact, I am. I came from in there," she pointed behind her, "and was trying to find the up."

"You came from where?"

"In the," she said politely.

Sam squinted. "The what?"

There was no response for a moment. Then the woman reached out and gently tapped Sam on the forehead. "Are you still in there," she called.

"In where? I am right here."

"You didn't say anything, so I was worried that you might have left," she explained patiently. "Do you know how I might go up?"

"Up?" he asked in confusion.

"Yes. I am trying to reach up, and then."

"And then what?" Sam asked.

Silence. As he waited for a reply, Sam saw, out of the corner of his eye, Od give the Everything a gentle squeeze. Waves of colour emerged, and Po shifted to let them pass undisturbed. When they were gone she struck the triangle again.

He turned his attention back to the woman, who seemed to be waiting patiently for him to speak.

"I'm sorry. I don't think I can help you. But can I ask you a question?"

"Of course," she replied, her voice sweet and soft.

"What do you see around you?"

"Well, I see you, of course, and there are" … pause … "with big frilly."

"What," Sam interrupted, "do I look like?"

"Well," she said, almost apologetically, "to be honest, you look like all of the other trees around here."

"I suppose you don't see the F sharp that is about to hit you in the stomach?"

The note passed through her midsection, and her stomach growled. From her pocket she withdrew a nutbar, took a bite. Between mouthfuls, she asked, "See a what?"

Sam shook his head. The woman shivered, as if struck by a chill. "Nothing," he said. "Never mind. Good luck finding your way."

"Thank you," she replied, and then started walking towards the edge of the room. Sam watched until she had passed through the drywall and was gone.

Sam pulled up a swirl of blue and sat down. He stared for a while at the Everything, which seemed different somehow, although it still hovered above the marble base as it always had. He scratched his leg.

When Po approached, he stood up and pushed the blue out of her way. She dinged her triangle at him in appreciation as she danced past. "You're feeling better," she noted.

It had not occurred to Sam until that moment, but she was right. When he had first arrived, the room was terrifyingly strange to him, and his stomach was tied in knots. Now, though, he felt more at peace. Po swayed her head to avoid a deep rumble, and Sam noted the grace with which she navigated.

Suddenly the slender woman burst back into the room through the wall where she had left. Sam could not see what it was that chased her, but his gaze followed the effect of its passage in the room as it pushed aside sounds and colours in its way. Except pink, which it always swerved to avoid.

The woman ran past him, and out another wall. Sam followed slowly. When he reached the wall, he cautiously put out his hand to feel the board. Unlike before, he did not black out immediately, but watched as his hand began to sink through. Then something jarred him harshly and everything disappeared.

REDUCTION

When Sam opened his eyes, he stared through his lenses to see a broad seascape. Beneath his feet, the deck swayed back and forth with the waves, and he put a hand on the gunwale to steady himself. Around him the crew was bustling as the ship prepared to drop anchor.

Staying out of the way, Sam watched the sailors work. Soon he heard the splash of the giant iron weight hitting the water's surface, but the sailors were already busy lowering a small skiff into the water. Once it was on its own, the captain and four other men shimmied down ropes onto the small boat, and began to row it towards shore.

The crew settled down, became idle. Some played cards, others just sat about talking or looking out over the swells. Now that the scene was over, Sam changed lenses.

This vision he nearly recognized from old war movies. A howitzer blared a little too close, and Sam fell to the ground in fear. All around him the ravages of battle churned, and he wasted no time in flipping down another pair of filters.

He stood up from the operating room floor covered in blood and gore. The noise had vanished, except for brief requests from the surgeon.

"Gauze," he said. "Wipe. Suture. Retract. Scalpel."

Sam listened and watched until the doctor had succeeded in removing the patient's appendix, and then changed scenes.

Three men and one woman stood at the back of a crowded auditorium. The men held cups of hot beverages, which they sipped slowly during the conversation.

"Momentum is still the key, of course. If we can measure the probability distribution of the electron's momentum before the interaction, and the same for the muons afterwards, we could narrow down the spectrum."

"Perhaps we could use your lab, Alice. You have a mass spec, right?"

The woman nodded. "Have you spoken with Walter, then? Is the NSF sufficiently on board to start drafting a proposal?"

"I had dinner with Kate last week, and she thinks that it would be well-received."

There was little that Sam could imagine that would be more boring than this, and he flipped down another set of lens.

Sam was shocked to find himself in exactly the same room, now standing on the other side of the group.

"No, with the overhead that the institute takes, I would need at least 400 K. More than that if we want to use some grad students, which I think would be a good idea."

"*Bullshit*," the young scientist across from Sam said, and at the same time he also said, "That would not leave very much for post-analysis". Sam shook his head, trying to sort out the double conversation.

"*Don't kid yourself, buddy. You are going to need a few more years and a lot more friends before you get a majority of the funding.*" And at the same time, "Well, we could always put in two proposals. That way the program manager would have the flexibility of funding those aspects that he feels are most valuable to the NSF."

"*What an ass.*" "That's not a bad idea, Frank."

Flip.

A speech therapy class.

Flip.

Lovers weaving towards each other through a crowded airport.

Flip.

An automatic coin sorting machine.

Flip.

A mirror.

Flip

"What?" Sam gaped in surprise. There had been something important in that mirror, but he was now finding the scenes so obvious and predictable that he no longer invested his full attention on them before flipping down the next pair of lenses. The vision currently before him was set near the bar of a pub, but he ignored it completely and started flipping back, trying to find the previous pair of lenses.

A woman in a grocery store selecting breakfast cereal.

A crime scene.

A young boy tuning a radio.

A graduation ceremony.

Scene after scene passed by Sam's eyes, but he could not find the mirror. After several minutes of fruitless searching he finally gave up and simply removed the glasses.

There was the mirror, and himself staring out of it. The glasses rested upon his face.

Sam nodded slowly, having decided that he had had enough. Reaching into the mirror, he took the glasses off his face.

The Everything deformed, and Od's hand was there with it. The triangle rang, and Po's hand swung the striker in concert. A strand of endearment and pineapple stretched out towards fourteen. Po shifted, Dwinkle became Po. The sound of cookies. Recycling reindeer ruefulness. Duality permeates. Is.

". . . what different types of beings see is different . . .
Is it that there are various ways of seeing one object? Or is it that
we have mistaken various images for one object? At the peak of our
concentrated effort on this, we should concentrate still more. Therefore,
our practice and verification, our pursuit of the way, must also be not
merely of one or two kinds, and the ultimate realm must also have
a thousand types and ten thousand kinds."

— FROM "THE MOUNTAINS AND WATERS SUTRA,"
DŌGEN, 13TH-CENTURY ZEN MASTER

www.ingramcontent.com/pod-product-compliance
Lightning Source LLC
Chambersburg PA
CBHW062200270326
41930CB00009B/1597